Second Edition

Inquire Within

Second Edition

Inquire Within

IMPLEMENTING INQUIRY-BASED SCIENCE STANDARDS IN GRADES 3-8

DOUGLAS LLEWELLYN

CORWIN PRESS
A SAGE Publications Company
Thousand Oaks, CA 91320

For information:

Corwin Press
A Sage Publications Company
2455 Teller Road
Thousand Oaks, California 91320
www.corwinpress.com

Sage Publications Ltd.
1 Oliver's Yard
55 City Road
London EC1Y 1SP
United Kingdom

Sage Publications India Pvt. Ltd.
B 1/I 1 Mohan Cooperative
    Industrial Area
Mathura Road, New Delhi 110 044
India

Sage Publications Asia-Pacific Pte. Ltd.
33 Pekin Street #02-01
Far East Square
Singapore 048763

Printed in the United States of America

Library of Congress Cataloging-in-Publication Data

Llewellyn, Douglas.
Inquire within : implementing inquiry-based science standards in grades 3–8/Douglas Llewellyn.—2nd ed.
        p. cm.
Includes bibliographical references and index.
ISBN 978-1-4129-3755-9 (cloth)
ISBN 978-1-4129-3756-6 (pbk.)
    1. Science—Study and teaching—Standards—United States. 2. Inquiry (Theory of knowledge) I. Title.

LB1585.3.L58 2007
507.1—dc22

2006021822

This book is printed on acid-free paper.

07 08 09 10 11 10 9 8 7 6 5 4 3 2

Acquisitions Editors:	Rachel Livsey and Cathy Hernandez
Editorial Assistants:	Phyllis Cappello and Megan Bedell
Production Editor:	Catherine M. Chilton
Copy Editors:	A. J. Sobczak and Barbara Ray
Typesetter:	C&M Digitals (P) Ltd.
Proofreader:	Doris Hus
Indexer:	Diggs Publication Services
Cover Designer:	Tracy Miller
Graphic Designer:	Scott Van Atta

Contents

Acknowledgments

Writing a book about inquiry is an inquiry in itself. I am profoundly indebted to many colleagues who have coached me through the writing process. A wholehearted thanks goes to Camille Perlo for guiding her fourth-grade class through the ice hand investigation. Also thanks to Douglas Brucker at Monroe-Orleans II BOCES for providing the illustration of the mealworm life cycle, to Alan Lacy for drawing the floating bananas, and to Dr. Larry Schafer at Syracuse University for allowing me to use the Bugs-o-Copter illustrations.

Through our conversations or their own writings, several colleagues have offered suggestions related to the background and investigations in this book and have helped me over the years to make sense of this thing called inquiry. They include Jay Costanza, Dr. Daniel Dobey, Dr. Hubert Dyasi, Dr. Lucia Guarino, Dr. Olaf Jorgenson, Inez Liftig, Michael Occhino, Helen Oosterveen, Rick Piercy, Dr. Dennis Showers, and Janis Tobin.

I am thankful to Christine Vernier at Vernier Software and Technology in Beaverton, Oregon, for providing the Logger Lite™ software, Go!™ Link, and sensors. For more information on Logger Lite and integrating technology into elementary and middle-school science inquiry, visit http://www.vernier.com.

I also appreciate the guidance that Ronald Bailey, Debbie Stack, and Dr. John Travers provided on the first and second editions by editing the manuscript and guiding me through the writing process. In addition, I am grateful to the Exploratorium in San Francisco for providing permission to use excerpts from the Institute for Inquiry.

I am indebted for the assistance I received from the Corwin Press team: Phyllis Cappello, Cathy Hernandez, Catherine Chilton, Robb Clouse, Rachel Livsey, Barbara Ray, and A. J. Sobczak.

Finally, a special word of gratitude goes to my wife, Ann, my daughter, Janice, and my son-in-law, Dr. Robert Fortuna. I sincerely appreciate their long-standing encouragement and support.

Corwin Press gratefully acknowledges the contributions of the following reviewers:

Robert Boram, Professor of Science
Morehead State University, Morehead, KY

Joan Commons, Academic Coordinator
University of California, San Diego, CA

Melanie L. Conaway, Fourth Grade Teacher
Tyler Run Elementary School, Powell, OH

Walter Glogowski, Science Teacher
Ridgewood High School, Norridge, IL

Marina Robles, First Grade Teacher
Hawthorne Elementary School, Riverside, CA

Sharon Schulze, Associate Director of the Science House
North Carolina State University, Raleigh, NC

About the Author

 **Douglas Llewellyn** teaches science education and educational leadership courses at St. John Fisher College (Rochester, NY). Previously, he was the K–12 Director of Science in the Rochester City School District, a mid-sized urban school district in upstate New York; a junior high school principal; and a middle school science teacher.

He has been involved with several National Science Foundation and Department of Education grants on systemic reform. He is a frequent speaker at National Science Teachers Association (NSTA) conferences and has written many articles on the culture of inquiry-based teaching, constructivist learning strategies, and leadership development for science education reform. He has two books published by Corwin Press: *Inquire Within: Implementing Inquiry-Based Science Standards in Grades 3–8* (2nd edition) and *Teaching High School Science Inquiry Through Inquiry*.

He is also a reviewer for *NSTA Recommends*, writes a leadership column for *NSTA Reports*, and serves on the NSTA Nominations Committee.

He enjoys boating on the New York State Finger Lakes and is an ardent Red Sox fan.

Douglas Llewellyn can be reached at

Home: dllewell@rochester.rr.com

or

Work: dllewellyn@sjfc.edu

Preface

Inquiry into authentic questions generated from student experiences is the central strategy for teaching science.

—National Research Council (1996)

WHY INQUIRY?

It's been just more than 10 years since the National Research Council (NRC) released its landmark publication, the *National Science Education Standards* (NRC, 1996). In that document, the NRC identified content and performance standards necessary for the United States to develop a scientifically literate society and regain a global presence in science and technology. Through committees of nationally recognized science educators, the *Standards* specifically identify what students need to know and to be able to do in the subject of science at all grade levels. Not only did the committees address the content of science, but they also stated how science should be taught, with implications for assessment, professional development, and recommendations for systemwide program reform at the local, state, and national levels. Today, the *Standards* serve as a guidepost for science teachers and curriculum developers recommending inquiry as a central strategy for teaching science. Moreover, the *Standards* encourage science teachers to plan ongoing, inquiry-based science programs for their students and to develop communities of learners who reflect the intellectual rigor of attitudes and social values conducive to scientific inquiry (NRC, 1996).

As a follow-up to the *Standards*, in 2000 the NRC published *Inquiry and the National Science Education Standards: A Guide for Teaching and Learning*. That document, through case studies and vignettes, made another strong argument for inquiry and serves as an excellent primer for preservice and practicing science educators at all levels, elementary school through college, interested in becoming inquiry-based teachers.

The National Science Teachers Association (NSTA) consistently and aggressively has supported inquiry instruction. In 1998, the NSTA adopted its position statement, *The National Science Education Standards: A Vision for the Improvement of Science Teaching and Learning*. In that statement, the NSTA strongly supports the *Standards* by asserting the following:

Teachers, regardless of grade level, should promote inquiry-based instruction and provide classroom environments and experiences that facilitate students' learning in science . . . professional development activities should involve teachers in the learning of science and pedagogy through inquiry . . . [and] inquiry should be viewed as an instructional outcome (knowing and doing) for students to achieve in addition to its use as a pedagogical approach. (pp. 32–33)

In 2000, the NSTA went even further in adopting a position statement focused on Scientific Inquiry. Readers may be interested in this and other NSTA position statements relating to inquiry, such as Elementary School Science, Laboratory Science, Science Education for Middle Level Students, the Nature of Science, and Science Teacher Preparation by searching online at http://www.nsta.org/position#list.

Throughout the past decade, blue-ribbon and congressional panels have advocated for education reform, especially in the areas of science. Most educators agree, however, that substantial reform will not materialize until it occurs at the school level. Today's science teachers, teacher-leaders, and supervisors need to seize an active role in implementing the national standards in every science classroom across this country (Llewellyn, 2006). This book focuses on teaching science through an inquiry-based process and implementing inquiry as called for by the *Standards*. It does not provide a plethora of inquiry activities. There are many other books that serve that purpose. *Inquire Within* will, however, challenge your values, beliefs, and biases about teaching and learning science. Although many activities and investigations are cited as examples, this book is not about doing activities; it is about raising your capacity to see questions within the activities and explorations you already provide so you can design further inquiries for your elementary or middle school students.

This book is also an opportunity for you to explore the connections between how children learn and teaching science through inquiry. By providing a historical perspective on constructivism, *Inquire Within* makes a strong point to understand constructivist principles and how these principles relate as the philosophical foundation, or the mind-set for scientific inquiry. It is the opinion of this author that to become an exemplary inquiry-based teacher, one must articulate his or her understanding about how children learn and be able to express how that philosophy guides the day-to-day classroom interactions and decisions made about guiding instruction, lesson planning, answering students' questions, assessment, and a whole host of other competencies.

This book is also about raising your IQ, your Inquiry Quotient. Again, the chapters will guide you through investigations and readings to raise your capacity to seek questions in an investigation. After all, if we, as teachers, can't see the questions, why should we expect those 20 to 25 students sitting in front of us to see them?

Last, this book is also about professional growth that modifies and transforms your teaching methods. Your trek may involve giving up on prior teaching strategies and engaging in new skills and competencies. For many, professional growth initiates a self-directed journey. The journey is not developed simply by assigning inquiry lessons to students. The process is more involved than that. It is an odyssey that originates with developing an inquiry-based mind-set and reflecting on your own present beliefs, practices, and understandings. You may begin your journey by accepting an invitation to inquire within the pages of this book.

Figure P.1   Levels of Teaching

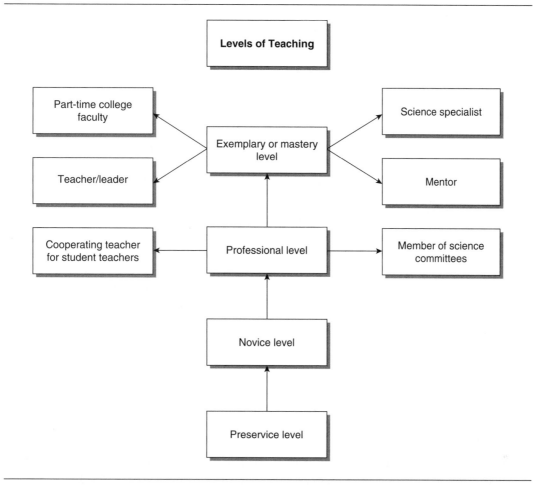

Your excursion into inquiry may start at different levels of the teaching profession (see Figure P.1). For some, the journey commences at the preservice level, where learning the rudimentary skills and methods of teaching elementary or middle school students takes place in the college classroom. Coupled with opportunities to observe and eventually practice-teach under a master teacher, many future teachers learn to teach science through inquiry as modeled by their education professors. Probably best of all, when you begin the job interview process, being able to articulate your understanding of the national science standards and your inquiry teaching techniques with a principal or interviewing committee, you are likely to strengthen your marketability in the hiring process.

Others may embark from the novice or professional levels. As a teacher at the novice level, you may want to polish specific inquiry strategies early in your career. As a teacher at the professional level, you may use your inquiry strategies to guide preservice teachers during their practice teaching experience or incorporate inquiry into work with school committees on curriculum, assessment, or other related matters.

This book may serve its greatest purpose for those teachers already at the professional level desiring to advance to the exemplary or mastery level. Master teachers who are proficient in inquiry-based instruction can use their expertise to act as teacher-leaders, mentors for those new to the profession, science specialists, or part-time college faculty. For many, professional growth becomes a passage ascending the steps to success.

Throughout this journey, you can expect to have gained enough confidence in inquiry-based instruction to invite your students to begin their own journeys, perhaps beginning with that same invitation; hanging a sign on the door of your classroom—"Inquire Within." The sign would communicate to students that they are about to enter a world of inquiry, where they will be invited to engage in meaningful investigations, where questions are as important as answers.

Often, we view inquiry as a set of activities that students are asked to do. During a recent teacher workshop, I asked the participating teachers to define inquiry. They responded by naming types of activities presented to students and described what students are expected to do. Their responses included descriptions that characterized student learning as "students are active learners," "students are asking questions and solving their own problems," "there is lots of activity about," or "students are encouraged to think for themselves." Although we might agree with these responses, before we can expect our students to inquire, we must raise our own understanding of how the *Standards* define scientific inquiry and the nature of science and how to carry out scientific investigations ourselves. The title's metaphor exists to stimulate our need to develop inquiring minds and strategies, and it further invites us to begin our journey by inquiring within ourselves.

WHAT'S NEW IN THE SECOND EDITION?

The second edition of *Inquire Within* takes several changes. First of all, with the publication of my high school book, *Teaching High School Science Through Inquiry*, which focuses on Grades 9–12, this book now exclusively targets the needs of elementary and middle school teachers at Grades 3–8. Also, more emphasis is placed on developing the prerequisite attitude and mind-set for becoming an inquiry-based teacher; balancing the *meaning* (the disposition) as well as the *mechanics* (the how-to) of inquiry. Background on self-directed learning and practice in climbing the ladder of professional improvement is an added central theme of the book.

Readers will also find many more case studies, investigations, and vignettes of inquiry-based activities. All the inquiry examples are correlated with the *National Science Education Standards* and are written in a teacher-friendly lesson format for easy implementation in your classroom. A section that ties inquiry-based instruction to scientific literacy, the nature of science, and naturalistic multiple intelligence is an added piece, as is a section on teaching inquiry to second language learners and students with special needs. A section on integrating inquiry with handheld technology rounds out the additional changes.

I trust that readers familiar with the previous edition will welcome the added information. For all readers of *Inquire Within*, I welcome your comments and suggestions, as well as your experiences and stories, as you create a culture of scientific inquiry in your own school or classroom. After all is said and done, it is you who will eventually determine whether inquiry-based instruction is a golden nugget for improving student motivation and ultimately academic achievement, or just fool's gold.

WHO SHOULD READ THIS BOOK?

You may be interested in this book for several reasons. As a preservice elementary or middle school science teacher, you may be studying teaching methods and strategies in your undergraduate science education courses. Your college professor may be introducing inquiry as you observe elementary or middle school classrooms and eventually complete your practice teaching. As mentioned earlier, being able to describe your preservice inquiry teaching experiences in up-to-date, inquiry-based language will certainly enhance your success as a future teacher.

As an elementary or middle school teacher, you may feel you are already a good hands-on teacher, but you want to take the next step in becoming an inquiry-based teacher. Maybe you have read articles about inquiry in *Science and Children*, or *Science Scope*, and wondered, "Am I an inquiry-based teacher?" Or maybe you already feel you are an inquiry-based teacher and you want to sharpen your present skills. In either case, this book will enable you to articulate, both theoretically and practically, your understandings, skills, and dispositions regarding why this method of teaching fits your own identity as a science teacher.

This book will also provide useful information and guidance for those teachers undergoing the process of National Board Certification for Early Adolescence (ages 11–15). As you prepare your portfolio submission for area VIII, *Science Inquiry*, you will need to be well versed in scientific inquiry and demonstrate competence in designing and implementing inquiry-based lessons. For more information about the National Board for Professional Teaching Standards and the National Board Certification, see www.NBPTS.org.

As a teacher-leader, mentor, science specialist, department head, or curriculum coordinator interested in improving science literacy in your school district, you will be provided with suggestions to facilitate professional development in inquiry-based instruction. You may also consider using *Inquire Within* for a collegial book study or supplementary reading for a summer institute on scientific inquiry.

CONTENTS

The chapters in this book will take you through a journey in constructing an understanding of scientific inquiry, the characteristics of inquiry-based lessons, and the skills and attitudes of those who foster inquiry in their classrooms.

Chapter 1 sets the context for becoming an inquiry-based teacher, while Chapter 2, "What Is Inquiry?" explores the meaning of inquiry through a constructivist approach. After writing your definition of inquiry, you will use several statements from the *National Science Education Standards*, *Benchmarks for Science Literacy*, and the Exploratorium (a hands-on science museum in San Francisco) to verify and modify your understanding of scientific inquiry and the processes scientists use in developing new knowledge. Later in the chapter, several myths of inquiry-based learning are uncovered to further your understanding of what inquiry is and what it is not.

Chapter 3, "Learning Through Inquiry," follows a fourth-grade class through a unit of study characterized by student-generated questions.

Chapter 4, "How Do Children Learn Science?" lays the foundation for constructivist learning strategies and how constructivism complements inquiry-based learning. Although constructivism has gained much support among science educators in the last 10 years, it is not a new idea. Its theoretical foundations began with the work of cognitive psychologists such as John Dewey, Jean Piaget, and Lev Vygotsky. Chapter 4 also addresses children's naive conceptions or misconceptions in science and how they influence the learning process. The chapter examines how children learn science through a constructivist approach and then compare them to how scientists do their work. Emphasis is placed on how science process skills such as observing, inferring, and model building enable students to construct knowledge and make meaning of science.

In Chapter 5, "Creating a Culture of Inquiry," traditional and inquiry-based classrooms are contrasted. By looking at the differences in the students, the teachers, and the classroom environments, you will further your understanding of inquiry-based classrooms and a culture of inquiry.

In Chapter 6, "What Are the Different Levels of Inquiry?" inquiry investigations are compared with other hands-on science activities using a grid that divides instructional strategies into four areas: demonstrations, activities, teacher-initiated inquiries, and student-initiated inquiries. The grid helps define inquiry-based investigations and assists teachers in selecting and sequencing the learning opportunities for students. The grid also shows that not all hands-on activities are inquiry-based.

Chapter 7, "Designing Investigations," compares scientific inquiry with problem solving, whereas Chapter 8 introduces the Learning Cycle, a five-step approach to designing lessons that facilitates inquiry.

Chapter 9, "Knowledge, Skills, and Attitudes of Inquiry-Based Teachers," presents a rubric for assessing and monitoring four stages of development in becoming an inquiry-based teacher. The rubric identifies several subsets: (a) curriculum and content, (b) lesson presentation, (c) communication, (d) engagement of students, (e) classroom organization, (f) questioning skills, (g) assessment procedures, and (h) professional development (see Resources C and D). In the inquiry process. Each subset is described in relation to teacher strategies from the basic awareness level to the practicing level. This chapter also addresses teaching suggestions for second language learners and students with special needs.

Chapter 10, "Using Questioning Skills in Inquiry," presents questioning strategies that enable inquiry-based learning. Questions are the language of inquiry; thus, competence in asking thought-provoking questions and responding to student questions is essential.

Chapter 11 provides sample inquiry lesson plans, with teachers' notes.

Becoming an Inquiry Teacher

When you inspire students to imagine beyond their expectations, to seek more questions than they will ever answer, and to persist when others concede, you are becoming an inquiry-based teacher.

—Douglas Llewellyn

Many teachers acquiesce that the journey in becoming an inquiry teacher is a very personal experience. We each make the excursion in diverse ways by constructing our own paths to instructional renewal and reform. Your journey may begin by assessing your prior experiences in becoming a teacher. Some teachers may have been educated with little or no experience in testing out their own ideas. For them, the shift must seem like climbing Mt. McKinley. For others, moving toward an inquiry approach is just good teaching. Thus the paradigm shift is different for different teachers.

Becoming an inquiry teacher requires creating and sustaining reflection practices and discourse with other teachers. As Sergiovanni (1996) puts it, "Good teaching requires that teachers reflect on their practice . . . (to) analyze problems, size up situations, and make decisions" (p. 151). For that reason, teachers should establish a network to offer encouragement and support. Inquiry support groups encourage teachers to share their lessons, accomplishments, and frustrations. A local college or university science education department can be a source for developing and facilitating a teacher study and support group. The school and the administration must also demonstrate trust that teachers can make the appropriate curricular decisions to bring inquiry-based instructional strategies and change to the classroom. Lack of support from peers and administrators has discouraged many teachers from building their capacity to develop inquiry-centered classrooms.

Regardless of how you plan to increase your ability to teach through inquiry, my best advice is not to do it alone. Seek out a friend or a group of people who share

Figure 1.1   Boyatzis' Theory of Self-Directed Learning

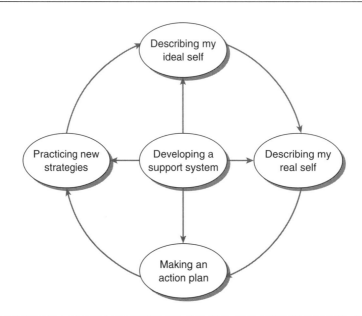

your values and beliefs about teaching. Ongoing conversations with colleagues will help you to develop and strengthen your skills and development.

Richard Boyatzis explains the five stages or "discoveries" in self-directed learning; that is, learning in which an individual intentionally develops and strengthens an aspect of his or her "self." According to Goleman, Boyatzis, and McKee (2002), "The steps do not unfold in a smooth, orderly way, but rather follow a sequence, with each step demanding different amounts of time and effort" (p. 109).

The first step involves forming an image of the ideal self, where you reflect on your professional aspirations and the kind of teacher you want to become. You may start by asking yourself, "What kind of a teacher do I want to be three years from now?" In the case of becoming an inquiry-based teacher, determining this desired state motivates you to develop your inquiry skills. As you begin to understand the type of teacher you want to be, you reflect on the values and commitment that will drive you toward this goal. Goleman et al. (2002) call this the "fuel" that drives one through the difficult and often frustrating process of change.

The second step of discovery is assessing your real self—who you are right now, how you teach, and your deep-seated beliefs about how children learn. This step includes reflecting on your strengths and weaknesses as a teacher and realizing the gap between the kind of teacher you are right now and what kind of teacher you want to become. Later in the book is a rubric for becoming an inquiry-based teacher. The rubric is a starting point in assessing your present and desired states. Identifying your strengths and weaknesses is an ideal way to plan a self-directed course of action.

In the third step, consider a professional development plan that leads you from the present state to the desired state. Whether your plan becomes a formal document that you commit to writing or is planted firmly in your mind, it is essential that you formalize your action plan and determine the professional development, additional reading, college courses, online resources, professional conferences, collegial study groups, or whatever else you need that will move you closer to where you want to be. The more you commit to the plan, the more intrinsically rewarding the plan will become.

The fourth step involves gaining new strategies and improving your performance through continuous practice and reflection. This trial-and-error phase requires patience and persistence because not everything you try may work out quite as you expect. Student inquiries need constant refining. You will find yourself trying a new investigation, noting what went well and what you plan to do differently the next time you present that activity.

The final step entails finding a support system. This, however, probably will occur throughout the process. A support system may include working with an experienced inquiry teacher, mentor, or role model. It may just be another teacher in your school who is as interested in inquiry as you are. Teaming makes the learning process easier. It provides a vehicle to share your accomplishments and frustrations in a nonthreatening way. It also provokes a trusting relationship where two or more teachers can professionally share and discuss their students' work.

Much to the consternation of those new to inquiry, developing one's inquiry-based teaching techniques and strategies is more than just searching for, and then implementing, inquiry activities in your classroom. Often, when I am asked to do an inquiry presentation for teachers, the request includes something like "just give them a lot of sample activities to take back to their classrooms." Becoming an inquiry-based teacher is far more than finding an inquiry science activity to do Monday morning. Becoming a truly effective inquiry teacher involves the three R's: *Restructuring*, *Retooling*, and *Reculturing*:

- Restructuring the school's science curriculum and daily science lessons, and modifying traditional labs,
- Retooling the teacher's instructional strategies and questioning skills, and
- Reculturing the classroom's norms and relationships that foster a learner-centered environment where questions, inquisitiveness, and risk-taking are valued.

The foremost purpose of this book is to introduce teachers to the three R's of inquiry and provide concrete suggestions for the journey in becoming an inquiry-based teacher.

As you work your way through this book, a word of caution: Don't expect to become an inquiry-based teacher overnight. Honing your skills and strategies takes time. I often say, "You need a Crock-Pot to cook inquiry, not a microwave!" In most cases, teachers may need three to five years to polish their inquiry teaching techniques. There are no shortcuts to expedite the journey. Be patient, and with a smidgen of persistence, tenacity, and peer coaching, you will find yourself becoming more comfortable using the strategies and techniques to bring about instructional change in your classroom.

According to the *National Science Education Standards* (NRC, 1996), "Teachers can be effective guides for students learning science only if they have the opportunity to examine their beliefs, as well as to develop an understanding of the tenets on which the Standards are based" (p. 28). This book was written to serve that purpose. The inquiry process starts with you, the reader, by inquiring within and examining your own ability to pose and pursue authentic questions.

INQ IRY
We can't spell inquiry without
U

What Is Inquiry?

All teachers of science have implicit and explicit beliefs about science, learning, and teaching. Teachers can be effective guides for students learning in science only if they have the opportunity to examine their own beliefs, as well as to develop an understanding of the tenets on which the Standards are based.

—National Research Council (1996)

Ask a roomful of science teachers to explain the meaning of inquiry and you will probably get a roomful of different answers. We should not be surprised, because each teacher would answer the question according to his or her prior knowledge and experience with inquiry-based instruction. The purpose of Chapter 2 is to assess your present understanding of inquiry and compare and contrast your understanding with the understanding of others in your course or study group, or those of your colleagues. You will also compare your understanding to statements from various national experts. This chapter is quite different from others you may have read about inquiry. In an attempt to model constructivist principles, I will not tell you what you should think inquiry is. Rather, you must construct your own meaning by stating your values, beliefs, and attitudes about inquiry and later making changes and accommodations on the basis of the readings. To begin constructing a definition of inquiry, you must start with your present understanding.

As an initial exercise, write down your present understanding or definition of inquiry. You may choose to write several statements on 3 × 5 cards (one statement per card), make a bulleted list, or make a concept map or graphic organizer to structure your thoughts. Concept maps (Novak & Gowin, 1989) are schematic diagrams illustrating the relationships and interconnections of concepts surrounding a particular topic. They are, in a way, *mental maps* that guide our thinking. Novak (1998) reports that when teachers and students frequently use concept maps, they learn how to negotiate meaning, organize ideas, and become more effective learners.

When constructing a concept map, it is important to

1. Place the main idea at the center or top of the map.

2. Organize the words or concepts from most general to most specific.

3. Use a *linking word* (verb, preposition, or short phrase) to connect and illustrate the relationships and linkages from one idea to another.

4. Use *crossing links* to make connections between words in different areas of the map.

5. Add to the map as new knowledge is constructed (see Figure 2.1).

Some readers may ask, "Why should I use a concept map?" According to the National Research Council (NRC), experts differ from novices in that "experts notice features and patterns of information . . . have acquired a great deal of content knowledge that is organized in ways that reflect deep understanding . . . and their knowledge cannot be reduced to a set of isolated facts or propositions but, instead, reflects contexts of applicability" (Bransford, Brown, & Cocking, 2000, p. 31) and "most important, they have efficiently coded and organized this information into well-connected schemas . . . [which] help experts interpret new information and notice features and meaningful patterns of information that might be overlooked by less competent learners" (Pellegrino, Chudowshy, & Glaser, 2001, p. 73). As we gain mastery in using concept maps, we develop an understanding of relationships among elements of a concept, ultimately making incremental gains in moving from novice to expert learners. Furthermore, by constructing concept maps, we enhance a metacognitive approach to learning by negotiating our ideas, taking control of our own learning, and monitoring our progress (Llewellyn, 2007). As we physically draw the connection between two subtopics, we reinforce that same connection mentally, thus using the map to monitor our progress of understanding through preassessments and postassessments.

Whether you use 3 × 5 cards, bulleted lists, or a concept map, it is important at this time to reflect on your presently held conceptions and cite your understanding in writing that is as explicit as possible. By committing your thoughts to paper, you solidify your ideas and make them available for deliberation at a later time. When your initial thought process is completed, take a few moments and reflect on your statements and definition of inquiry. You may want to add or modify the statements. Save the statements and return to them several times throughout the course of this book. You may even save them to read in a year, or three years from now. Later in this chapter, you will use other statements from the Exploratorium, the National Research Council, and the American Association for the Advancement of Science (AAAS) to tweak and refine your definition. As you continue through this book, you will use a constructivist approach to assimilate new information about inquiry and make accommodations in your own mental model while constructing a personal meaning for inquiry. Throughout this book, you will be asked to meditate on your statements and definitions for the purpose of assessing your "pre" and "post" understanding and determining how, if any, they are evolving.

If you need a suggested starting point, this simple graphic method may help you organize your thoughts (see Figure 2.2).

Figure 2.1 Concept Map

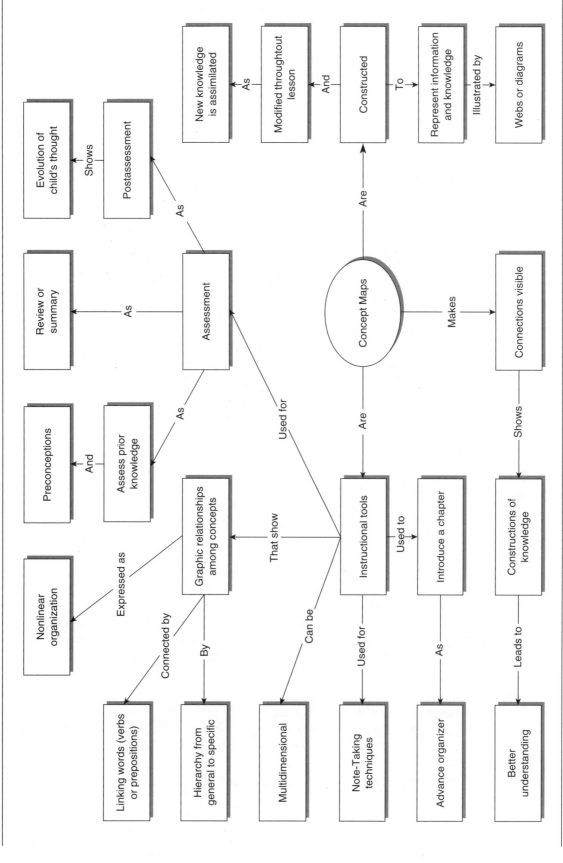

WHAT THE EXPERTS SAY

The Exploratorium in San Francisco is a hands-on science museum and professional development center for inquiry-based learning. In the fall of 1996, the Exploratorium's Institute for Inquiry held a forum in which researchers, teachers, and professional development specialists examined the topic of inquiry from the perspective of their different disciplines—science, mathematics, history, writing, and the arts. Prior to the forum, participants were asked to write short descriptions of inquiry from their professional perspectives. The following are selected descriptions[1] that pertain specifically to science.

> Philosophically, I find inquiry a wonderful metaphor for life. Interacting with phenomena in open-ended ways, following individualized learning paths and noticing everything that occurs, especially the oddities, is a fitting way to go through one's days whether practicing science, the arts, or life. . . . I have become convinced that although inquiry can be a highly personalized experience, it has structures and elements that can be explored and described. The "magic" can be examined and transformed into tools for those who want to teach it and practice it. (Doris Ash, science educator, Exploratorium)

> Inquiry . . . is a process of exploration which is guided by a personal interest or question. It involves risk taking and experimenting which can lead to pathways where the learner may discover meaningful concepts and understandings. (Marilyn Austin, teacher-in-residence, Exploratorium)

> Inquiry, to me, means pursuing a question and figuring out the solutions to problems through a process of observation, development of explanations (theories), testing these through experimentation, discussing the outcomes and adjusting theories based on the outcomes. These various steps are developed with the participation of all members of the class and always shared and debated in group discussions. . . . By listening to one another, and working to make sense of what others say, students are invited to broaden their notions of the topic and consider new ideas. (Mary DiSchino, teacher, Graham & Parks Alternative School, Cambridge, MA)

> Curiosity is the centerpiece of inquiry. . . . To inquire is to seek, obtain and make meaning from answers to one's questions. (Hubert Dyasi, Director, Workshop Center, City College of New York, School of Education)

> An inquiry approach to teaching stimulates curiosity by teaching children how to observe very closely, encourages children to take more than one quick look, provides adequate materials for exploration, and makes it safer for students to ask questions and to take risks. It helps them to make connections to events in their own lives, and gives them ownership of their learning. I believe that using inquiry can be a means for significant change in teaching in the schools, from providing an education that relies on memorization of facts to one that teaches thinking and problem-solving, and enhances the ability of students to relate what they learn to new problems that come up later. Equally important, teachers need to inquire into their own teaching

Figure 2.2 Scientific Inquiry

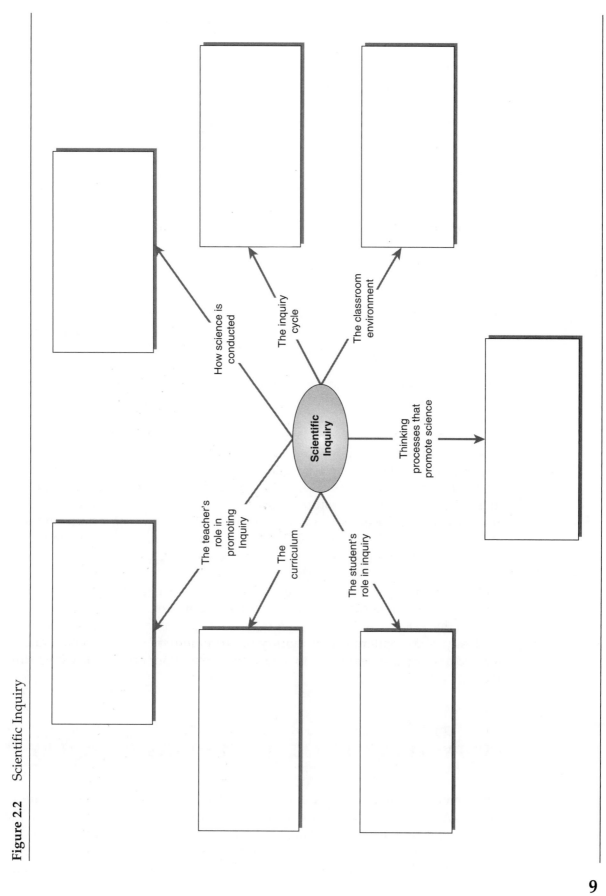

methods . . . constantly reflecting on their own teaching. (Cappy Greene, science educator, Exploratorium)

Inquiry is a major means for learners to extend their understanding of the natural and made environment. It is essentially active learning, inseparably combining mental and physical activity. The motivation for inquiry is within the learner and the learner's relation to the things around him or her. Inquiry starts with something that intrigues, that raises a question—something that is not presently understood, that does not fit with expectations, or just something that the learner wants to know about. . . . The process of inquiry involves linking previous information to the new experience in an attempt to make sense of the new. (Wynne Harlen, Director, Scottish Council for Research in Education, Edinburgh, Scotland)

Science inquiry consists of actions in the world that allow for multiple results. Any activity that is intended to lead to one result only should not be considered inquiry. The definition excludes almost all school laboratory work, because that usually is intended to demonstrate a concept, not general, novel or diverse activity. (George Hein, Director, Program Evaluation and Research Group, Lesley College, Cambridge, MA)

We were born doing science. By randomly touching objects and placing them in our mouths, we learned as toddlers what is hot or cold, sweet or sour, sharp or dull, rough or smooth. We learned almost everything through inquiry. Watching toys sink or float in the bathtub is/was a chance to investigate the principle of buoyancy. By playing catch, we made discoveries about gravity and trajectories. By building towers out of blocks, we explored principles of size, scale and center of mass. . . . Unfortunately, somewhere along the way we lose our natural curiosity about the world. It seems to happen when we are faced with our first science class. Science becomes a list of facts and formulas to memorize. Our natural instincts to do inquiry are suppressed. (Linda Shore, Co-Director, Teacher Institute, Exploratorium)

Did you find the statements interesting? Were the Exploratorium statements similar to yours? Go back to your definition and compare and contrast what you wrote with the statements you just read. How are your statements or definitions similar to those of the Exploratorium participants? How are they different? If you especially liked any of the statements you read, add them to your bulleted list, 3 × 5 cards, or concept map.

WHAT THE EXPLORATORIUM MEANS BY INQUIRY

The Exploratorium (n.d.) also provides several statements regarding the definition of inquiry. As you read these statements below, use them to reflect on your own thoughts about inquiry and to enhance your understanding. Again, you will be asked to reflect on the Exploratorium's definition of inquiry-based learning and compare it with the statements you wrote earlier. According to the Exploratorium:

Inquiry is an approach to learning that involves a process of exploring the natural or material world, and that leads to asking questions, making discoveries, and testing those discoveries in the search for new understanding. Inquiry, as it relates to science education, should mirror as closely as possible the enterprise of doing real science.

The inquiry process is driven by one's own curiosity, wonder, interest, or passion to understand an observation or to solve a problem.

The process begins when the learner notices something that intrigues, surprises, or stimulates a question—something that is new, or something that may not make sense in relationship to the learner's previous experience or current understanding.

The next step is to take action—through continued observing, raising questions, making predictions, testing hypotheses, and creating conceptual models.

The learner must find her or his own pathway through this process. It is rarely a linear progression, but rather more of a back-and-forth, or cyclical, series of events.

As the process unfolds, more observations and questions emerge, providing for deeper interaction with the phenomena—and greater potential for further development of understanding.

Along the way, the inquirer collects and records data, makes representations of results and explanations, and draws upon other resources such as books, videos, and the expertise or insights of others.

Making meaning from the experience requires reflection, conversation, comparison of findings with others, interpretation of data and observations, and the application of new conceptions to other contexts. All of these serve to help the learner construct an improved mental framework of the world.

Effective teachers rely on many different ways of teaching science. At the Institute for Inquiry we focus on inquiry learning, a powerful tool in learning science and in keeping wonder and curiosity alive in the classroom.

WHAT THE *NATIONAL SCIENCE EDUCATION STANDARDS* SAY ABOUT INQUIRY

In 1996, the NRC released the *National Science Education Standards* (NSES). In regard to the inquiry standards, the NRC states:

Inquiry is a multifaceted activity that involves making observations; posing questions; examining books and other sources of information to see what is already known in light of experimental evidence; using tools to gather, analyze, and interpret data; proposing answers, explanations, and predictions; and communicating the results. Inquiry requires identification of assumptions, use of critical and logical thinking, and consideration of alternative explanations. (p. 23)

The NRC (1996) standards highlight the ability to conduct inquiry and develop an understanding about scientific inquiry:

Students in all grade levels and in every domain of science should have the opportunity to use scientific inquiry and develop the ability to think and act in ways associated with inquiry, including asking questions, planning and conducting investigations, using appropriate tools and techniques to gather data, thinking critically and logically about the relationships between evidence and explanations, constructing and analyzing alternative explanations, and communicating scientific arguments. (p. 105)

The inquiry standards set forth by the NRC (1996) are divided into three separate grade levels or junctures: K–4, 5–8, and 9–12. Each juncture identifies content standards specific to those grade levels. The standards help science educators identify what students should know and be able to do at particular junctures. Reading and analyzing the standards for a particular juncture will result in a deeper understanding of inquiry. The standards can be ordered online from the National Academy Press (www.nap.edu/bookstore). You may also be interested in reading the NRC's accompanying text, *Inquiry and the National Science Education Standards: A Guide for Teaching and Learning* (2000; see Resource A).

The NSES clearly differentiates inquiry between a content goal and a teaching strategy. By reading the content standards for K–4 and 5–8, inquiry is presented as the abilities to do scientific inquiry as well as the understanding about scientific inquiry. According to the standards, "scientific inquiry refers to the diverse ways in which scientists study the natural world and propose explanations based on the evidence derived from their work. Inquiry also refers to the activities of students in which they develop knowledge and understanding of scientific ideas, as well as an understanding of how scientists study the natural world." (NRC, 1996, p. 23)

The abilities to do scientific inquiry include:

- Asking or identifying questions
- Planning and carrying out investigations
- Using equipment and tools to collect, analyze, and interpret data
- Using data and evidence to develop explanations and models
- Communicating the procedures of an investigation as well as the explanations

Whereas the understanding about scientific inquiry includes the following:

- Investigations involve asking questions
- Scientists use different kinds of investigations depending on the question being posed
- Scientists use simple equipment and tools, as well as advanced technology, to gather and analyze data
- Scientists develop explanations from observations and evidence
- Scientists communicate their finding so it can be skeptically reviewed by others
- Scientists review and ask questions of other scientists' work

The standards also refer to scientific inquiry as the way in which teachers teach science. The "Science Teaching Standards" outline key ideas in providing inquiry-based instruction. They include:

- Planning an inquiry-based program for students
- Guiding and facilitating instruction
- Engaging students in ongoing assessments
- Designing and managing an effective learning environment
- Developing a community of learners that reflects the rigor of scientific inquiry and the attitudes and values conducive to learning
- Actively planning and developing the science program

For further elaboration of NRC's meaning of inquiry, readers should consult the *National Science Education Standards* and other sources identified in Resource A.

WHAT THE AMERICAN ASSOCIATION FOR THE ADVANCEMENT OF SCIENCE SAYS ABOUT INQUIRY

In 1990, the AAAS published the first of two documents, *Science for All Americans*, which outlined a long-term view for instructional reform in science. It also marked the beginning of Project 2061 by the AAAS, which proposed recommendations for moving toward the goal of nationwide scientific literacy by 2061 (the year of the return of Halley's Comet). Following *Science for All Americans*, in 1993 the AAAS released *Benchmarks for Science Literacy*. It did not define curricular needs but instead identified specific outcomes for science education. Like the *NSES*, *Benchmarks* provided local school districts, state education agencies, and national science educational organizations with a blueprint for systemic reform.

Like the *NSES*, Project 2061 addressed the need for integrating scientific inquiry and content. Both the NRC (1996) *Standards* and the AAAS (1993) *Benchmarks* are divided into separate grade levels or junctures. The AAAS uses four junctures, as opposed to the three used by the NRC: Grades K–2, 3–5, 6–8, and 9–12. Both sets of standards are similar in approach and help educators identify what students should know and be able to do for the particular content area and juncture. At Grades 3–5, the AAAS (1993) says:

> Children's strategies for finding out more and more about their surroundings improve as they gain experience in conducting simple investigations of their own and working in small groups. They should be encouraged to observe more and more carefully, measure things with increasing accuracy, record data clearly in logs and journals, and communicate their results in charts and simple graphs as well as in prose. Time should be provided to let students run enough trials to be confident of their results. Investigations should often be followed up with presentations to the entire class to emphasize the importance of clear communication in science. Class discussions of the procedures and findings can provide the beginning of scientific argument and debate. Students' investigations at this level can be expected to bear on detecting the similarities and differences among the things they collect and examine. They should come to see that in trying to identify and explain the likenesses and differences, they are doing what goes on in science all the time. (p. 9)

At Grades 6–8, *Benchmarks* state, "Students need to become more systematic and sophisticated in conducting their investigations, some which may last for weeks or more. . . . The concept of controlling variables is straightforward but achieving it in practice is difficult" (p. 12). "By this level, students must assess the risks associated with an investigation before being permission to proceed . . . [and use] computers to collect, store, and retrieve data, to help in data analysis, to prepare tables and graphs and to write summary reports" (p. 17).

Reading the inquiry statements from *Benchmarks for Science Literacy* is strongly recommended, as is reading *Standards*. *Benchmarks* can be purchased through or downloaded from the AAAS Web site (www.aaas.org). You may also be interested in the AAAS's accompanying text, *Inquiring Into Inquiry Learning and Teaching in Science* (Minstrell & Van Zee, 2000) (see Resource A).

WHAT THE NATIONAL SCIENCE TEACHERS ASSOCIATION SAYS ABOUT INQUIRY

As mentioned in the Preface, in 2000 the National Science Teachers Association (NSTA) adopted a position statement on Scientific Inquiry. I highly recommend reading this NSTA position statement.

After reading the position statement, go back once again to your definition of inquiry and compare it with the statements from the NRC, the AAAS, and the NSTA. How is your definition of inquiry similar to and different from those of the *NSES*, the AAAS *Benchmarks*, and the position statement? This time, make your additions or corrections to your concept map by using a different color. With successive additions and corrections, continue to use a different color. This will allow you to capture, visually and over time, how your understanding about inquiry is evolving.

MYTHS ABOUT SCIENTIFIC INQUIRY

So far we have been reading what scientific inquiry is. Now, we will address what inquiry is not by exploring several commonly held myths and misconceptions. If your statements or concept map reveals any of the myths and misconceptions described next, you can alter them accordingly.

1. Doing hands-on science is the same as doing scientific inquiry.

Providing students with an opportunity to do hands-on science does not necessarily mean they are doing inquiry. Many science activities are very structured. They tell the students what question to answer, what materials to use, and how to go about solving the question or problem. In most cases, they even provide charts or tables to record the observations, measurements, or data. This type of *cookbook* activity provides step-by-step procedures and follows a linear path to a solution. Although most inquiry activities are hands-on, not all hands-on activities are inquiry-oriented. Others may even suggest that some student inquiries, like those involving Internet researching, can be minds-on and not hands-on.

2. Doing scientific inquiry results in students knowing about scientific inquiry.

An implicit assumption teachers may hold is that if they provide their students with opportunities to do inquiry, students will come to know about inquiry. This idea likely parallels the Nike saying, "Just do it!" Lederman (2006) suggests, however, that "such an expectation is equivalent to assuming that individuals will come to understand . . . photosynthesis by watching a plant grow" (p. 315). Students come to know about scientific inquiry by modeling the process, reflecting on the scientific endeavor itself, and engaging in constructive arguments, negotiation, and skepticism regarding the evidence and explanations provided and the role the findings play within the community of science.

3. Inquiry is using the scientific method.

As stated by the AAAS (1993), doing inquiry does not necessarily imply following the steps of the scientific method. Many contemporary science educators will argue that there is no *one* scientific method; in fact, there are many methods to do science. While Schwartz and Crawford (2006) suggest a multiplicity of scientific methods, others (Lederman, Abd-El-Khalick, Bell, & Schwartz, 2002) go so far as to say that the scientific method is actually a myth, despite what many science textbooks propose. Inquiry uses a logical approach to solving scientific questions but does not necessarily use the delineated, specific steps of a scientific method. Understanding the overall intention of a scientific method has a role in planning investigations; however, there is more to inquiry than a sequential set of procedures. As stated by the NRC (1996), "In the vision presented by the *Standards*, inquiry is a step beyond "science as a process," in which students learn skills, such as observation, inference, and experimentation. The new vision includes the 'processes of science' and requires that students combine processes and scientific knowledge as they use scientific reasoning and critical thinking to develop their understanding of science" (p. 105). Chapter 7 further explains how teachers use the logic of the organized thought processes to plan scientific investigations.

4. Inquiry is unstructured and chaotic.

In some schools, the sign of a good teacher is a classroom that is quiet and under control. Classroom management skills are essential for inquiry learning, but an active, child-centered classroom should not be equated with chaos or unstructured instruction. When students do hands-on and manipulation-based science, we can expect the noise level to rise somewhat. On the surface, inquiry may appear to be open-ended and unstructured; however, as student involvement increases, so does the need for the teacher to manage classroom movement and communication. When teachers use inquiry-based strategies, they may find that teaching requires more preparation and anticipation of possible student questions than do traditional teaching approaches. Bell and Gilbert (1996) report that teachers new to inquiry often feel less in control when students move about the room, make decisions about their work, and are encouraged to challenge the work of others. Although most teachers actually maintain control, they may perceive otherwise. To establish inquiry-centered environments, teachers must accept changes in their role and changes in the culture of the classroom.

5. Inquiry is asking students a lot of questions.

A common misconception held by science teachers is that inquiry requires asking a battery of questions. You may have sat in many science classrooms where the teacher fired off question after question. Asking a lot of questions does not neces-sarily make an inquiry lesson. Chapter 10 presents several examples of effective questioning strategies, such as probing, prompting, and redirecting, that support inquiry settings. In inquiry-centered classrooms, teachers provide open-ended expe-riences that lead students to raise their own questions and design investigations to answer them.

*6. If I provide opportunities for my students to **do** inquiry, they will be learning **about** inquiry.*

This is a typical belief of many elementary and middle school teachers. Contrary to this popular, yet naïve, conception, no substantial research indicates that when students are actively engaged in scientific inquiry they are implicitly learning about scientific inquiry and the nature of science. To promote a deep understanding of scientific inquiry and nature of science, teachers must follow up an investigation with explicit "coaching" explanations and scaffolding discussions about the selec-tion of the questions, the procedures selected, and thus evaluating and debating the evidence and claims generated from the investigation. Furthermore, teachers need to vary the inquiry landscape by providing natural opportunities for both low-level and high-level interventions. In the vignettes that follow, look for instances in which the teacher concludes an exploration or investigation with explicit science language and instruction to enhance students' abilities about scientific inquiry. Balancing the "implicit-explicit continuum" (Holliday, 2006) within science inquiry teaching should be a goal of all effective inquiry-based teachers.

7. Inquiry is fine for elementary school students, but middle school science teachers don't have extra time in their courses.

For many secondary school science teachers, lecture and discussion methods are the primary means of delivering content instruction to students. These teachers per-ceive lecturing as the most effective and efficient way to transmit large amounts of science information to their students in a relatively short period of time. Lecturing is the method by which many teachers learned science when they were in high school and college. With this as their prior experience, why should we be surprised that so many science classes are lecture-based?

Secondary school science teachers often talk about time constraints. With more and more concepts being added to the curriculum, many middle school science teachers say they are hard pressed to cover a great number of concepts within the school year. It is true that inquiry-based learning takes more time; however, devel-oping higher-level thinking skills and having students pose questions, plan solu-tions, and collect and organize data are skills that must be practiced and nurtured over time. There are no shortcuts to developing critical thinking skills. To create inquiry-based curricula or classrooms, teachers need to use their instructional time effectively while presenting topics and concepts at the core of the curriculum.

8. You can't assess inquiry-based learning.

Inquiry-based learning can be assessed like any other concept or topic in science. To assess student progress in inquiry-based learning, teachers need to use alternative methods of evaluation. For inquiry-based learning, popular objective-type multiple-choice questions do not provide adequate assessments of student progress. Inquiry-based teachers often rely on student portfolios, student journal entries, student self-assessments, and rubrics in conjunction with objective-type questions to assess students' academic progress. Examples of each of these alternative assessment measures are presented in Chapter 8.

9. Inquiry is the latest "fad" for science education.

Those who have studied the history of science education know that questioning, discovery learning, and inquiry date back to the early days of the Greek scholar Socrates. Progressive education reformer John Dewey is credited as being one of the first American educators to stress the importance of discovery learning and inquiry (Dewey, 1900, 1902, 1916). In his early work, Dewey proposed that learning does not start and intelligence is not engaged until the learner is confronted with a problematic situation. Inquiry was also the basis for several elementary school science programs funded by the National Science Foundation in the mid-1960s, based in part on the work of Joseph Schwab (1962). During this "golden age" of science education, programs such as Science—A Process Approach (SAPA), Elementary Science Study (ESS), and Science Curriculum Improvement Study (SCIS) were all based on the philosophy of integrating inquiry teaching and learning with science process skills. On the secondary school level, premier high school biology programs such as the Biological Sciences Curriculum Study (BSCS) (1970) are deeply rooted in instructional methods of learning that stress the importance of inquiry-based instruction. Today, nearly every elementary and middle school science textbook or hands-on science program proclaims inquiry as some aspect of the program.

10. Inquiry is "soft science" and not content related.

We sometimes hear critics of inquiry-based instruction call inquiry "science lite." Inquiry, according to both the *NSES* and *Benchmarks for Science Literacy*, is one of the areas identified as content. That elevates inquiry to the same level as knowing the concepts, principles, and theories of life, earth, or the physical sciences. According to the AAAS (1990), "Science teaching that attempts solely to impart to students the accumulated knowledge of a field leads to very little understanding and certainly . . . science teachers should help students to acquire both scientific knowledge of the world and scientific habits of mind at the same time" (p. 203).

If students are to gain an appreciation for science and compete in a scientific and technical society in this new millennium, they will require a program that promotes active learning, raising questions, opportunities to solve their questions as well as discourse and reflection. Within the last several years, much has been written about inquiry-based science as an effective means to enhance scientific literacy (Bybee, 1997, 2002). Additional research has led to the conclusion that inquiry promotes critical thinking skills and positive attitudes toward science. Although inquiry is no panacea, it is one more strategy teachers can use, at the appropriate time, to engage students in investigations and satisfy their curiosity for learning (Haury, 1993).

11. Inquiry is for high-achieving students and not for students with special needs or learning disabilities.

The recommendations set forth by both the NRC (1996) and the AAAS (1993) apply to all students regardless of age, cultural or ethnic heritage, gender, physical or academic ability, interest, or aspirations. The AAAS (1990) stresses that the recommendations apply in particular to those who historically have been underrepresented in the fields of science—mainly students of color, female students, limited English proficiency students, and persons with disabilities. According to *NSES*,

"Given this diversity of student needs, experiences and backgrounds, and the goal that all students will achieve a common set of standards, schools must support high-quality, diverse, and varied opportunities to learn science" (NRC, 1996, p. 221). The ability to think creatively and critically is not solely for the high-achieving student. Inquiry-based instruction can and should be taught equitably at all levels.

12. Doing school-based science inquiry is the same as authentic scientific inquiry as practiced by career scientists.

Although teachers often tell students during their science investigations they are "acting and thinking like scientists," in reality, given the obvious limitations in time, materials, and the curriculum, classroom or school-based inquiries are quite different from authentic inquiries practiced in the scientific community. The apparent differences include the level of knowledge, sophistication, and level of scientific reasoning one brings to the activity. Although we encourage students to think like a scientist, use the scientific processes scientists use, and foster critical thinking skills, we need to understand classroom constraints. For that reason, all the scientific investigations in this book fall under the category of school-based science inquiry.

INQUIRY AS A THINKING SKILL

Learning through inquiry empowers students with the skills and knowledge to become independent, lifelong learners. Finding solutions to their own questions also allows students to gain an appreciation for scientific knowledge and the discovery process. Through inquiry, students are easily able to assimilate and anchor their prior experiences and knowledge with newly formed experiences and knowledge.

Hunkins (1995) says:

The good thinker, possessing attributes enabling him or her to create and use meaning—to add to knowledge and culture—possesses a spirit of inquiry, a desire to pose questions central to [his or her] world. The good thinker ponders [his or her] world, actual and desired, querying things valued and desired. (p. 18)

Hunkins goes on to say:

These individuals realize that productive inquiry essentially starts with the articulation of personal concerns or questions. In many ways, this is a major shift, for students have been taught to wait for the authority, usually the teacher or textbook author, to furnish the problem, define the questions, and suggest the solutions. Indeed, in many schools, students are not challenged to make meaning; rather, they are asked to remember the meaning of others. (p. 19)

Hester (1994) reminds us that inquiry involves

critical thinking processes such as methods of diagnosis, speculation and hypothesis testing. The method of inquiry gives students the opportunity to confront problems and generate and test ideas for themselves. . . . The emphasis is on ways of examining and explaining information (events, facts, situations, behaviors, etc.). Students, when taught for the purposes embodied in inquiry, are encouraged to evaluate the usefulness of their beliefs and ideas by applying them to new problem situations and inferring from them implications for future courses of action. (pp. 116–117)

"INQUIRING WITH FRUIT"

Now that we have expanded our understanding of inquiry, let's consider a group of seventh-grade students exploring the properties of fruit, raising questions, testing their ideas, and discovering new concepts in density. The objective of this lesson is to allow students to explore the properties of fruit and raise questions to investigate. In this session, students are given the task of predicting whether a particular group of fruits will float or sink when placed in a two-gallon tub of water. (The names of the teacher and students are fictitious.)

"Inquiring With Fruit" aligns with the *National Science Education Standards* (NSES) (NRC, 1996) for Grades 5–8:

Science as Inquiry Standards

Students will

- Identify questions that can be answered through scientific inquiry (p. 145)
- Design and conduct a scientific investigation (p. 145)
- Think critically and logically to make the relationship between evidence and explanations (p. 145)
- Communicate scientific procedures and explanations (p. 148)

Physical Science Standard

- A substance has characteristic properties (such as density), all of which are independent of the amount of the sample. (p. 154)

As the lesson begins, Mr. Roberts assesses the students' prior knowledge and preconceptions about fruits that float and sink. He poses the question, "What would happen if I place this apple in the tub of water?" The unanimous response is that the apple would float. As Mr. Roberts lowers the apple into the tub, the students' prediction proves correct. "Now," he says, "what would happen if I cut the apple in half and placed it back into the tub?" He goes on to say, "Take time to predict whether you think the apple will float, sink, or maintain a position half way down the tub." Mr. Roberts encourages them to record a prediction and to provide the reasoning for the prediction. He then takes time for students to share their predictions in small groups and discuss the reasoning for their answers. Mr. Roberts circulates from one group to another listening to their conversations and noting any misconceptions that arise. After a while Mr. Roberts says, "Let's test our half apple." He lowers the apple into the tub and the students observe that the half apple still floats.

After the demonstration, Mr. Roberts says, "It's time to move on to less familiar fruits." Each student has an opportunity to observe (using all five senses) a lemon, a kiwi, a grape, a banana, an orange, and a mango and make predictions about whether each one will float or sink when placed in a tub of water. After the students assign each fruit with either an "F" or an "S" marked on their worksheets, they *pair and share*, exchanging their fruit predictions. During this part of the activity, Mr. Roberts encourages students to provide explanations of their thinking to support their individual predictions. Students then rearrange their desks in groups to discuss their different predictions. After 10 minutes, the groups are told to produce a group consensus for each fruit. Each group is then asked to record its predictions, test each fruit, and record the results.

As the students test each prediction, they record their data by constructing a table with two columns, *floaters* and *sinkers* (see Figure 2.3).

Figure 2.3 Floaters and Sinkers

Inquiring with fruit results

Floaters	Sinkers

At this point, Mr. Roberts encourages the students to go beyond the initial exploration and raise their own "What if" and "I wonder" questions. In one group, Kayla asks, "Does the outer peel of a fruit affect whether it will float or sink?" She leads her group through a brainstorming session to determine ways to test whether a peeled banana versus an unpeeled banana will float or sink. They decide to place one peeled and one unpeeled banana in the tub and compare the results. They soon observe that both bananas float and conclude that the peel makes no difference.

As Kayla observes the floating banana with the ends pointed downward in the water, she calls Mr. Roberts over to her table and asks, "Why is the banana floating upside down?" (see Figure 2.4).

Mr. Roberts probes her thinking to determine the root of the question. Kayla admits that she thought the banana would float with the ends upright, like a "banana boat" (see Figure 2.5). Mr. Roberts quickly realizes that she was using her prior understanding about bananas and boats to predict that the ends of the banana would float upright, like a boat!

Figure 2.4   Banana Floating With Pointed Ends Down

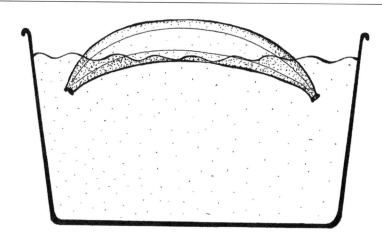

Figure 2.5   Banana Floating With Pointed Ends Up

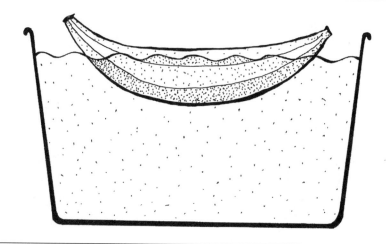

Kayla's group proceeds to discuss floating and sinking in relation to the term *density*. They all know that objects less dense than water float and objects denser than water sink. Mr. Roberts suggests that they apply the principle to the floating banana. There is still confusion, however, about why the banana doesn't float like a boat. Frank, another member of the group, poses the question to the teacher, "What would happen if we cut the banana in half?" Rather than answering the question, Mr. Roberts assumes that the group can answer the question without his help, so he responds, "How could you find out?" Frank shares his thoughts about the floating banana and suggests a procedure to test his question.

As the group decides on a plan of action, Frank pulls the banana from the tub and cuts it in half. Just before Frank is about to place the two halves back in the water, Mr. Roberts says, "Wait! What do you think will happen to each half of the banana?" Debbie predicts that each half will float with the pointed end downward.

Figure 2.6   Two Halves of a Banana Floating

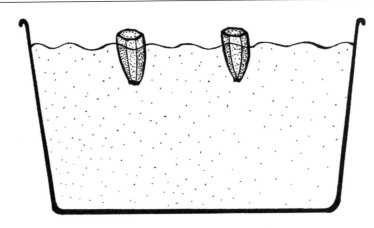

Then Rob asks her to support her prediction. Debbie responds by saying that the ends probably will act the same as they did when the banana was whole. Figure 2.6 shows how the two halves look after they're placed in the water.

The observation spurs "Wows" and more "What if" questions. Next, Sara asks, "What if we cut each of the halves in half again?" Frank then cuts each banana in half again and, just before lowering the banana quarters into the water, he jokingly asks the other group members, "What is going to happen when I drop these pieces into the water?" Their inquiry leads to more observations (see Figure 2.7).

Seeing the ends of the banana at the bottom of the tub and the two middle quarters floating on top leads the group to conclude that the banana must be denser at the ends and less dense in the middle. They analyze their results and use an illustration to draw a model of the density of a banana (see Figure 2.8).

Having their observations fit their newly developed model, the group members are confident that they understand why the banana floated "upside down."

Figure 2.7   Banana Pieces Floating and Sinking

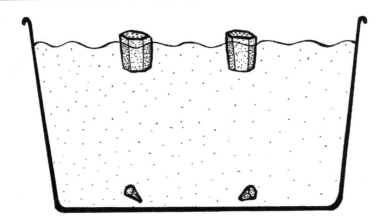

Figure 2.8   Model of Banana Density

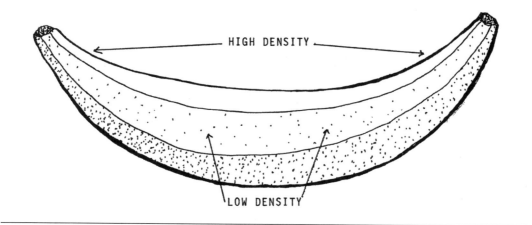

Mr. Roberts suggests that the group members look up the formula for density and actually measure the mass and volume of the banana pieces to confirm their model mathematically and share their discovery with the rest of the class. Excited with their new findings, Kayla, Frank, Debbie, Rob, and Sara search their textbooks for a way to calculate density.

The following day, Mr. Roberts reviews the investigation skills the group used as part of their inquiries. He also spends time clarifying their understanding about scientific inquiry and the newly acquired content regarding density. Mr. Roberts knows he needs to provide closure to this investigation by explicitly discussing and reflecting with his students on the procedures they developed. He suggests they consider alternative explanations based on the evidence collected and how different groups in the class may have made different conclusions from the same investigations.

Not surprisingly, his students have more inquiries to explore. Kayla wants to know if fresh bananas float differently from overripe ones. Frank suggests they test larger bananas versus smaller ones. Debbie and Sara suggest they test bananas versus plantains, and Rob intends to find out how a banana would float if he placed it in saltwater as compared with fresh water. Although their questions will keep them busy for several days, it's time for Mr. Roberts to provide a teacher-led lesson on density and how to calculate the density of a solid object using the formula $D = M/V$.

As a paper-and-pencil assessment, Mr. Roberts provides students with the formula for density along with the mass and volume of several fruits. Their task is to use the formula and data to calculate the density of each fruit and sequence the fruits from the least to the most dense. The second part of the assessment involves an application-level question where students are given the problem: Suppose you have a bar of candy. If you cut the bar of candy in half, what will happen to the candy's density? Will it increase, decrease, or remain the same? Provide a justification for your answer. The third part of the assessment involves a performance task. Here the students are shown how to calculate the volume of an irregular solid (the fruit) by displacement. Given a triple beam balance and the equipment for measuring volume by displacement, each student is given three different pieces of fruit and must determine the density of each fruit and again sequence the fruits from the least to the most dense.

THE INQUIRY CYCLE

"Inquiring With Fruit" is just one example of an exploration that encourages students to raise questions and think critically. Although different kinds of questions require different kinds of investigations, in analyzing the group's work, the *inquiry cycle* shown in Figure 2.9 represents aspects of many scientific investigations:

1. *Inquisition*—stating a "What if" or "I wonder" question to be investigated

2. *Acquisition*—brainstorming possible procedures

3. *Supposition*—identifying an "I think" statement to test

4. *Implementation*—designing and carrying out a plan

5. *Summation*—collecting evidence and drawing explanations

6. *Exhibition*—communicating and sharing explanations with others

During the inquisition phase, students usually initiate their inquiry by posing a question. It is often stated as a "What if" question and can originate from observing an open-ended exploration, a discrepant event, a demonstration, or a teacher-directed activity. Teachers often plan explorations that end with an observation that

Figure 2.9　The Inquiry Cycle

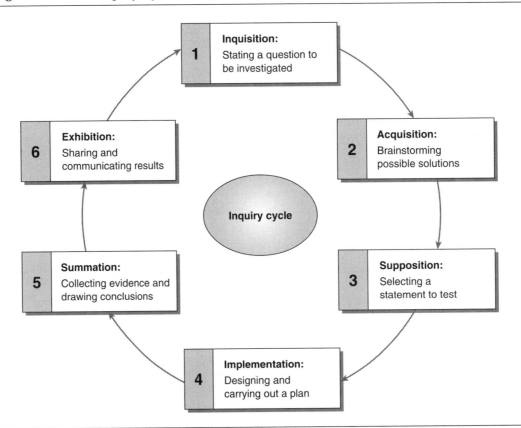

is counterintuitive to students' normal experience. The event seeds disequilibrium in the students' minds and causes them to ask "Why?" Educators often call this a teachable moment, when a student raises a question and opens his or her mind to imagination. In the "Inquiring With Fruit" investigation, the inquisition phase is initiated by the predicting activity.

During the acquisition phase, students rely on their prior experience to brainstorm possible solutions to the inquiry. Here students ask, "What do I already know about this situation that could help answer the question?" In the acquisition phase of the fruit activity, Kayla's prior conceptions about bananas and floating affect how she perceives the outcome of the group's question.

During the supposition phase, students consolidate the information under study to propose an "I think" statement. This phase generally includes a design of the plan to answer the question under investigation. During the fruit activity, Frank provides leadership to the group in identifying possible statements to test.

During the implementation phase, students design a plan to investigate the phenomenon in question and carry out the plan.

During the summation phase, students record and analyze their observations to use them to address the original "What if" question. Mr. Roberts also encourages further investigations by suggesting that the group confirm its results by calculating the density of each banana piece. During the summation phase, students are often led to other discrepancies and "What if" questions, returning the group to the inquisition phase.

During the exhibition phase, the students communicate their findings and new information in the form of a written report, a poster or trifold display, or an oral or PowerPoint presentation. In the fruit activity lesson, the group is eager to share its discovery and new knowledge about density.

The inquiry cycle can serve as a general format for teachers planning inquiry-based investigations for their students. You should be reminded that the model serves as a general approach to raising and answering questions. Following the inquiry cycle, students often enter and reenter the phases at different aspects of their inquiry process. Thus, the cycle serves as a model to guide students through their investigations, rather than a linear, sequential, "step-by-step" procedure.

Similarly, Hubert Dyasi and Karen Worth (n.d.) describe the process through which knowledge about the natural world is developed. Figure 2.10 shows the dynamic and cyclical nature of scientific inquiry.

A DEFINITION OF INQUIRY

From the previous readings we see that inquiry has a three-prong meaning. According to Flick and Lederman (2006), "inquiry stands for a fundamental principle of how modern science is conducted. Inquiry refers to a variety of processes and ways of thinking that support the development of new knowledge in science. In addition to the *doing* of science, inquiry also refers to knowledge *about* the processes scientists use to develop knowledge that is the *nature of science itself*. Thus, inquiry is viewed as two different student outcomes, ability to *do* scientific processes and the knowledge *about* the processes" (p. ix).

Figure 2.10 The Scientific Inquiry Cycle

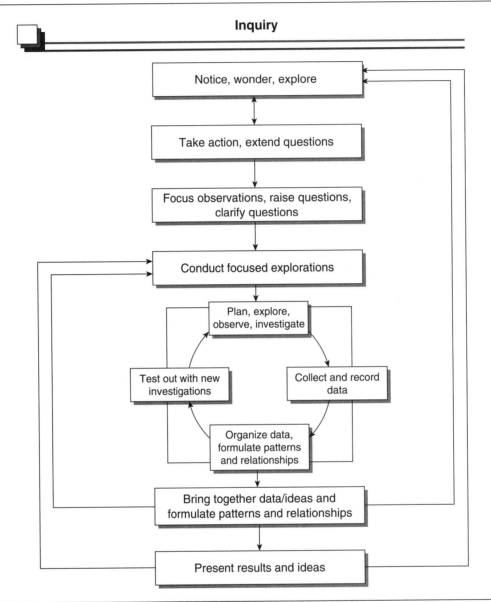

SOURCE: Dyasi and Worth (n.d., http://cse.edc.org/products/inquiryscienceelemclassroom/Inquiry.pdf).

The third prong of its meaning has to do with teachers using an inquiry approach as a means to teach students science content and the methods and processes scientists use. Flick and Lederman (2006) go on to say that "the logic here is that students will best learn science if they learn using a reasonable facsimile of the processes scientists follow" (p. x). Thus for effective inquiry instruction, science teachers need to balance both the understanding *about* scientific inquiry and the abilities in *doing* scientific inquiry.

Inquiry involves the science, art, and spirit of curiosity. It can be further explained as the scientific process of active exploration by which we use critical, logical, and creative thinking skills to raise and engage in questions of personal interest. Driven by our curiosity and wonder about observed phenomena, doing inquiry investigations usually involves eight essential aspects:

1. Generating a science-related question or problem to be solved, one that physically, mentally, and personally engages the student

2. Brainstorming possible solutions

3. Formulating a statement to investigate

4. Designing an action plan and carrying out the procedures of the investigation

5. Gathering and recording evidence and data through observation and instrumentation

6. Drawing appropriate conclusions and explanations from the evidence

7. Connecting the explanation to previously held knowledge

8. Communicating the conclusions and explanations with others

As we communicate and share our explanations, inquiry assists in (a) connecting our prior understanding to new experiences, (b) modifying and accommodating our previously held beliefs and conceptual models, (c) providing opportunities for discourse, and (d) constructing new knowledge. In constructing newly formed knowledge, students generally are cycled back into the processes and pathways of inquiry with new questions and discrepancies to investigate.

Finally, learning through inquiry empowers students with the knowledge, skills, and attitudes to become independent thinkers. In many ways, it is a preparation for lifelong learning, fostering curiosity and creativity. Teachers can encourage students to use communication, manipulation, and problem-solving skills to increase their awareness and interest in science, setting them on the path to becoming scientifically literate citizens. For science teachers, the inquiry approach requires a different mindset and expectations. At first, inquiry can be both seductive and intimidating to the novice teacher. As teachers come to understand the role they play in facilitating an inquiry-based classroom, the transition from a teacher-centered to a learner-centered classroom becomes promising. For this reason, rather than just providing a compendium of inquiry activities, the book principally emphasizes understanding the philosophical ideology and role-changing process considered necessary for inquiry instruction.

INQUIRY AND SCIENTIFIC LITERACY

When we define a scientifically literate individual, Flick and Lederman (2006) suggest that contemporary conceptions include the foundations of scientific inquiry and the nature of science. When we think of a literate person, we may also picture one educated with specific knowledge and skills, and having certain dispositions in a particular subject matter. It is the intention, therefore, to provide some discussion on the relationship among all three ideas. Having defined scientific inquiry, we now move on to scientific literacy and the nature of science.

In the area of science, the AAAS, in *Science for All Americans* (1990), defines a scientifically literate person as possessing several facets: a familiarity with the natural world and its unity; an understanding of key laws, principles, and theories that govern science; the capacity to think scientifically, knowing that science, like mathematics and technology, is a human endeavor with its own strengths and limitations; and the ability to use scientific knowledge and process to address personal and societal challenges. The *Standards* take a similar approach, stating "Scientific literacy is the knowledge and understanding of scientific concepts and process required for personal decision making, participation in civic and cultural affairs, and economics productivity" (NRC, 1996, p. 22). As a lifelong process, developing from the school years and throughout adulthood, attaining scientific literacy, as the *Standards* go on to state, means "a person can ask, find, or determine answers to questions derived from curiosity about everyday experiences. It means the individual has the ability to describe, explain, and predict natural phenomenon" (NRC, 1996, p. 22). From these definitions, we begin to appreciate the impossibility of divorcing inquiry from its underpinning, that of scientific literacy. Becoming scientifically literate equates to understanding scientific inquiry; the two are tightly coupled.

As do many others, Bybee (1997) and the NRC (1998) suggest that achieving science literacy means achieving for *all* students, not different standards or different instructional programs for particular groups of students. In a democratic society, we should seek attainment for all equally, and without exception. Given this goal, the challenges facing teachers today put a tremendous burden on them, especially when considering the amount of subject content being pushed into the schools' curricula and loaded into high-stakes standardized testing throughout America's schools. Just looking at the number of pages in a typical middle school science textbook today causes us to think about how much content is demanded of today's students. It is not unusual to find a middle-school science textbook with 400 to 500 pages these days.

Despite these demands, science educators need to look no further than the morning newspaper to read about the new technological advances and potential hazards we encounter each day: acid rain, global warming, environmental pollution, cloning, new semiconductors, new viruses, new galaxies, new fuels, and new practically everything else. The rational decision-making process about these growing issues and technologies will necessitate a scientifically literate population.

James Trefil provides us with a broadened scope of the issue. According to Trefil (2003):

> a person is scientifically literate if he or she can deal with scientific matters that come across the horizon of public life with the same ease as an educated person would exhibit in dealing with matters political, legal, or economic. In a society that is becoming increasingly driven by science and technology, a society in which the citizenry is increasingly called upon to deal with issues that contain a large scientific or technical component, this kind of literacy isn't a luxury—it's a necessity. (p. 151)

Several proponents of science literacy (DeBoer, 2000; Shamos, 1995; Sutman, 1996, 2001) suggest that achieving a citizenry that is scientifically literate will be difficult, if not impossible, unless educators at the elementary and secondary school levels become clear themselves about the meaning of literacy for their particular field, and practice the reform efforts proclaimed by the *Benchmarks* and the *National Science Education Standards*. So what needs to happen? At the K–12 level, teachers need to hone their understanding of what it means to be scientifically literate, read books and articles on the subject, and have in-depth discussions about its impact in today's classrooms. Curriculum coordinators need to emphasize an inquiry-based approach for all students throughout all levels of the district's learning outcomes. Science supervisors need to provide teachers with effective and ongoing professional development that advances the *Standards*, science literacy, and inquiry-based learning. School administrators need to hire teachers familiar with the *Standards*, with the competencies to teach through inquiry-based and problem-solving modes, and with the ability to create learner-centered classrooms. It is only through a multifaceted approach that school districts will achieve literacy in science for their students.

On July 20, 1999, the 30th anniversary of the first landing on the moon, then Secretary of Education Richard Riley appointed former astronaut and senator from Ohio, John Glenn, to chair a 25-member commission of blue-ribbon educators charged with the task to investigate and report on the state of mathematics and science in the nation. In *Before It's Too Late* (U.S. Department of Education, 2000), the commission suggested ways to improve the recruitment, preparation, retention, and professional growth for America's K–12 math and science teachers. In addressing mathematical and scientific literacy, the commission made targeted recommendations for school boards and superintendents, principals, teachers, parents, state education leaders, institutions of higher education, and businesses to raise student achievement. In the report, the commission set forth three goals:

1. To establish an ongoing system to improve the quality of mathematics and science teaching in Grades K–12

2. To increase significantly the number of mathematics and science teachers and improve the quality of their preparation

3. To improve the working environment and make the teaching profession more attractive for K–12 mathematics and science teachers

The full report with a supplementary video identifies the need for scientific literacy and is available free online at www.ed.gov/pubs/edpubs.html or at www .ed.gov/inits/Math/glenn/index.html.

Readers may be interested in the NSTA position statement on *Science, Technology, and Society* (STS), which addresses several aspects of science literacy, making it a goal for all students. For the STS position statement, go to www.nsta.org/position statement&psid=34.

INQUIRY AND THE NATURE OF SCIENCE

Understanding how science works is vital to understanding how scientific inquiry works. Recently, the nature of science (NOS) has received an unpretentious rebirth in its place and influence in science instruction; part of this renewed emphasis is due to the *National Science Education Standards* (see NRC, 1996, pp. 141 and 170-171). The *Standards* devote one section specifically to the history and nature of science and encourage elementary and middle school teachers to teach science as a human endeavor, focusing on how people of all backgrounds have applied their skills of insight, inquiry, and investigation to contribute to our understanding of how the natural world works.

The nature of science, according to McComas (2004), "is the sum total of the 'rules of the game' leading to knowledge production and the evaluation of truth claims in the natural sciences" (p. 25). McClough and Olsen (2004) add, "Understanding how science works is crucial to scientific literacy because bound up in the content and public decisions involving science are issues regarding what science is, how knowledge comes to be accepted, and what science can and cannot do" (p. 28). Similarly, Lederman (2006) says "The phrase 'nature of science' typically refers to the epistemology of science, science as a way of knowing, or the values and beliefs inherent to scientific knowledge" (p. 303) and that several aspects of nature of science are viewed as important to include in science curriculum and instruction:

- Science knowledge is tentative and subject to change,
- Science knowledge is empirically based and in part derived from observations of the natural world,
- Science knowledge is human enterprise, subjective, and based on individual or group interpretations, and
- Science knowledge may be interpreted through several possible explanations for a particular phenomenon.

Scientific inquiry is often confused with the nature of science (Lederman & Lederman, 2004), although they overlap and share many similar principles. Both rely on empirical evidence to formulate and justify conclusions. As with inquiry, the nature of science involves interpreting data and evidence; however, two researchers (or students) can derive conflicting results from the same set of data. According to the *Standards*, "although scientists may disagree about the explanations of phenomena . . . they do agree that questioning . . . and open communication are integral to the process of science" (NRC, 1996, p. 171).

For a further explanation of the NOS, read the NSTA's position statement on the *Nature of Science* at www.nsta.org/positionstatement&psid=22.

It is important that teachers encourage habits of mind that complement scientific inquiry and the nature of science. These habits include attitudes and behaviors in a creative and humanistic endeavor: commitment, curiosity, diligence, fairness, imagination, innovation, integrity, persistence, and patience, as well as skepticism—all the attributes we want children to demonstrate as they investigate their natural world.

As previously mentioned, inquiry and the nature of science have a subjective element (McComas, 2004). As with the construction of knowledge, science itself is tentative at best. Ideas and theories are constantly evolving based on newly discovered evidence. Every day, new species of organisms are being found in remote corners of the world, new remedies and drugs are being formulated to control diseases once thought to be uncontrollable, and new discoveries in space test our understanding of the cosmos. From an understanding of science as a human activity, scientific inquiry and the nature of science both provide avenues to bring historical relevance to our lessons. By discussing the biographies of scientists in class, history tells the story of discoveries and dispels the stereotypic notion of what a scientist looks like or that scientists work alone in isolated laboratories. Adding the human aspect to our lessons also provides opportunities to explain the contributions made by people representing historically underrepresented groups in science: women, African Americans, Hispanics, Latinos, and physically disabled scientists. According to the

Standards, "Many people have contributed to the traditions of science. Studying some of these individuals provides further understanding of scientific inquiry, science as a human endeavor, the nature of science, and the relationships between science and society" (NRC, 1996, p. 171).

INQUIRY AND NATURALISTIC INTELLIGENCE

Theories on learning and human intelligence have been around throughout the twentieth century and continue to develop. With recent research on brain functioning and cognitive development, however, new theories on intelligence have emerged. This section of the chapter will focus on Howard Gardner and his work with Project Zero at Harvard University. In 1983, Gardner published his landmark book, *Frames of Mind*, and proposed that human intellect was far more involved than what can be measured by a single test determining intelligence, the IQ score. Utilizing research from cognitive development, psychology, and sociology, Gardner proposed that questions from an IQ test too narrowly define intelligence. According to Gardner, IQ is reliable in predicting mental reasoning but does not take into account other abilities and talents that individuals possess. In *Frames of Mind*, Gardner proposes that humans can demonstrate multiple intelligences (MI), other than linguistic forms, and he suggested that human intellect is not fixed throughout one's lifetime. He put forward seven types of intelligence, each with its own distinctiveness. Gardner's theory of multiple intelligences discusses various types of intelligence:

Verbal/linguistic

Logical/mathematical

Visual/spatial

Bodily/kinesthetic

Musical

Interpersonal

Intrapersonal

People with *verbal/linguistic* intelligence are skilled with the spoken and written word. Although everyone has some degree of verbal/linguistic intelligence, Gardner believes that certain individuals demonstrate an ability to understand and manipulate words and language with greater ease. These people enjoy all forms of verbal and written communication: reading, writing, and speaking. Students with verbal/linguistic intelligence like to keep journals, read and write stories for pleasure, do crossword and jumble puzzles, talk aloud as they think, and recite poetry. Students with high verbal/linguistic skills often do well on the verbal portion of the SAT and other standardized tests. They seek careers in communications and become authors, journalists, teachers, and attorneys.

Those with *logical/mathematical* intelligence do well collecting, organizing, and interpreting data. They are also good at seeing numerical relationships, sequences (such as playing Sudoku), and patterns among discrete variables.

Logical/mathematical individuals think both inductively and deductively. They use strategic logic in solving abstract math problems and games. Students with logical/mathematical intelligence are good in math and science and pursue careers in engineering, applied technology, statistics, computer programming, and the sciences. Students with high logical/mathematical skills often do well on the mathematical portion of the SAT and other standardized tests.

Visual/spatial intelligence involves the ability to construct concrete and mental models. People with visual/spatial intelligence are especially good at reading and interpreting maps, drawing, playing chess, and solving maze puzzles. Students with visual/spatial intelligence prefer to have lectures supplemented with PowerPoint slides, graphs, charts, illustrations, computer graphics, concept maps, and graphic organizers. Students caught doodling in class are often masquerading their visual/spatial intelligence. Individuals with high visual/spatial intelligence usually go on to careers in architecture, planning, and design.

People can also express their intelligence using *bodily/kinesthetic* channels. Students with bodily/kinesthetic intelligence are gifted with natural fine and large-motor coordination skills and are very physical and tactile. They like observing and examining objects through physical and haptic sensations such as touching, feeling, and hands-on manipulation. Teachers often plan hands-on science activities to complement students' bodily/kinesthetic urges. Because this type of intelligence often is played out as squirming, wiggling, or acting out, teachers often mistake these behaviors as problems rather than habits to express one's physical needs. People with bodily/kinesthetic intelligence go on to become athletes, dancers, and performers.

Many of us are very familiar with *musical* intelligence. These are people with talents to carry a pitch or song, create and interpret rhythm, compose music, and write lyrics. Understanding sound, timing, and voice are aspects of someone with musical abilities. Students with high musical intelligence play in the school band or orchestra, sing in the choir at school or church, and perform in musicals. Many teachers often allow students with creative, musical intelligence to demonstrate their understanding about an academic concept by performing a song or rap.

Interpersonal intelligence involves interacting and communicating with others. People with interpersonal intelligence demonstrate an ability to "read" the moods and emotions of people around them. They excel when participating in group processes and cooperative learning situations, and they display compassion and empathy for the feelings of family members and friends. Descriptions such as sensitive and sentimental apply to individuals with interpersonal intelligence. These people often seek careers in counseling and social work. By providing opportunities for students to work in cooperative learning groups during science class, teachers promote and encourage interpersonal intelligence.

When one understands his or her own emotions, motivations, strengths, and weaknesses, he or she demonstrates *intrapersonal* intelligence. People with intrapersonal intelligence seek opportunities to reflect on their thoughts and feelings. Students with intrapersonal intelligence like to connect new knowledge with preexisting knowledge. Teachers promote intrapersonal intelligence by having students write in journals and use self-assessment strategies. Children with high intrapersonal intelligence like to use their "private time" in such activities as taking solitary walks or building forts and tree houses, and they prefer secretive play places for reading or listening to music. They take extra time to contemplate actions and decisions that affect them personally, directly or indirectly.

In *Frames of Mind*, Gardner explains that each of us has one or more dominant intelligences that profile our human intellect, but he points out that all humans have varying degrees of all seven intelligences. He goes on to propose that each intelligence occupies a distinct and separate area of the brain and that injury to the brain can result in impairment to the intelligence associated with that affected section.

Gardner's theory, although not originally formulated for instructional use, has had a dominant place in education. Teachers who embrace his ideas apply multiple intelligence theory to classroom settings by designing lessons and assessments in which students can demonstrate competence through a variety of intelligences. To integrate inquiry-based instruction and multiple intelligences in the science classroom, consider setting up seven stations or learning centers for a particular unit of study, with each station emphasizing the need to use a different intelligence to complete the task. Other projects in this unit of study may involve students working in cooperative groups (interpersonal), doing hands-on activities (bodily/kinesthetic), writing in science journals (verbal/linguistic), classifying objects (logical/mathematical), completing remedial or enrichment excursions at their own pace (intrapersonal), listening to songs (musical), or creating a concrete model of the phenomenon observed (visual/spatial).

In 1999, Howard Gardner followed up his 1983 work, *Frames of Mind*, with *Intelligence Reframed*. In this publication, Gardner added *naturalistic intelligence* to the original list of seven intelligences. People with naturalistic intelligence are gifted with the ability to see patterns and distinctions in the natural world. These individuals keenly recognize relationships among the flora and fauna in a community and focus on existing phenomena that others disregard. Naturalistic intelligence fosters caring and sensitivity to the environment.

Although little has been written on the connection between scientific inquiry and naturalistic intelligence, a "natural" link seems to exist. In inquiry, students can enhance their naturalistic intelligence through observing and recognizing patterns from the environment and surroundings. Thus, inquiry becomes an ideal vehicle for students to explore their natural world, heightening the senses that allow them to discern similarities and differences in organisms. This exploration may lead to carefully observing and recording the behaviors of various species of plants and animals. In *Inquiry at the Window: Pursuing the Wonders of Learning*, Phyllis and David Whitin (1997) provide an excellent reading for a yearlong inquiry of primary-level students observing birds drawn to a bird feeder outside a classroom window. The authors weave a brilliant story wherein the teacher encourages students' naturalistic intelligences to observe patterns in nature and to record the various species and their frequent visits to the feeder, while undergoing a school-year science project; in other words, learning to appreciate the world of nature. In *Taking Inquiry Outdoors* (Bourne, 2000), classroom teachers reflect on coming to understand science through reading, writing, and outdoor inquiry—the perfect blend of verbal/linguistic, bodily/kinesthetic, visual/special, and naturalistic intelligences.

Teachers of environmental science have an "open invitation" to incorporate scientific inquiry and naturalistic intelligence (Barkman, 1999). Consider designing an ecology unit appropriate for your grade level and the district's content standards, a unit in which students have the opportunity to use their sensory skills to observe nature. In that unit, students may create collections of woodland organisms and make drawings of the specimens in their science logs or journals. Some students may be interested in making a scrapbook of their collection. Others may use the science references and field guides to identify the common and scientific names for the organisms.

For a Web site on Howard Gardner's multiple intelligences application to the classroom, see www.thirteen.org/edonline/concept2class/mi/index.html

QUESTIONS FOR REFLECTION AND DISCUSSION

At the end of each chapter are questions designed for reflection and discussion. Whether you are reading the book alone, collaborating in a small study group, or participating in a college course or summer institute, the questions are designed to evoke thoughts, opinions, viewpoints, and personal feelings. Even though we tend to "gloss over" end-of-chapter questions, read each one and make notations and reflections in the margin. Your comments will become beneficial as you progress on your journey into inquiry.

1. Leon Lederman, renowned scientist and Nobel laureate, has said "Scientific literacy may likely determine whether or not democratic society will survive into the 21st century." What do you think he meant by this?

2. What role do science literacy and inquiry-based instruction play in making our country and its citizens globally competitive?

3. Chapter 2 suggested 12 misconceptions about inquiry. Can you think of other misconceptions teachers may have about scientific inquiry?

4. Return to the opening quote for this chapter. How does the statement from the National Research Council resonate with your thinking now that you have read sections on scientific inquiry and nature of science?

NOTE

1. Excerpts from Exploratorium, *Inquiry Descriptions*. Reproduced with permission. © Exploratorium®, http://www.exploratorium.edu/ifi/index.html

Learning Through Inquiry

Inquiry is a multi-faceted activity that involves making observations; posing questions; examining books and other sources of information to see what is already known; planning investigations; reviewing what is already known in light of experimental evidence; using tools to gather, analyze, and interpret data; proposing answers, explanations, and predictions; and communicating the results.

—National Research Council, *National Science Education Standards*

Real classroom case studies can show how inquiry-based lessons progress. This is the story of a fourth-grade teacher who introduces an exploration to her class that allows students to investigate the properties of ice and provides them with opportunities to generate questions to investigate.

"Exploring Ice Hands" aligns to the *National Science Education Standards* (NSES) (NRC, 1996) for Grades K–4.

Science as Inquiry Standards

Students will:

- Ask questions about objects, organisms, and events in the environment (p. 122) Plan and conduct simple investigations (p. 122)
- Employ simple equipment and tools to gather data and extend the senses (p. 122)
- Use data to construct a reasonable explanation (p. 122)
- Communicate investigations and explanations (p. 122)

Physical Science Standards

- Objects have many observable properties (p. 127)
- Materials can exist in different states—solid, liquid, and gas (p. 127)

DAY 1: EXPLORING ICE HANDS

"I hope they're ready," Ms. Camille Perlo thought as she opened the freezer door. There, she saw seven frozen hands. Actually, they were ice hands she had made the night before by filling latex surgical gloves with water and tying the ends with twist ties. Ms. Perlo took the ice hands out of the freezer, wrapped each one in a kitchen towel, and carefully laid them in a red picnic cooler. Then, it was time to leave for school.

As the bell rang at 9 a.m., 22 fourth graders made their way to Ms. Perlo's class in Room 139. "Today," Ms. Perlo said, "we are going to start a special science unit. We are going to investigate ice hands and see what we can discover about ice. This is going to be a very special unit because all of you will become young scientists and think like real scientists do. To start us off, let's first think about what we already know about ice. Take out your science journals and write down five things you know about ice."

The students quickly opened their journals and began to write. After a few minutes, Ms. Perlo had students "pair and share." This activity gave each student an opportunity to exchange what he or she knew about ice with another person in the class. After a few minutes, Ms. Perlo said, "Okay, who would like to share with the rest of the class and tell them what you know about ice? Michael?"

"It's cold and slippery," he answered.

"Good," Ms. Perlo said. "I'll write that on the board. Anyone else?" Several hands went up. Nicole said that ice floats in water. Robbie said that ice is the solid form of water. As all the students were given an opportunity to answer, Ms. Perlo wrote and arranged their comments on a concept map on a poster board (see Figure 3.1). Pointing to the concept map, Ms. Perlo said, "See, as a class, we already know a lot about ice." Ms. Perlo further encouraged students to share how they have come to know about their understandings about ice. Did they experience it through direct observation? Did they hear about it from a friend or family member? Or did they read about it in a book? Did they learn it in school? By doing so she facilitates their prior knowledge and promotes metacognition.

During the second part of the preassessment, Ms. Perlo showed the students a clear plastic tub of water and measured the height of the water in the tub. "If I add a block of ice to the water," she asked, "what will happen to the level of the water? Will it go up, or down, or remain the same? Record your prediction in your science journal and provide a reason for your answer." Then she posed the question, "As the ice melts, what will happen to the level of the water? Will it go up, or down, or remain the same? Again, record your prediction in your science journal and provide a reason for your answer." Finally she asked, "If I now place the tub of water near a sunny window and leave the tub sitting for several sunny days, what will happen to the level of the water? Will it go up, or down, or remain the same? Again, record your prediction in your science journal and provide a reason for your answer."

Ms. Perlo used the questions to solicit students' prior knowledge about the three states of matter and how one form can change into another. This information, she thought to herself, will be valuable later in the unit.

Figure 3.1   Concept Map Showing Students' Prior Knowledge About Ice

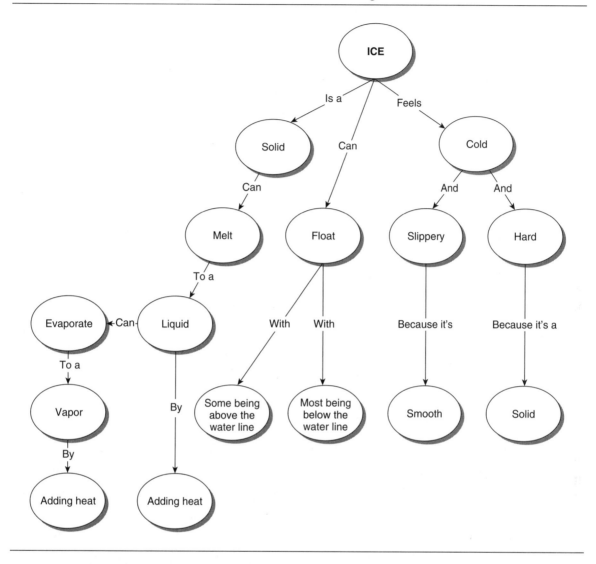

"Today," Ms. Perlo continued, "you are going to use the information you already have to make investigations about ice hands." Although Ms. Perlo's class had prior experience with doing hands-on science, this was their first full inquiry-based scientific investigation of the school year. She divided the students into six groups, with three or four students to a group. Ms. Perlo gave each group a plastic kitty litter pan and one ice hand. After removing the latex glove that formed the hand, she placed the ice hand in the pan and instructed the students to start to make observations. "Magnifying lenses and rulers are available at the science center for those who want to make closer observations and measurements," she said. The young scientists began making observations and recording data in their science journals. As Ms. Perlo moved about to the room to observe each group, she noticed the observations and measurements the children were recording in their journals:

"There are little bubbles and streaks inside." (Karima)

"Inside the ice hand, little tiny swiggly lines look like hair strings or bacteria." (Terry)

"One side is flat and the other is rounded." (Renee)

"It's 5½ inches wide." (Savannah)

"From the pointer finger to the end of the hand it's about 7 inches." (Dominick)

The students then shared their observations by reading them aloud.

After giving the students 15 minutes to record, then share, their observations and data, Ms. Perlo said, "I'm going to come around to each of your groups and fill your pan about half full with water. After I do this, you need to place your ice hand in the water and continue to make observations and measurements about your ice hand. Keep recording your results in your science journals." She suggested that they may want to add drawings or illustrations to show how their ice hands change (see Figures 3.2 and 3.3).

While observing the hands in the water, students continued to record their observations:

"It floats in water." (Nicole)

"In water the fingers and hand are starting to melt, but slowly." (Emanuel)

"The little pointy finger is shrinking." (Kyle)

"The fingers are getting pointy." (Katie)

While the students were making their observations, Ms. Perlo suggested the students make a T-chart to list their observations and questions. "Think of several questions you would like to investigate about ice from your observations. Also be prepared to state why that question is important to you. Your questions may be about the melting or freezing rates of ice, for example. Then write them down in your T-chart. Later, we will review all the questions and decide which ones you want

Figure 3.2   Students During Ice Hands Activity: Observation

Figure 3.3 Students During Ice Hands Activity: Recording

to investigate. We will also discuss how the question should be investigated since different questions require different means of investigation."

As she rotated from group to group, the students shared their observations and investigative questions. In about 20 minutes, all the ice hands had melted, and it was time to share discoveries. One by one, each group shared what it had observed and what questions members wanted to investigate. Ms. Perlo wrote all their questions on a poster board.

After all the questions were recorded on the poster board, she reviewed each question and, with the students' help, sorted them into three categories: (a) questions that were ready to be investigated, (b) questions that needed further revision, and (c) questions that could be answered only with assistance from outside experts or print or online resources.

Each young scientist then had an opportunity to choose an appropriate question to investigate. "I want to see if crushed ice melts faster than block ice," Ariene said. Katie was certain she wanted to be with the group that tried to freeze a bubble.

"Now," Ms. Perlo said, "since this might be the first time you have done a real science investigation on your own, let's take one question and work it through as an example." She took one question and led the class through a lesson on how to design a fair "experiment"—designed so only one variable would affect the results of the investigation.

Ms. Perlo: Let's take the question, "Does the amount of water affect the time it takes water to freeze?" Tony, how would you start to answer that question?

Tony: I'd try to see which takes longer to freeze, a lot of water or a little water.

Ms. Perlo: Good. How could you do that?

Tony: I'd take a big jar and a little jar and fill them both with water.

Ms. Perlo: And then what would you do next? Robbie?

Figure 3.4   T-Chart

Observations	Questions

Figure 3.5 Thermometers During an Ice Investigation

Robbie:	I'd place them both in the freezer and see how long it takes for each one to freeze.
Ms. Perlo:	That's good. How could you measure the freezing rate?
Robbie:	I don't know. Watch it, I guess.
Ms. Perlo:	Is there any way to measure the freezing rate?
Students:	[No response]
Ms. Perlo:	Maybe use a small stick or something like that?
Renee:	Yeah, you could use a little toothpick and poke the ice to see if it's frozen or not.
Ms. Perlo:	That's a good idea. Now, would you use the same shape containers for both? Kayleigh?
Kayleigh:	I guess so. Yeah. One container would be full with water and the other would only be, say, half full.
Ms. Perlo:	But why would you have to use the same shape container in both cases?
Nicole:	Because the shape of the container might affect how the ice freezes.
Ms. Perlo:	[Silence]
Nicole:	And it would make it fair.
Ms. Perlo:	Good! Now, would you put them in the freezer at the same time?
Class:	[In unison] Yessss.
Ms. Perlo:	Would you put regular tap water in one container and bottled water in the other?

Class: [In unison] Noooo.

Ms. Perlo: Would you put the containers in two separate freezers?

Class: [In unison] Noooo.

After the children understood how to set up a controlled science investigation, it was time to move on to their own inquiries. The class formed groups consisting of three to four students, each with a different question to be investigated. Mark, Justin, Emanuel, and John wanted to find out how long it took ice to melt in regular water versus saltwater. Dominick, Terry, Jesse, and Thomas wondered if ice melts more quickly in your hand or in water. Kathy, Katie, and Kayleigh wanted to figure out if they could make soap bubbles freeze. Savannah, Nicole, Renee, and Elizabeth decided to investigate whether ice melts faster in or out of water. Robbie, Michael, Kyle, and Tony wondered if ice would float or sink in regular water versus saltwater; and Karima, Ariene, and Regina wanted to know if crushed ice melted faster than block ice.

DAY 2: PLANNING AN INVESTIGATION

On the second day, the children worked in small groups, deciding how they would go about answering their investigative questions. "Use your scientific minds to brainstorm a list of steps of your own investigation. You may also want to draw a picture showing how you plan to conduct your inquiry" Ms. Perlo told them. "And remember to make a list of the materials you will need to complete your investigation."

As the groups discussed how to design the procedures for their investigations, Ms. Perlo circulated around the room checking their progress. She reminded the students to think ahead about how they were going to make their observations and collect their evidence. "When you do that," she reminded them, "it helps you to think about how you are going to organize your data in a table or chart."

By the end of the science lesson's second day, all the groups had completed their plans and were excited about their investigations. They had thought about their questions and were ready to put their ideas to the test!

DAY 3: CARRYING OUT THE PLAN

On the third day, the students were eager to perform their investigations. As soon as morning announcements were completed, the students started assembling their materials and carrying out their inquiries.

In one corner, Kathy, Katie, and Kayleigh blew soap bubbles into plastic containers. They thought that if they put the container in a freezer, the bubbles would freeze. They decided to try containers that were dry inside and others that had been moistened inside with bubble solution. They soon discovered on their own that the container had to be moist inside in order to keep the bubble from popping.

Across the room, Dominick, Terry, Jesse, and Thomas were putting an ice cube in a glass of water. They placed another ice cube in each of their hands and held it there. They measured the time it took for ice to melt for both situations.

Savannah, Nicole, Renee, and Elizabeth were busy setting up a way to measure whether ice melts faster in or out of water. They decided to place one ice cube in a glass of water and another ice cube in an empty glass of the same size (see Figures 3.6 and 3.7).

Figure 3.6   Students Conducting Ice Investigations

Figure 3.7   Students Conducting Ice Investigations

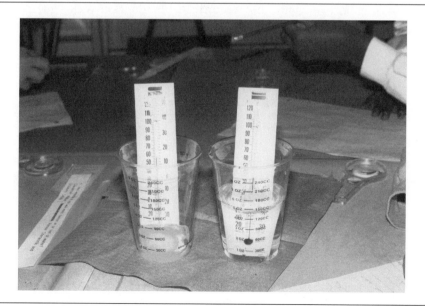

Figure 3.8 Students Completing a Display Board

Robbie, Michael, Kyle, and Tony investigated whether ice would float or sink when placed in regular water versus saltwater. Their question came from a prior discussion in which one of the group members shared his understanding that objects float "better" in saltwater than in regular water.

Next to them, Mark, Justin, Emanuel, and John wondered whether melting rates are different for ice placed in saltwater versus ordinary water. They were busy measuring equal amounts of water to be used for both cases (see Figure 3.8).

Hammering sounds came from the area where Karima, Ariene, and Regina were working. They wanted to know if crushed ice melts faster than block ice, and they were crushing ice to use in their experiment.

As Ms. Perlo looked around the classroom, she saw each group busy carrying out its investigation, collecting data, and recording results. She was very proud of her fourth-grade scientists as they worked together, enjoying a morning of discovery.

DAY 4: ORGANIZING THE DATA

By the fourth day of the lesson, all the investigations had been completed and the data had been collected. Now, it was time to start the sharing and communicating phase of the inquiry. "Review the observations and evidence from your investigation and discuss it critically within your group. Draw a conclusion and an explanation based on the data and be prepared to share your claim with the rest of the students." Ms. Perlo told the class. "Remember, all your notes go in your science journals." Ms. Perlo suggested that the groups organize the information from their investigations on trifold display boards.

"The left side of your display boards should state the question you were investigating and your prediction," she explained. "The middle section lists the materials

Figure 3.9   Students Presenting Their Findings

used and the procedure of the investigation. The right side of the board has the data table and results. Don't forget to write a concluding statement about your prediction," she added. "Be ready to give your presentations tomorrow. The entire class will hear your claim and determine if the evidence you collected fully supports your claim or not." (See Figure 3.9.) Ms. Perlo also provided a rubric for making an oral presentation. On it were levels of suggested behaviors for voice projection, eye contact, and participation.

DAY 5: COMMUNICATING THE RESULTS

The day of the inquiry presentations was a special one for Room 139. One at a time, each group made its way to the front of the room, eager to share what it had learned. As each group made its presentation, Ms. Perlo carefully recorded on a separate sheet of paper all the new information the class had learned about ice for the next, and final, day's lesson (see Figure 3.10). Later, the students were debriefed on their investigations and reviewed what they had learned. They carefully discussed the meaning of their inquiries and the evidence and claims they produced. Ms. Perlo reinforced the difference between the results of an investigation and the conclusions we draw from it. Acting as reflective friends, they gave one another comments on the procedures of the inquiries and the oral presentations of the investigations.

Ms. Perlo brought out the original concept map depicting what the students knew about ice on Day 1 (see Figure 3.10). Students added their newly acquired knowledge about ice to the concept map. Ms. Perlo also made a list of the vocabulary terms that had arisen during the investigations and wrote them on the chalkboard. These terms became part of the students' spelling words for the week: density, expansion, weight,

Figure 3.10 Concept Map Showing Students' Knowledge About Ice

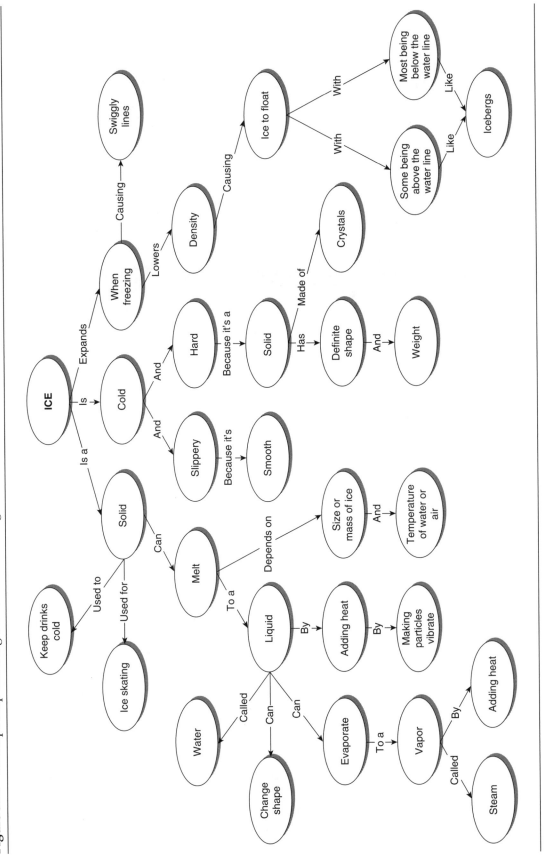

color, melting, solid, luster, hypothesis, liquid, size, temperature, width, float, ruler, and height.

The students then applied their new knowledge to other situations. For example, they wanted to know how icebergs were formed and how big they are. That led to students wanting to know more about the ocean liner *Titanic* and what caused the "unsinkable" ship to go down on the night of April 14, 1912.

Students also raised other questions about ice:

Why does ice float?

Would having a fan blow on an ice cube affect the time it took the ice to melt?

Does an ice hand melt faster in or out of the latex glove?

How long does it take water to freeze?

Does the size of the container affect the time needed to freeze?

Does hot water freeze faster or more slowly than cold water?

Does salt in the water affect the freezing rate?

How do freezing rates compare among water, milk, detergent, and soda?

Does the size of an ice cube affect how fast it will melt?

Does the temperature of the air affect how fast an ice cube will melt?

Does stirring water that contains an ice cube make the ice cube melt faster?

Does the temperature of the water affect the melting rate?

Does an ice cube melt faster in or out of its container?

How can you make an ice cube melt faster?

How can you keep an ice cube from melting?

Will twice as much ice melt half as quickly?

Will ice melt faster in a gallon of water or a quart of water?

Ms. Perlo encouraged the students to continue satisfying their curiosity by investigating these questions through further investigations and using the Internet during their free time and after school.

CONCLUSION

At the close of the ice hand inquiry, Ms. Perlo collected the students' science journals. She used the journals as a way of assessing their progress on writing and note taking. She also distributed a self-evaluation form (see Form 3.1) to help students reflect on how well they had worked during the ice hand investigation and how well they presented their results. Following the ice hand inquiry, she engaged students in a reflective discussion of their investigations. She began the activity by having each student reflect in his or her science journals by completing the starter sentence, "During the ice hand investigation I learned. . . ." and recap the connection between the evidence collected and the claims made. During this time the class discussed how different kinds of questions required different kinds of investigations and why they designed the procedures the way they did. Ms. Perlo then led a dialogue on how their individual prior knowledge may have affected the way they interpreted the evidence gathered and how the class moved beyond their prior understanding about the properties of matter. The next day, Ms. Perlo presented a teacher-led lesson from the district intermediate grade-level science standards on "Observable Properties of Matter."

As the unit concluded, Ms. Perlo gave an assessment that included multiple-choice questions on the content portion of the unit including the three states of matter and the properties of ice. As an alternative assessment, students were given an ice hand investigation with five procedural errors. The students' task was to identify the five errors and suggest appropriate changes.

Success in learning science can best take place when students are actively and thoughtfully immersed in the learning process. Ms. Perlo summed up her experience by saying, "This investigation certainly aroused the students' interest and curiosity about ice. Now they are more apt to investigate and discover on their own because the students were genuinely engaged in the subject."

Inviting inquiry in the classroom provides students with opportunities to raise their own questions, plan the procedures, collect evidence, and communicate the results of their investigations. This is just one story about how teachers can use an open-ended exploration to facilitate inquiry-based learning. We will refer to the ice hand investigation again in a later chapter to demonstrate how students can explore and investigate science in meaningful ways.

In the next chapter, you will use the ice hand story to blend your personal understanding of inquiry with constructivism, a theory on how children learn.

AN INTERVIEW WITH CAMILLE PERLO

Teachers who use an inquiry-based approach in science can offer guidance to others who also use inquiry in their classrooms. In the following interview, Ms. Perlo elaborates on her understanding of implementing an inquiry investigation.

Author: What does inquiry mean to you?

Camille: Well, let's start from the students' point of view. I've posed this question to my classes several times, and most often the response is searching for an understanding about something we don't know. Exploration is usually based on what we already know and discovering what more we need to know to solve the question or problem. I also impress upon them that sometimes disappointments may be part of inquiry. Not every scientist and not every student will design an investigation that yields the evidence to solve the question he or she is asking. That's just reality. When the investigation doesn't produce the expected results, it opens new avenues for further investigations. I suspect my meaning of inquiry is not much different from theirs.

Form 3.1   Self-Evaluation Form for "Ice Hands": An Inquiry Unit

Self-Evaluation Form for "Ice Hands": An Inquiry Unit

Name:_____

Shade in the circle that best describes your experience.

	Almost Always	Often	Sometimes	Rarely
I handled the ice hands properly.	O	O	O	O
I made accurate observations of the ice hands.	O	O	O	O
I made accurate drawings of the ice hands.	O	O	O	O
I followed the procedures in my inquiry plan.	O	O	O	O
I participated in the group discussions productively.	O	O	O	O
I listened to other members of my group and respected their ideas.	O	O	O	O
I did my share of the group work.	O	O	O	O
I used my journal to record my observations and measurements.	O	O	O	O
I used the supplies and materials appropriately.	O	O	O	O
I used many sources to collect information about ice hands.	O	O	O	O
I shared what I learned about ice hands with others in my class.	O	O	O	O
I shared responsibility during the ice hand presentation.	O	O	O	O
I made good eye contact during the ice hand presentation.	O	O	O	O
I projected my voice during the ice hand presentation.	O	O	O	O

Author: How would you describe your classroom?

Camille: It's truly a culture of inquiry I attempt to promote. In every unit I teach, I preplan ways to incorporate investigations and thinking skills into the curriculum. So each unit comprises some aspect of inquiry, regardless of the subject matter. Students are constantly working in groups to discover on their own. For example, when individuals asked me a question, I point to a sign in the room that reads: *Ask three before me.* They are reminded to ask three other people before they ask me. This helps to reinforce peer learning, and it places more emphasis on them learning together rather than seeing me as the "eternal source" of all knowledge—which I'm certainly not! I want them to become both good students and teachers to one another.

Author: If a visitor came into your classroom, what would he or she see students doing?

Camille: First of all, you would see students working predominantly in groups. I impress upon them that collaborating in groups is something they will do their entire life. Group work offers them the opportunity to develop habits of mind and dispositions such as fairness, sensitivity to others, group commitment, shared responsibility, and openness to the ideas of others. Sometimes I assign the groups, and other times the groups are self-selected. I am aware that on occasions I need to assign equity in the groups so that the same boys or girls aren't working together all the time. I consciously mix the groups on the basis of status, gender, and reading proficiency.

You would also see students using primary sources of information. Sure, textbooks are fine, but having newspapers, magazines, and fiction and nonfiction literature organized in bins makes knowledge readily available. The material is not locked up in cabinets or drawers; it's out in the open and accessible.

I also have what I call "silent teachers." Those are the poster papers from our daily work, students' work, and exemplary models of excellent work throughout the classroom. Using the overhead projector is fine, but when the acetate sheet is taken away, so is the idea. That's why I prefer to use poster papers. I can keep their ideas posted on the walls for many days after the lesson.

Author: What would he or she [the classroom visitor] see you doing?

Camille: You would see me observing and recording their interactions in their groups. I constantly monitor their organizational skills, their group responsibilities, and record any misconceptions I overhear. I also want to make sure everybody is being courteous and respectful of each other. Most of all I'm listening to the conversations and determining their progress. I listen to the vocabulary they are using.

Say there is a group of four. I look for signs of understanding. Are individuals making eye contact when answering questions? Are they giving me an answer they truly understand or the answer they think

I am looking for? It's not always easy to do, but I have to be cognizant of outward signs that they are moving toward understanding the content standards for that particular unit.

Author: If inquiry-based teaching takes more time, how do you balance your teaching style with meeting the district's standards, curriculum, and testing requirements?

Camille: (Chuckle) Not always that well. That's something that concerns every good teacher. It's sometimes discouraging that I don't feel as free to do many of the science activities I used to do. With all the new content standards needed to be taught, choice seems to be taken away. I find I have to be very effective and efficient with my instructional time to "squeeze" long-term projects into the curriculum. If the teacher values students doing explorations and investigations, you need to be "time conscious."

Since the schedule calls for half the class going to art once a week, I use that time with the remaining class to do hands-on science. It becomes easier to balance the investigations with 11 students in the room rather than 22.

I also limit the instructional classroom time for doing homework and avoid assigning "skill sheets" and "busy work" for homework. Some teachers see them as skill builders; I see them as classic time-wasters.

Author: Inquiry teaching is often characterized as valuing the students' points of view and encouraging them to engage in raising and answering their own questions. How do you deal with the questions your students ask?

Camille: First of all, I rarely interrupt a student in the middle of his or her answer. I avoid posing "guess what I'm thinking of" type questions. If I constantly cut off the students in the middle of their responses, then I would subliminally communicate that brief, effortless answers are sufficient. Students need ample time to clearly articulate what they are thinking. When we pay meticulous attention to their answers, those which are either right or wrong, we connect to their thinking processes.

Author: What special skills do students experience when learning through inquiry?

Camille: Students certainly do acquire lifelong skills through inquiry. One skill acquired is the ability to state your point of view. Through inquiry-based learning, students hone their abilities to communicate their models and ideas about the natural world. They may not know that's what they are doing, but as educators, we do. Inquiry fosters critical or higher-order thinking skills. It also helps develop a sense of responsibility, perseverance, and skepticism. Inquiry also allows them to practice defining distinct and divergent strategies to attack a problem; all skills that will prepare them for the workforce or college, whichever they choose.

Author: What advice would you give to other teachers just starting out in establishing an inquiry-based classroom?

Camille: I think we have a moral and professional responsibility to nurture inquiring minds for the world that lies ahead of them. And being good inquirers is part of that preparation. Inquiry takes time. Kids need time to practice and demonstrate inquiry skills, especially if they have not had the opportunity in previous grades. I would suggest using inquiry-based instruction as often as you can fit it in and in all subject areas, not just science. I would also suggest finding a partner to work with. Becoming an inquiry-based teacher becomes easier when you can share your successes and challenges with a colleague. Last, don't get caught in the rut of teaching just basic skills. Stretch your curriculum and your students' minds and imaginations beyond the minimum level of expectation.

QUESTIONS FOR REFLECTION AND DISCUSSION

1. How is the ice hand investigation characteristic of the opening quotation in this chapter?

2. What is the importance of using a T-chart for students to record their observations and questions?

3. How would you assess students' understanding before, during, and after an inquiry like ice hands? What content, skills, or attitudes would you assess?

4. What is the importance of having students record their investigations, data, and evidence in a science journal rather than writing a prescribed lab report?

5. How would you grade the students' journals at the conclusion of the ice hand investigation?

6. What extension activity or lesson would you plan after the ice hand investigation?

7. Teachers often use prompts to guide students toward desired outcomes. How does Ms. Perlo guide individual students toward an understanding of how to plan an investigation for their question?

How Do Children Learn Science?

If [the teacher] is indeed wise he does not bid you enter the house of his wisdom, but rather leads you to the threshold of your own mind.

—Kahlil Gibran, *The Prophet*

DEVELOPING A MIND-SET FOR INQUIRY

Developing an appropriate philosophical mind-set to complement inquiry is a prerequisite in becoming an inquiry-based teacher. For many teachers, the principles of *constructivism* lay the foundation for understanding and implementing inquiry-based learning. This chapter introduces the philosophical and historical developments that have shaped our perception of how children learn science and presents a learning theory aligned with inquiry- and learner-centered classrooms.

Becoming an inquiry-based teacher usually starts with a "gut feeling" about good, hands-on instruction. Sooner or later, however, it becomes similarly important to appreciate what it is about the notion of inquiry that complements your style of teaching. Teachers interested in inquiry are highly encouraged to articulate their ideology and philosophy of teaching; that is, to get the feeling out of their gut and into their head. This chapter will align how children learn science with your teaching behaviors. In essence, the classroom behavior that a teacher demonstrates is a reflection of that teacher's values and beliefs about how children learn. The better one can articulate his or her understanding of learning, the better that teacher can express how inquiry, problem solving, and other active teaching strategies align to one's ideology. Thus, as a teacher, your classroom behavior is a function of your ideology within a given learning environment, and where your ideology is expressed as a sum total of your beliefs, biases, and prejudices about how children learn.

This chapter introduces constructivism, one perspective on how children learn, and how naïve conceptions can influence learning. The chapter will assist you in verbalizing your thoughts about how learning occurs. Through the works of psychologists such as Dewey, Piaget, Vygotsky, and Ausubel, this chapter also presents the historical developments of constructivism and orients constructivist principles in practice.

WHAT IS CONSTRUCTIVISM?

To *construct* an understanding of constructivism takes considerable reflection. Before we discuss what constructivism is, let's start with what constructivism is not. First, constructivism is not about how to *teach*. More accurately, it's about how children *learn*, although it does have implications for instruction. Let's consider a traditional, teacher-centered science classroom in which communication flows from the teacher to the student and teacher talk dominates the lesson. In this classroom, students sit in straight rows of desks facing the front of the class and have few opportunities to interact or work in cooperative learning groups. Let's call the teacher in this class Mrs. Jones.

In Mrs. Jones' classroom, students are passive learners and receive information based on a rigidly fixed curriculum. Information is dispensed to students predominantly in a didactic manner. The students' seat time is consumed with note taking, handouts, and completing worksheets that emphasize basic thinking skills. Mrs. Jones relies on a single textbook that, along with lectures and drill and practice, serves to disseminate information to students from the body of knowledge that exists within the world of science. The activities and laboratory experiences serve as recipes to verify or confirm already-stated knowledge and show how a set of scientific principles or truths applies to life. In the end, all students are expected to learn the same information at the same time. Ultimately, the unit test relies on objective, multiple-choice questions designed to elicit desired responses and inform the teacher about which facts and concepts the students have retained—likely only to be forgotten days after the test.

Although the example of Mrs. Jones is purposely overgeneralized and exaggerated, most of us can recall times when we sat in classes like hers. In traditional classes, the teacher breaks down the curriculum into preplanned smaller bits of information to be presented. The teacher then determines how to evaluate and reward (or punish) the student for his or her performance in understanding the new content material. Whether traditional classrooms are superior or inferior, teacher-centeredness has dominated educational practices for most of the past century. It is based on the belief that learning can be predicted and manipulated by the teacher through sequencing the content or skills of the lesson, from simple to more complex. According to the classical teaching model, knowledge is *imparted* or *transferred* from the teacher to the student; the teacher sees the student's mind as an empty vessel or a sponge, absorbing what's said.

Contrary to teacher-centered classrooms, constructivism takes a more *cognitive* or brain-based approach. Constructivism is premised on the ideas that knowledge is "constructed" by thinking individuals and that knowledge is self-regulated and self-mediated on the basis of a person's prior experiences. In constructivist classrooms, emphasis is placed on first *acknowledging* that prior conceptions students bring to the classroom have a profound effect on how they interpret the teacher's language and *believing* that knowledge is not transmitted from the teacher to the student. Rather, knowledge is fashioned individually according to the prior experiences and the previously held understanding one brings to the lesson. Let's call the teacher in this class Mrs. Fisher.

> In contrast to Mrs. Jones' classroom, constructivist teachers, such as Mrs. Fisher, recognize that students bring a varied set of personal experiences and understandings to the unit. Mrs. Fisher realizes that prior conceptions brought to class often are based on misinformation or naïve understandings of complex subjects. Uncovering these misconceptions or naïve conceptions and replacing them with evidence-supported concepts forms the foundation of her lessons. To accomplish this task, Mrs. Fisher provides experiences and opportunities where students share their presently held theories and models with their peers. Students can then test their understandings through discussions, cooperative group work, and inquiry-based investigations.

We now see that constructivism is a theory about how we come to know what we know. It is founded on the premise that we search for and construct meaning from the world around us. We do this by reflecting on our everyday experiences. In this way, each of us constantly constructs and reconstructs our own mental models to accommodate and make sense of our new experiences.

In constructivist classrooms, the teacher envisions the student as an active participant in the learning process, attempting to search for meaning and interpret the natural world. Through mental and physical manipulation, students link prior knowledge and familiarities with new ideas and concepts being presented. Because constructivist teachers value and pursue student questions and points of view, there is a natural, inherent link between constructivism and scientific inquiry.

Last, for most of us, teaching and learning entails a combination of both approaches. At times, our teaching may be more teacher-centered, and at other times more student-centered. It often depends on the time of the school year, the topic being studied, the level of the students, and the culture and climate of the school. It is not an all-or-nothing approach. Learning, in and out of the classroom, can encompass aspects of both thoughts. There are always aspects and degrees of difference across the continuum of learning.

THE CONSTRUCTIVIST LEARNING MODEL

Lorsbach and Tobin (1992; see http://www.exploratorium.edu/IFI/resources/research/constructivism.html) believe that constructivism can be useful to teachers when used as a referent to make sense of what students see, think, say, and do.

Regardless of whether you lean toward the traditional or the constructivist end of the instructional spectrum, your personal beliefs affect and reflect your professional practice in the classroom. Take, for example, the metaphor of an iceberg. Only 10% of the ice is visible above the waterline; 90% is below the surface. Our teaching represents the visible part of the iceberg. The part we cannot see comprises our values, beliefs, biases, and prejudices; these are consciously or subconsciously below the surface. These values and beliefs determine how we design and operate our classrooms, our lessons, our language, and our interactions with students. By challenging our philosophical beliefs about how children learn, we can see how those beliefs guide our teaching.

Unlike the traditional approach, which focuses on factors *external* to the learner, the constructivist approach places a high priority on the cognitive aspects *internal* to the learner.

A constructivist learning model begins with an active and engaging process that provides an opportunity for the learner to create meaning from an experience. That process may include involving the individual's senses with parts of a particular phenomenon. Through exploration and "messing about," the student uses present cognitive structures, ideas, theories, and beliefs to act on and interpret the experience. The student can also make predictions about the phenomenon by applying prior learning to the new experience. Often, the experience matches the student's past experience, and the new information is assimilated into the learner's understanding. Other times, the student raises a question, makes a prediction, and tests an understanding—but goes on to record observations and measurements that point out a *discrepancy* between the predicted and the observable results. This causes *disequilibrium*, forcing the individual either to (a) discard the observable results because they don't fit into his or her present beliefs, or (b) make accommodations within his or her present cognitive structure to allow the new knowledge to replace the previous. Thus, the individual has made changes in the way he or she perceives and understands a particular concept or phenomenon. This is called the *conceptual change model*.

THE CONCEPTUAL CHANGE MODEL

To provide a nonscientific yet simple example of conceptual change, consider a child's belief in Santa Claus. Young children often hold on to this belief for many years because what is said and shown to them about Santa fits their present beliefs. Seeing images of Santa on television or in magazines and newspapers or visiting Santa in the mall helps children assimilate reality into their cognitive structure. In cognitive theory terms, all is well, and a state of *equilibrium* exists. The "reality" of the outside world matches the children's cognitive beliefs.

Sooner or later, children hear conflicting stories from other kids on the bus or from friends at school that there really isn't a Santa Claus. Or maybe they begin to question how Santa can get around the entire world in one night. Because peers exert considerable influence on how one develops and forms beliefs, children begin to question their theories. What results is a discrepancy between their present beliefs and the contradictory beliefs of friends. By comparing and contrasting their own beliefs with those of their peers, children begin to recognize other possible models and points of view. This conceptual change results in *accommodations* or changes in their understanding of a concept. When the new model appears to fit their observations better than the old one, the prior conception is replaced or modified.

In the classroom, some students may state the answer they believe the teacher expects, yet still personally embrace their own beliefs. We frequently observe this type of behavior in science classrooms. The award-winning Annenberg video *A Private Universe* (see Resource A) provides an excellent example for middle school teachers of how stubborn misconceptions, specifically those relating to planetary orbits, can be. Unfortunately, without extended probing, teachers may not be able to determine whether students are actually stating their understanding of a concept or instead are simply providing the answer they believe the teacher wants to hear.

CAN I CHANGE MY MIND?

From their earliest years, children develop an understanding about the world around them through observation, inquiry, and discovery. They observe drops of liquids, pushes and pulls, earthworms on a sidewalk after a rain, shadows, and just about everything around them. They formulate their understanding through sensory experiences. This knowledge enables individuals to make interpretations about the world around them as they view the world through their personal lenses. Constructivist teachers believe these lenses attempt to filter out all experiences that do not fit with presently held beliefs. As stated earlier, children are personally and emotionally attached to their beliefs and do not easily give them up. The authority of a teacher often is not strong enough to change many of the misconceptions held by students. That is to say, just because words come out of a teacher's mouth and go into the ears of students does not mean that students will accept what is said.

Challenging children and causing them to modify misconceptions takes a considerable amount of patience and persistence. What we do know is that peers sometimes can be strong motivators for giving up misconceptions and undergoing cognitive conceptual change. We must also remember that peers have their own naïve conceptions and often share them in social settings. In classroom situations involving constructivist and inquiry-based learning, engaging in discussion at the start of the lesson is one way to understand students' beliefs and possibly uncover their misconceptions. But simply uncovering misconceptions may not be enough. We need to become aware of students' misconceptions and adjust our teaching accordingly.

Children come to understand and interpret their world through observing and inquiring with the help of their peers. Dialogue, discussion, and communication with peers during inquiry make the construction of knowledge a *social* experience. Discussion provides a forum in which previously implicit beliefs can be shared, made explicit, tested, and reflected on. It provides a situation in which students can clarify their own notions in the process of discussing their ideas with others. The student often modifies, reorganizes, and reconstructs his or her ideas through dialogue coupled with the interaction and manipulation of materials.

Students will change their conceptual structures and misconceptions when there are adequate incentives. According to Posner, Strike, Hewson, and Gertzog (1982), students will change their conceptions when

- They become dissatisfied with their existing conditions,
- The new scientific concept is intelligible,
- The new scientific concept appears plausible, and
- The new scientific concept is useful in a variety of new situations.

MISCONCEPTIONS: WHAT YOU
KNOW MAY NOT BE SO

Each one of us has our own values, beliefs, and biases. They influence, in part, the information and understanding we hold at any given time. One example of how children construct meaning occurred this past summer with my seven-year-old nephew, Brandon, while we visited my family cottage at the lake. Brandon was spending the weekend with me, and I had promised that I would take him fishing. So, early Saturday morning, we packed up our fishing poles, the tackle box, and a Styrofoam cup filled with earthworms and headed down to the lake. Arriving at the dock, we found a spot where the fish certainly were going to be. After all, it was breakfast time, as Brandon told me, and the fish had to be hungry.

As we sat on the edge of the dock with our poles dangling just above the surface of the still morning water, Brandon looked down at the worm on his hook and asked, "How long does it take worms to grow up to be snakes?"

"What?" I asked, astonished.

"The worms, you know, the baby snakes. How long does it take the worms to grow up to be snakes?"

"Wow," I thought to myself, what a unique thought for a seven-year-old: worms growing up to become snakes!

For many individuals, especially young children, such concepts are often derived from commonsense interpretations of experience, thus forming what are called naïve concepts or misconceptions. For Brandon, it made perfect sense to connect earthworms and snakes. After all, they looked and acted alike. It would seem to be a logical conclusion.

Many kids enter our classrooms with a host of naïve misconceptions about the world around them. Uncovering and addressing the misconceptions that kids bring into our schools has received much attention in modern education theories. Duit and Treagust (1995) suggest that "at all ages students hold conceptions about many phenomena and concepts before they are presented in science class. These conceptions stem from and are deeply rooted in daily experiences because they have proved to be helpful and valuable in daily life" (p. 47). In fact, children are often quite satisfied with what they think they know and don't question their present notions. Duit and Treagust go on to say, "Very often, however, these conceptions are not in accord with science concepts. Research has shown that students do not switch easily from their old pre-instructional conceptions to the new science concepts taught" (p. 47).

Scores of examples of misconceptions have been identified in recent literature. The common idea that it's warmer in the summer because Earth is closer to the Sun seems to be the "immaculate misconception"! Phillips and Soltis (1991, p. 21), in identifying misconceptions in earth science, point out that before beginning classroom instruction, the teacher should attempt to uncover misconceptions commonly held by students. However, with 20 to 30 students in a class, this can be a daunting and sometimes impossible task.

Let's take the study of comets as an example. Most elementary and middle school students have seen pictures of comets in science textbooks and magazines. When asked to determine the direction in which a comet is traveling, students often draw on the "tail" of the comet to answer the question. Because prior experiences about rockets show a stream of gases and fumes escaping from the base of the rocket, a stream is always opposite the direction the rocket is traveling. Many students apply that same logic to comets and assume the tail is behind the comet. Actually, the tail of the comet is formed by solar winds blowing back on the evaporating gases as the comet "melts." The comet's tail tells us where the sun is in relation to the comet because the tail is always pointing away from the sun (see Figure 4.1).

To accurately and visually demonstrate this phenomenon to young children, the teacher can stand in front of a floodlight or some other bright light source and have students observe the position of the teacher's shadow. Whether the teacher is walking toward or away from the light (or sun), the shadow (or tail) is always pointing away from the light source. Thus, the tail of the comet does not indicate the direction the comet is moving; it indicates only where the sun is in relation to the comet. When students can actually see the shadow and compare it with their prior experiences with light and shadow, their misconceptions about comet tails may be dispelled.

Figure 4.1   Comet's Tail Pointing Away From the Sun

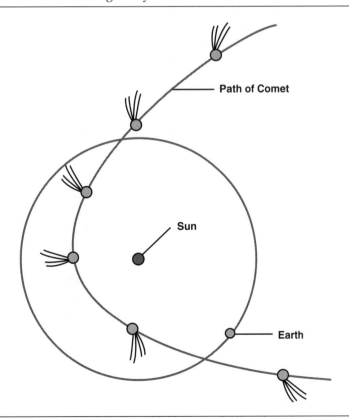

WHERE DO MISCONCEPTIONS COME FROM?

As children begin to make sense of their natural world, they start by observing and interpreting phenomena. These experiences are processed and recorded in various locations of the brain—in the visual, auditory, and motor cortices—not just in one specific place (Wolfe, 1998). Interpretations are sometimes based on deductive reasoning. When the deductive reasoning results in an understanding that is not matched to a scientific explanation, the interpretation is called a naïve conception or misconception. Misconceptions can come from a variety of sources: direct experience, television, books, peers, and even adults. Because these misconceptions are usually based on personal experiences, they are often deeply rooted and difficult to modify.

Even teachers can foster misunderstandings and misconceptions. In one classroom activity, third-grade students were following the directions from a teacher for making a collage on the phases of the Moon. To complete the collage, students were instructed to make cardboard cutouts representing the various phases of the Moon: full moons, half moons, and crescents. In the procedure of the activity, the students were directed to tie the cardboard moon phases to strings and hang them on a clothes hanger (see Figure 4.2).

The teacher questioned one student, Marsheka, about the moon's phases and how they change. Marsheka explained that the Moon gets larger and smaller. Although Marsheka could not explain where the rest of the Moon went or where it came from, she just knew that it changed shape.

This misconception was probably brought about by some prior experience and reinforced by the collage activity. A suggestion for the revision of the activity would be to cut out full circles to represent the Moon and darken the areas of the Moon that

Figure 4.2   Cut-Out Moon Phases on Hanger

Figure 4.3 Darkened Moon Phases on Hanger

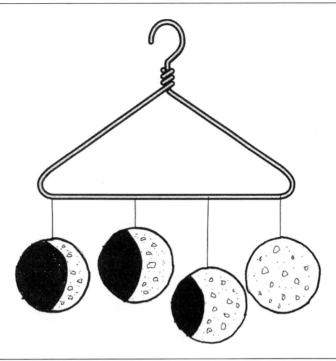

are not lighted (see Figure 4.3). This way, Marsheka could see that the entire Moon is present, although some of its surface is not completely visible on the unlit side. The activity could be followed by the teacher using a light source, a globe, and a Styrofoam ball to simulate the rotation of the Moon and the cause of its phases. Many science resource books and Web sites contain information for setting up this demonstration.

Peers are another primary source of information for children and sometimes can also be sources of misconceptions. Consider the conversation between two fourth-grade girls as they plant bean seeds in a container:

Genna: We have to put lots of dirt in the container if we want the seed to grow into a plant.

Karen: How do you know?

Genna: 'Cause when we add the water and fertilizer, the dirt will give the plant food to grow.

Karen: Oh yeah?

Genna: Yeah. That's how the plant gets its food . . . from the dirt. It's the same as earthworms eating the dirt.

Karen: That's awesome. I didn't know that.

In this case, the students appear to have a common yet limited knowledge of plant growth and food production. The relationship between the plant's basic needs (air, water, and minerals) and the production of food still needs to be developed during additional science lessons. Rather than the teacher telling the students that the plant manufactures its own food in the leaves by photosynthesis, the teacher could prompt the students into an inquiry to discover if plant seeds can grow in a medium other than soil. After posing the question "How can you find out if plants need soil to grow?" the students can plant seeds in cotton balls or paper towels and observe the seeds germinating without soil. This inquiry, coupled with a conversation between teacher and students to refine their understanding, may be the first step in dispelling the notion that plants need soil to grow.

Everyday language, among both peers and adults, can contribute to shaping one's understanding of the world. Take, for example, the statement, "The sun rises in the east and sets in the west." It conveys a basic contradiction of the simplest laws of planetary physics and reinforces the notion of a helio-centered universe.

COMPARING THE EARTH AND THE MOON

The relative sizes and distances of the Earth and the Moon are other examples of misconceptions that children and even adults have about our solar system. Through a simple demonstration using a globe and various balls, the size and distance relationships between the Earth and the Moon can be easily understood.

Picture an eighth-grade science class studying the solar system. The teacher, Mrs. Braun, uses an inflatable globe, 16 inches in diameter, to represent the Earth. This globe works especially well because it shows an actual image of the Earth instead of lines of latitude and longitude. Alongside the globe are four balls: one ball is one inch in diameter, the second two inches, the third, three inches, and the last, four inches in diameter. Her lesson involves students understanding the relative size of the Earth compared with the Moon and the distance between them. Her lesson aligns with the *National Science Education Standards* content for Earth and Space Science, which states that students "can begin to construct a model that explains the visual and physical relationships among the earth, sun, moon, and the solar system" (NRC, 1996, p. 159).

Showing the Earth and the four smaller balls, Mrs. Braun assesses students' prior conceptions and presents this question to her students: "If the Earth is represented by the inflatable globe, which of the four balls represents the size of the Moon, so that the Earth and the Moon are in correct proportion in terms of their relative sizes?" She asks each student to make an individual prediction and record that prediction in his or her science journal. She then asks students to pair and share their predictions and give reasons for choosing the sizes each recorded. In doing this, students rely on prior knowledge and provide details in support of their predictions—possibly exposing some commonly held misconceptions or naïve conceptions about the relative sizes of the Earth and the Moon. As the students work in pairs, Mrs. Braun circulates about the room, listening to the comments being made and mentally noting possible misconceptions. As expected, there is a great deal of variation in the responses of the students.

After the students share their predictions with their partners, Mrs. Braun takes a poll of the responses. Of the 25 students, 11 chose the one-inch ball, six chose the two-inch ball, five chose the three-inch ball, and two chose the four-inch ball. One

Figure 4.4   Globe and Moons

student thinks it was a trick question because he thought the Earth and the Moon were the same size.

After recording the predictions on a chart, Mrs. Braun asks several students to explain, elaborate, and justify their predictions. Most of them respond by telling about how small the Moon is and that the smallest ball seems the best choice. The class is obviously eager to find out which ball is correct. Rather than giving the answer, Mrs. Braun probes further by asking, "What information do you need to know which ball is the correct one?" They respond that they need to know the diameters of the Earth and Moon in miles. She provides information to show that the Earth's diameter is approximately 8,000 miles and the Moon's diameter is approximately 2,000 miles. One student, Maria, concludes that the ratio of the size of the Earth to the Moon is approximately 4:1. Maria now asks for the size of the inflatable globe. Rather than giving the answer, Mrs. Braun hands Maria a ruler. Maria measures the diameter of the globe as 16 inches and explains that because the ratio is about 4:1, and because the globe is 16 inches, the correct ball must be four inches. The other 24 students break out in applause!

HOW FAR IS THE MOON?

Mrs. Braun's next question builds on the students' knowledge of the size problem. She asks them, "If the Earth is represented by a globe 16 inches in diameter, and the Moon is represented by a ball four inches in diameter, how far does the four-inch Moon have to be from the 16-inch Earth to place them in relative proportion to their distances? Would it be 10, 15, 20, 30, or even 40 feet?" Again, Mrs. Braun asks them to make individual predictions. To help them in making their predictions, one student holds the Earth and another holds the Moon. The student holding the Moon walks across the room to estimate her distance in feet from the Earth.

Once again, Mrs. Braun uses the pair and share procedure to have students explain their predictions to their partners. Later, the class poll shows that most of the students predicted that the distance between the Earth and the Moon would be 10 to 15 feet. Again, Mrs. Braun asks them, "What information do you need to know to determine the correct distance?"

Several students conclude that they need to know the distance from the Earth to the Moon. Students are then encouraged to do a quick search using the Internet, and they find that the distance between the Earth and the Moon is 240,000 miles. They determine that because the 16-inch globe represents 8,000 miles, 12 inches or one foot would represent 6,000 miles. By dividing 6,000 into 240,000, they determine that the accurate distance between the Earth and the Moon should be 40 feet! They measure 40 feet and position the inflatable globe and the four-inch Moon appropriately—the length of the entire room apart.

Mrs. Braun leads the class into a follow-up discussion about how demonstrations and group work can help overcome naïve conceptions and build new, accurate knowledge.

By developing visual models of size and distance, students learn to express the structure and relationship among planetary objects. Mrs. Braun concludes the lesson by explaining how this activity helps students to hone their spatial thinking and reasoning skills as well as their understanding. According to the National Research Council (2006) in *Learning to Think Spatially*, "spatial thinking in *not* an add-on to an already crowded school curriculum, but rather a missing link across that curriculum. Integration and infusion of spatial thinking can help to achieve existing curriculum objectives. Spatial thinking is another level to enable students to achieve a deeper and more insightful understanding of subjects across the curriculum" (p. 7).

WHY TEACH TO MISCONCEPTIONS?

In classrooms, misconceptions often go undetected. Unfortunately, teachers receive little or no professional development in identifying and addressing misconceptions. Addressing misconceptions is an important part of teaching and learning. If we don't attempt to uncover and teach to students' misconceptions, chances are that students will leave our classrooms with the same misconceptions they had when they entered the room.

Changing a child's long-held belief about a concept can sometimes be easier said than done. A student's misconception is often challenged when a discomfort level or disequilibrium exists between the student's present notion of a concept and new information being presented. Once again, consider a child's belief in Santa Claus. Most young children hold on to this belief for many years, although they may question just how someone Santa's size could fit down a chimney or get around to all the houses in the world in just one night. Although their friends may talk about the nonexistence of Santa Claus, children may refuse to stop believing in this red-suited character. In fact, when questioned, children often defend their belief in Santa Claus, as opposed to giving it up. Finally, after realizing that not all houses have chimneys, and testing their theories (and misconceptions) against their peers', they begin to recognize the possibility of other models and beliefs and start to make changes and accommodations in their understanding.

Other beliefs commonly held by young children are just as difficult for them to give up. These may include the Easter Bunny or the Tooth Fairy. Think about the various early ideas children have about how babies are born. Initially, some children believe in the "stork" model, while after conversations with others, the "Cabbage Patch" model takes its place. Other ideas children may hold are the model that the baby grows in mommy's tummy or that mommy and daddy go to the hospital and pick a baby out from behind a glass wall. If you are a parent, your child may have asked you, "Where do babies come from?" The question may have been prompted by a contradiction between what the child believed and the beliefs held by someone else. The talk young children are given by parents about the "birds and the bees" often creates disequilibrium in their understanding of reproduction. Yet that little talk, as awkward and uncomfortable as it may have been, may not have been influential enough for children to change their beliefs or give up their prior conceptions. But don't fret; sooner or later, students get the right story!

In any case, children and young adolescents should not be laughed at or ridiculed when stating their beliefs, especially when their prior knowledge may be naïve conceptions. When children are embarrassed about sharing their ideas, they often withdraw and are reluctant to risk sharing again. This causes them to hold on to their prior knowledge and not expose their ideas to peers or teachers. Thus, for teachers to assess and identify misconceptions, students need an atmosphere in which they can freely express their thinking without being laughed at or ridiculed.

UNCOVERING MISCONCEPTIONS IN SCIENCE

Several instructional strategies can be used to unveil prior knowledge and misconceptions held by students. Beginning a lesson by asking students "What do you know about . . ?" is a technique often used by teachers using the *KWL* method (Ogle, 1986). In this method, the teacher organizes the lesson or a chart into three questions: What do you *know* (about the topic)? What do you *wonder* (questions to investigate)? and, at the conclusion of the lesson or unit, What have you *learned*?

By posing the first question, What do you know? the teacher can assess students' prior knowledge about the topic they are about to study and adjust the lesson accordingly. This strategy can be carried out at the beginning of any lesson through individual writing or group discussion and charting the responses (see Form 4.1).

The Learning Cycle (Karplus & Thier, 1967) is a teaching and learning model based on Jean Piaget's work in cognitive development. The Learning Cycle was also used as the instructional model for an exemplary elementary science program funded by the National Science Foundation—the Science Curriculum Improvement Study (SCIS)—in the early 1960s. More detailed information on the Learning Cycle is presented in Chapter 8.

Form 4.1   A KWL Chart

What do you **KNOW?**	*What do you* **WANT** *to know?*	*What have you* **LEARNED?**

The model includes a five-step approach to lesson development. The five steps are

- Engagement
- Exploration
- Explanation
- Elaboration
- Evaluation

During the Engagement stage, the teacher introduces students to the learning task and focuses on connecting prior knowledge to the new knowledge being presented in the lesson. As the teacher makes this connection, it is an opportune time to find out what prior knowledge and possible misconceptions the children bring to the lesson. Thus, the Engagement stage provides an excellent opportunity for the teacher to access prior knowledge and understanding, identify what students' already know about the topic, and modify the lesson.

A third way to assess prior understanding is to administer a *misconception interview* prior to starting a new unit of study. During a misconception interview (see Form 4.2), the teacher or another adult asks three to five previously identified questions to a small group of students. The purpose of the interview is to reveal and uncover any misconceptions the students may have about the new topic being taught. As the students respond to the questions, the teacher records their responses. The teacher later analyzes the responses and makes accommodations to the lesson on the basis of the responses.

Addressing a student's misconceptions is not a simple process. First, the teacher needs a firm grasp of the concepts being studied to be able to recognize subtle misconceptions. Next, the teacher needs to pose questions and carefully listen for misconceptions. Because a student usually answers a question on the basis of his or her prior knowledge and experiences, teachers need to pay close attention to all student responses—both right and wrong answers. Wrong answers generally reflect naïve understandings or misconceptions held by students. Although we tend to "blow off" wrong answers, they often tell us more about prior understanding than correct answers do. Wrong answers can be an "open door" to student misconceptions. They send up a red flag to us.

HISTORICAL DEVELOPMENT TO CONSTRUCTIVISM

We begin our look at the development of education by turning our attention to *epistemology*, the structure and origin of knowledge. We must understand how knowledge is engendered to appreciate the potential of inquiry-based learning as a means for students to attain knowledge. We start by examining some early education philosophers and possibly reliving some recollections from "Ed Psych 101." Before the groans of reading about educational psychologists get too loud, understand that it is my belief that teachers make a quantum leap in their practice of inquiry once they have a solid foundation of how children learn.

Form 4.2   Misconception Interview

Misconception Interview

Title of Unit or Lesson:

Grade Level:

Name of Interviewer:

Description of Student A:

Description of Student B:

Description of Student C:

Question #1:

Student A Response:

Student B Response:

Student C Response:

Question #2:

Student A Response:

Student B Response:

Student C Response:

Question #3:

Student A Response:

Student B Response:

Student C Response:

Analysis/Misconceptions Uncovered:

Accommodations to Lesson Based on Responses:

The Constructivists

The latter half of the twentieth century produced an interest in understanding cognitive psychology and metacognition. The new theorists argued that learning develops as structures within a child's mind. Recent research on the brain and children's cognitive and social experience has opened the door to understanding how one comes to learn and communicate knowledge. This new era in educational psychology ushered in the cognitive and constructivist theorists.

The earliest constructivist writing, *De antiquissima Italorum sapientia*, dates back to an Italian philosopher, Giambattista Vico, in 1710. Here, we examine the research and philosophy of several twentieth-century reformers to learn how they have shaped modern theories about learning.

John Dewey

John Dewey (1859-1952) is considered one of the twentieth century's most influential education theorists and philosophers. His work at the University of Chicago helped shape modern education. Dewey's ideas about education were closely tied to the natural world. Dewey believed that teaching should be an active process, including solving problems that interested students. He believed that problems posed to pupils too often involved the interests of the teacher rather than those of the students. In Dewey's mind, learning had to have personal meaning for the student. Although he did not deny that some knowledge could be presented to students by their teachers, he did emphasize that each learner needs to make use of knowledge for it to be meaningful and retained. Dewey believed that thinking arises when a person confronts a given problem. The mind actively engages in a struggle to find an appropriate solution to the problem by drawing on the person's prior knowledge and experience, formulating a strategy to solve the problem, and, finally, weighing the consequences of that action (Phillips & Soltis, 1991, p. 39). In short, Dewey wanted schools to engage students in meaningful problems.

In applying Dewey's philosophy to today's science classrooms, DeBoer (1991) says that Dewey believed all instruction should be organized in such a way that it takes account of what the student knows. Prior student experience is restructured in the mind through a process of interacting with the teacher and the other students. Learning always involves present understanding as a starting point. Insistence on relevance of subject matter to enhance meaningful learning has been part of science education discussions since the late nineteenth century and continues to be a large part of good science teaching today.

Jean Piaget

Jean Piaget (1896-1980) was a Swiss scientist who began his scientific career studying bivalved mollusks. While working at the Binet Institute in the early 1920s, translating intelligence tests from English to French, he became interested in the mistakes children made on the tests. Piaget concentrated his work and research on humans, not animals. Although Piaget began researching cognitive development in the 1930s, his theories on cognitive development didn't catch the attention of American educators until the 1960s, partly because his writings were in French. By studying how children make sense of their world, his work became a turning point in our thinking about how knowledge is acquired and had a great impact on educators over the last half of the twentieth century.

Piaget (1970) believed that knowledge is not out there somewhere, waiting to be discovered, but rather is acquired and constructed through a process of interaction with materials. He studied a number of learners through clinical interviews in which he posed questions and provided problems (later to be called Piagetian tasks) for them to solve. He then made careful observations about their solutions and analyzed their comments. Piaget focused his study on the cognitive structures that enable a child to solve a problem. On the basis of his research, he identified four developmental stages of mental reasoning that characterize the development of knowledge and use of logical thinking. He believed that children construct cognitive representations from their experiences that he termed *schemas*. Schemas are personal mental models that enable us to actively interpret and assess phenomena and incoming information from existing conditions. These schemas are often naïve, incomplete, and imprecise. Sometimes, mental models represent scientific views, and sometimes they represent presently held misconceptions. As children experience new information, they use these schemas to assimilate new ideas in constructing knowledge. Driscoll (1994) suggests that schemas are used to make inferences and predictions about other unobserved events. Unlike some of his predecessors who believed that knowledge is *imparted*, Piaget (1970) theorized that children *construct* their own knowledge on the basis of their explorations and interactions with peers, adults, and objects within their environments. In other words, we come to know an object by acting on it.

Piaget's theory is largely based on three assumptions:

1. Knowledge is a result of ever-changing interactions between individuals and their environments.

2. Knowledge is constantly being constructed and reconstructed from prior and new experiences.

3. Cognitive growth is self-regulating within the individual and between the individual and the interaction of the physical and social environment.

Although Piaget's theory was never intended specifically for academic teaching, it holds a special interest for teachers, especially science teachers. In studying the transition that children make from concrete to formal operations, teachers understand that students need to explore a new concept through hands-on experiences before being introduced to the terminology and vocabulary associated with the concept. Introducing concrete inquiry investigations first and saving the terminology and vocabulary development for later allows children to explore new experiences, test theories and ideas against their peers, and assimilate their understanding.

According to Piaget, the process of *adaptation* occurs through *assimilation* and *accommodation*. Assimilation involves making use of new information and transforming new knowledge to fit existing schemas and mental models. In accommodation, mental models are altered, modified, or changed to accept or fit the newly perceived knowledge. Adaptation occurs when individuals encounter phenomena that are contrary to their presently held understanding. They judge the new events and make adjustments in their cognitive structures to accommodate the new situations. This results in new learning. In most cases, assimilation and accommodation function simultaneously. Piaget refers to this as *equilibrium*. That is, the individual is self-regulating his or her understanding and maintaining stability. At equilibrium, we are at ease with our presently held notions. All is well with the world.

Disequilibrium occurs when one experiences a new phenomenon that does not neatly fit into his or her presently held schemas or models. Piaget called this *cognitive conflict*. Causing disequilibrium and cognitive conflict is not all destructive. Often, constructivist teachers instill degrees of disequilibrium to cause individuals to give up misconceptions or undergo cognitive change.

Constructivists believe that when a new event doesn't fit a child's presently held belief, it can possibly be discarded because it doesn't fit with the child's cognitive model of understanding. Assimilation, accommodation, and disequilibrium are the bases for constructivist thinking and conceptual change and are constantly at work. According to Piaget, for conceptual change to occur, the child must be faced with new conceptions that are inconsistent with the child's presently held beliefs. The child must also acknowledge dissatisfaction with his or her present schema and accept the plausibility of the new concept, thus substituting the new concept for the previously held one.

Piaget's theory has been widely accepted in the field of cognitive development as well as in education circles. Applications of Piaget's theory include the following:

- Learning should be active and discovery-based.
- Children should be given many opportunities to interact with their peers.
- Instructional strategies should be adapted to fit the cognitive structures of children.
- Conceptual change should be promoted by allowing children to test their presently held theories and become aware of inconsistencies in their thinking when compared with scientific models.

Lev Semenovich Vygotsky

The Russian psychologist Lev S. Vygotsky (1896-1934) was born near Minsk in western Russia in 1896, the same year as Jean Piaget. He received a law degree in 1917 from Moscow University but later turned his attention to medicine and psychology, with a specific focus on learning disabilities. In 1924, the outspoken young psychologist took exception to Pavlov and Gestalt. With the prevailing notion that animal behavior can be applied to understand how humans learn, Vygotsky (1924/1979) contrasted animal and human behavior by describing the abilities of humans as uniquely specific to the species. According to Bodrova and Leong (1996), Vygotsky's theories on cognitive development were unique and distinct from those of his contemporaries, and although under extreme pressure to be politically correct, he never gave in to that pressure. Although many of his theories on teaching and learning were never backed up with empirical data due to his early death, researchers recently have expanded on his theories and framework on preschool and early childhood education to innovation in teaching at all grade levels.

Vygotsky made a significant contribution to cognitive development and the theory of constructivism by writing frantically for his last 3 years before his death from tuberculosis at the age of 37. Most of his writings were still incomplete at the time of his death and weren't translated into English until the early 1960s. His work *Thought and Language* (1934/1962) did not capture the attention of Western constructivists until its translation in 1962. Vygotsky and Piaget shared similar thoughts on constructivism; however, Vygotsky was not concerned with identifying stages of mental development. He explored the influence of language and social processes on cognitive development, as well as the accomplishments a child could achieve when solving a problem alone as compared with assistance from an adult.

Two basic principles from the Vygotskian framework include the role language plays in mental development and the importance of social interaction within the context of learning. Whereas Piaget's theory about learning focused mainly on interaction with physical objects, Vygotsky believed that the construction of knowledge is predicated on manipulation but additionally is socially mediated. In his work, Vygotsky emphasized the importance of social interaction between the learner and his or her peers; thus, he was given the label of "social constructivist." According to Vygotsky (1978), an "important factor in social learning was the young person's ability to learn by imitating and modeling. Interacting with adults and peers in cooperative settings gave young children ample opportunity to observe, imitate, and model" (pp. 79-80).

One of his foremost known theories is the *Zone of Proximal Development* (ZPD). According to Vygotsky, students' abilities and skills in solving problems or accomplishing tasks can be categorized into two levels:

- Skills the student possesses to perform tasks independently and
- Skills the student lacks (at an independent level), so tasks can be performed only with assistance from another student or adult.

The independent level is a lower or minimum level of performance where students can operate unassisted. The assisted level is a higher or maximum level where children can achieve more complex performance with help or assistance from another. The zone is an arbitrary continuum or area between these two levels. Although most of traditional teaching is focused more closely on what students can achieve independently, a constructivist teacher instructs to the upper zone by providing assistance to the performance through prompts, leading questions, hints and clues, or asking the student to clarify his or her position about the phenomenon being studied. Although this interaction can be interpreted as an "expert-novice" relationship, Vygotsky believed that all students could enhance their learning through social mediation with peers or an adult.

One instructional strategy based upon the idea of the ZPD is *scaffolding* (Wood, Bruner, & Ross, 1976). Using the metaphor of a scaffold in building construction, scaffolding provides a level of support that enables the learner to accomplish a task normally beyond his or her current capabilities. In scaffolding situations, the teacher purposefully and intentionally designs a performance task just beyond the independent level. Providing guidance at first, the teacher then gradually decreases assistance until the student can take more responsibility for completing the task. Vygotsky suggests that teachers provide problems and tasks just beyond the student's present capabilities and, through cooperative learning groups and modeling from adults, the student is scaffolded to high levels of thinking and performance.

To provide an example of scaffolding, I'll use the day I taught my daughter, Janice, to ride a two-wheel bike. She was the only one in her fourth-grade class who was riding a bike with training wheels. That was enough of an incentive for Janice to ask me for help. We got the bike out of the garage and headed for the street. At first, she practiced balancing on the bike without the training wheels while I held the bike upright. Next, we moved on to short spurts where Janice pedaled and I ran alongside, holding the bike upright. With one hand on the back of the seat, I held the bike while she pedaled down the street. I can still recall her saying, "Daddy, don't let me go!" Well, what she didn't know, as I ran alongside the bike for what seemed an eternity, was that I sporadically let go of the bicycle seat, allowing Janice to ride on her own. "I've got you," I said. "Just keep pedaling!" Nearly out of breath, she began to gain confidence in balancing without assistance. After a few spills and some scraped knees, she gained more confidence and achieved the goal of riding the bike on her own.

In many ways, good constructivist teachers teach in the same way. They are consciously aware of the prompts and assistance they need to provide to have their students achieve at higher levels of academic performance. Constructivist and inquiry-based teachers do not make the task easier; rather, they provide the appropriate level of support and assistance for students to acquire the necessary knowledge and skills in science. Constructivist and inquiry-based teachers are also constantly aware of shifting the onus of responsibility from the teacher to the student, enabling the student to become a more independent learner. Sometimes unknowingly, elementary and middle school teachers use Vygotskian principles by implementing *guided*, *semi-guided*, and *independent* approaches to proving tasks to students.

The teacher begins by providing a mental challenge task to the student. With help from the teacher or a peer, the student is guided to the solution and begins to understand the nature of the concept. With the second problem, the student is provided a semi-guided practice to gain confidence and control over the task. Presented with a third problem, the student functions independently in solving the task. The teacher models appropriate behaviors and assists students to work at levels that stretch their imagination, thinking, and abilities. As the communication exchanges between the student and the teacher continue, the student begins to construct and mediate understanding of the topic.

David Ausubel

Ausubel (1918–), like other constructivists, viewed cognition as the framework for organizing hierarchical concepts (1968). Ausubel believed that with meaningful learning, links are formed or *subsumed* between previous, more general concepts and new knowledge. Meaningful learning occurs when new information is linked (or assimilated) to existing or previous concepts (Novak, 1977, 1998). Often, information derived without meaningful learning is not retained for long periods after the initial introduction. In the words of the old Chinese proverb, "Tell me and I forget, show me and I remember, let me do it and I understand."

Along the same lines as our previous discussion on accessing prior knowledge at the start of a lesson or unit, Ausubel, Novak, and Hanensian (1978) wrote, "The most important single factor influencing learning is what the learner already knows; ascertain this, and teach him accordingly" (p. iv). This serves as a reminder for teachers interested in constructivist learning strategies to begin with the child's perspective as a departure for instruction.

CONSTRUCTIVISM TODAY

Traditionalism so dominated educational culture during most of the twentieth century that constructivist principles were not readily accepted, even in the realm of research. Modern brain research offered much to sway the general acceptance toward constructivism during the 1980s and 1990s.

Constructivism today has an increasingly significant impact on educational reform and is increasingly being adopted as the accepted theory on how children learn. The ideas of Dewey, Piaget, Vygotsky, and Ausubel are largely responsible for the new era of enlightenment in science education that began during the 1960s and continued through the beginning of the new millennium.

In summary, key points in constructivism include the following:

1. The senses are conduits to assimilating new knowledge.

2. The learner's existing or presently held understanding determines which new ideas are accepted, rejected, or ignored.

3. The learner's existing or presently held understanding determines how new ideas are interpreted.

4. Knowledge is not transmitted or imparted from one individual to another. Communication, in the form of language, is transmitted, and the learner has to make sense of that language.

5. Knowledge is constructed by the learner making links to previously stored knowledge.

6. The learner uses mental links to construct new knowledge.

7. The learner's models are constantly undergoing construction and reconstruction.

8. Learning is a personally and socially constructed process.

9. Inquiry is a viable teaching strategy to test the degree of fit between one's theories and scientific explanations.

BACK TO THE ICE HANDS

We now have a better understanding of how inquiry and constructivism accompany one another. Let's turn back to the ice hands in Chapter 3 and analyze the investigation from an inquiry and constructivist perspective. Here is a summary of the ice hands investigation, in which Camille Perlo enacted the following sequence:

1. She introduced the investigation by saying it was going to be an opportunity for students to do the things scientists do.

2. She assessed prior knowledge by having students write in their journals what knowledge they brought to the lesson and then had students discuss through a think-pair-share activity. The information was then shared with the entire class by designing a concept map or listing their ideas on poster board to include all their presently held understanding about ice.

3. She provided materials with which the students could observe and explore an ice hand in a dry pan while recording observations in their science journals. Later, she added water to the pan so that students could observe the ice hand floating and melting.

4. She encouraged the students to raise and record "What if" and "I wonder" questions.

5. She categorized student questions according to which ones could be answered through experimentation, which ones needed revising before investigating, which ones could be answered best through expert resources (or books), and which ones couldn't be answered at that time.

6. She had students select questions and grouped students around the questions to be investigated.

7. She provided time for students to discuss and brainstorm their investigations through group dialogue and identify specifically what they wanted to find out.

8. She had students write statements to test, in the form of predictions.

9. She provided time for students to design plans to carry out their investigations.

10. She had students collect evidence and data, organize data in tables and charts to look for patterns and relationships, and draw claims and conclusions about their stated predictions.

11. She encouraged students to communicate their evidence and claims by having each group make an oral presentation with a trifold board.

12. She compared new knowledge gained through the investigations with prior knowledge by revising and modifying the concept maps made during Day 1.

13. She applied newly acquired knowledge to other situations.

14. She encouraged students to pursue and explore additional questions, thus beginning the inquiry cycle all over again.

15. She explicitly focused a discussion on the critical thinking skills and processes inherent in inquiry-based learning.

The process followed during the ice hands investigation represents attributes of both constructivist principles and the inquiry cycle. The process can be summarized by illustrating the "constructivist" inquiry cycle (see Figure 4.5).

A CONSTRUCTIVIST UNIT OF STUDY

Through the ice hand example, you can see how the notion of constructivism has implications for teaching and learning using inquiry-based science. How many of the following characteristics can you identify from the ice hand investigation that portray a constructivist unit of study?

1. Knowing how children learn and its relevance to how we approach teaching and learning

2. Knowing that educational theory places meaning on our understanding about teaching and learning

Figure 4.5   The Constructivist Inquiry Cycle

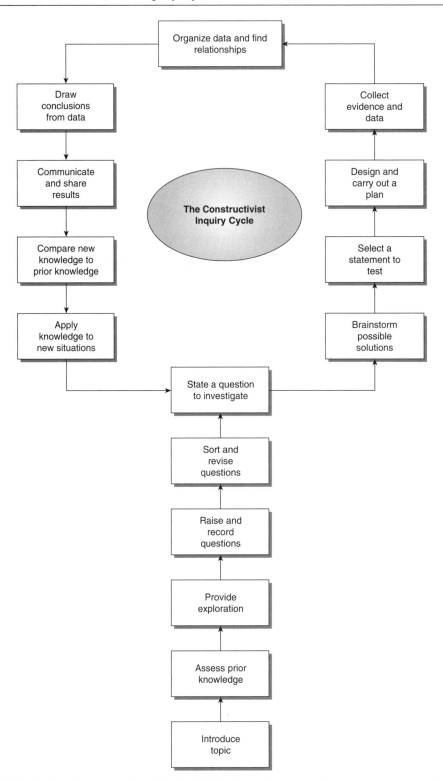

3. Demonstrating that it is essential to use concrete and manipulative materials to introduce formal concepts

4. Starting with what a child knows as an effective departure point for any science lesson

5. Allowing explorations and "time to mess about" to introduce and sequence new knowledge

6. Encouraging inductive and discovery learning to open the doors to problem solving and higher-level thinking skills

7. Providing activities that challenge students' thinking and problem-solving skills

8. Using active learning in which the student can discover and construct new knowledge

9. Posing "What if" and "I wonder" questions to facilitate assimilation and accommodation

10. Encouraging students to work in groups to share and communicate knowledge and to test one another's ideas and theories, making learning a personal and social experience

Again, whether you are reading the book alone, collaborating in a small study group, or participating in a college course or summer institute, take time to reflect and discuss the 10 characteristics listed above. How many of the following characteristics can you identify in a lesson you recently observed or taught? Make notations and reflections in the margin alongside each statement.

HOW SCIENTISTS USE MODELS IN SCIENCE

When elementary school children draw a scientist, quite often they portray a white male with frizzy white hair and a white lab coat mixing chemicals in a laboratory—resembling the image of a stereotypical "mad scientist" (Barman, 1996, 1997; Bodzin & Gehringer, 2001; McDuffie, 2001). A more mature notion of a scientist evokes a person who seeks a broad *explanation* of a particular unexplained phenomenon, formulated through repeated testing and scrutiny. This explanation is sometimes called a *theory*. A theory, in turn, may be represented as a physical or mental *model*. Model building is an important aspect of the work of scientists. Models are especially useful tools in science because they convey what we can and cannot directly observe. According to Gilbert and Watt Ireton (2003), "using models is a form of communication. . . . [M]odel building can help students assemble their seemingly fragmented knowledge about concepts and relationships into larger, more clearly understood constructs" (p. vii). Gilbert and Watt Ireton further state that "when we are conscious of our surroundings, we may believe that we are seeing the world as it exists, like a projection on a screen: In fact, we are not; we are seeing a mental model of a world we have constructed from information our senses, sense receptors, and memories give us" (p. 4).

The child who draws an image of a mad scientist probably bases that image on his or her previous experiences from movies or cartoons. As distorted or incorrect the image or naïve conception may be, it is still based on reality from the individual's perspective. We know that over time the child's notion of what a scientist is and what a scientist does will change as the child matures into an adolescent and then an adult, and develops a normative reality of science. Our understanding of the natural world is an ever-evolving mental construct, containing perceptions and models that are constantly being modified or discarded to reflect additional experiences and new information.

Models and model building are so essential to the study of science that both the *National Science Education Standards* (NRC, 1996, pp. 145, 219) and the *Benchmarks for Science Literacy* (AAAS, 1993, pp. 267-269) embrace models as one of the overarching, common themes in organizing an understanding of science. Scientists usually begin an investigation by observing a specific phenomenon in the natural world. These observations lead to inferences from the observations, which in turn lead to theory building, testing the theory under meticulous conditions, and repeating the test for reliability. As repeated conditions produce consistent results, a model is constructed to explain the theory. Over time, as our abilities to observe and measure are enhanced, so are our explanations, theories, and models. Our understanding of the atom is one example of how models change through applying our ability to observe and measure. In this section, we will see how scientists (and children) use models to explain abstract concepts and phenomena.

The early Greeks thought that all matter was made of four elements: air, fire, earth, and water. Although limited by human intuition, this was one of the first "models" of atomic theory. The first "modern" atomic model was proposed in 1911 by British physicist Ernest Rutherford. Rutherford proposed that atoms were composed mostly of empty space. Rutherford's model included a positively charged center surrounded by negatively charged particles called electrons. Later, Niels Bohr proposed a model that became the modern theory of atomic structure. Many of us were taught the Bohr model in high school chemistry class and can recall electrons pictured as particles orbiting around the nucleus like planets in our solar system. With new technological advances in electronic imagery and quantum mechanics, today's atomic model includes subatomic particles, called *quarks*, in various clouds around the nucleus.

Mental and physical models are constructed through direct and indirect observations. Although models help scientists explain scientific phenomena, they are always limited by human senses, tools, and abilities. These observations lead to inferences, and inferences help build theories. Scientists then use these theories to construct models that fit their observations and inferences. As said earlier, as our abilities to make observations are enhanced, so are the models that stem from those observations and inferences. In other words, models are evolving explanations of our natural world. Thus, it is best to be cautious about assuming that any one model represents reality. As Karl Popper (1972) once said, "Whenever a theory appears to you as the only possible one, take this as a sign that you have neither understood the theory nor the problem which it was intended to solve." Models do not exist forever. The history books of science are filled with outdated theories and models that were once thought to be true (Youngson, 1998). Consider for a moment the second-century astronomer Ptolemy, who proposed the theory that the Earth was the center of the solar system, or the French biologist Jean-Baptiste Lamarck, who proposed the theory that the giraffe got its long neck by stretching it to reach the leaves on branches of tall trees. Both of these prominent scientists formulated popular models, only to have them later disproved.

Although some models become outdated on the basis of new observations, other phenomena may be explained by several possible models because of the limited way in which models can be tested. Consider what may have caused dinosaurs to become extinct. Several models exist to explain the disappearance of dinosaurs. The model of an asteroid hitting the Earth's surface 65 million years ago near the Yucatán Peninsula in Mexico appears to be one of the most accepted.

In studying dinosaurs, paleontologists continue to rewrite the pages of science. In the past, many of us have visited museums and seen dinosaurs as fierce animals, with their tails on the ground. Recently, new observations indicate that dinosaurs may have been warm-blooded and quite maternal. Many science museums exhibiting *Tyrannosaurus rex* skeletons have had to "redesign" their extinct creatures by repositioning the tails as extensions of the backbone.

In one third-grade class, the teacher explained to her students how scientists now know that *T. rex* didn't drag its tail. She explained that because of the lack of tail marks between the footprints of dinosaurs, left in mud fields and preserved as fossils, scientists have concluded that dinosaurs held their tails up—above the ground. The class went on to find more than 50 pictures of dinosaurs shown dragging their tails behind or resting on them. The students later displayed their findings on a poster titled "Misconceptions About Dinosaurs."

Thomas Kuhn (1962/1996), in his landmark book *The Structure of Scientific Revolutions*, introduced the phrase *paradigm* to describe the laws, theories, and applications from which "normal science" (research-based knowledge) springs. Thirty years later, *paradigm shift* became popular in describing a change of position in thinking. Corporate leaders use the term "paradigm shift" to refer to a new way of thinking or doing business. Undergoing a paradigm shift means taking on a new way of looking at something. Paradigm shifts are analogous to the way scientists rethink theories and models on the basis of new observations and evidence.

HOW CHILDREN LEARN

Although some educators often describe a child's learning like "a sponge soaking up knowledge," constructivist teachers see learning quite differently. Constructivist teachers see learning as a process by which the child acts as a *theory builder*. As children use their senses to make observations about the natural world, they draw inferences about the cause-and-effect phenomena they experience. These inferences lead children to form theories about how the world operates. Thus, a child's present understanding or theories are, again, largely based on his or her prior experiences. These experiences allow the child to form models and store them as memories within various areas of the brain.

Children continue to test their ideas, beliefs, and models through ongoing observations. Children often test their theories and models through interaction with their peers, one of the most influential aspects of their life. When their observations and experiences continue to match their presently held theories and those of their peers, the experiences are assimilated and the model is reinforced. When their observations and experiences do not match their presently held theories, either (a) the experiences can be discounted because they don't align with the present understandings, or (b) their model can be accommodated by a conceptual change to include new experiences and observations. In other words, they would undergo a paradigm shift!

Recall the process you went through in Chapter 2, in which you wrote a statement about your understanding of inquiry. The statement was meant to help you reflect on your present understanding and make changes and modifications to your model of inquiry by considering the ideas of other experts. Using various colors for each time you revised your concept map provides visual evidence that new meaning was being constructed. In other words, you were constructing an understanding of inquiry.

According to constructivist philosophy, meaning is continually being negotiated by means of assimilation and accommodation in the minds of thinking beings through verbal communication with others. In other words, language plays a key role in learning. How often do teachers find themselves presenting a concept one day and discovering the next day that the students just didn't "get it"? If your teaching philosophy is based on assumptive learning, you might assume that learning occurs because the students are listening to the teacher. But just because students are listening to me does not mean they can make sense of my language. The words may be part of the sender's (the teacher's) experience but not part of the receiver's (the student's) experience.

Recently, a seventh-grade life science teacher was giving a lecture on the parts of a cell. Thinking she had to prepare the students for high school biology, the teacher repeatedly tossed out terms like mitochondria, endoplasmic reticulum, Gogli bodies, lysosomes, and ribosomes. Most of the students in the class were completely baffled and unfamiliar with the utterance of the new vocabulary posted on the blackboard. Although the terms made sense to the sender (the teacher), they made little sense to most of the receivers (the students). For many students, those cell terms were not part of their prior experience and made as little sense to them as would the words in a foreign language class. This is not to suggest that students can't learn rigorous vocabulary terms, but rather that the introduction of such new and unfamiliar terms might be better linked to the students' prior knowledge by drawing an analogy between the "cell" and a "city," with the teacher explaining the cell organelles in relation to services provided by a city.

In this example the teacher is not imparting or transferring knowledge to the class. Likewise, the students are not soaking up the information like little sponges. The teacher, however, is sharing communication, but in the form of oral language that makes little sense to the students if the language is not part of their everyday language. For learning to occur from a constructivist point of view, the teacher needs to communicate in a language familiar to the student, make meaning out of the new information, and initiate the replacement of the child's everyday language with the new scientific language.

MOTHER GOOSE MEETS THE MAD SCIENTIST

To emphasize the importance of language, consider the following scientific nursery rhymes. Again, the emphasis here is to understand the role language plays in communication and the learning process. If you don't understand the language, gaining new knowledge becomes a difficult task. These scientific nursery rhymes may make sense to you because you understand the scientific language from your previous familiarity with the scientific terms. Can you name the following scientific nursery rhymes? (The original author is unknown.)

1. A research duo proceeded toward the apex of a natural geologic protuberance. The purpose of their expedition was the procurement of a sample of fluid hydride of oxygen in a large vessel, the exact size of which was unspecified. One member of the team precipitately descended, sustaining severe fractural damage to the upper cranial portion of his anatomical structure. Subsequently, the second member of the team performed a self-rotational translation, oriented in the direction taken by the first member.

2. A triumvirate of murine rodents totally devoid of ophthalmic acuity was observed in a state of rapid progression in pursuit of an agriculturalist's marital spouse. The aforementioned spouse then proceeded to perform a triple caudectomy utilizing an acutely honed bladed instrument generally used for the subdivision of edible tissue.

3. A female of the species *Homo sapiens* possessed of a small immature ruminant of the genus *Ovis*. The outermost covering of the ruminant reflected all the wavelengths of visible light with the luminosity equal to that of a mass of naturally occurring microscopically crystalline water. Regardless of the translational pathway chosen by the *Homo sapiens*, the probability that the aforementioned ruminant would select the same pathway was 1.

THE CHILD AS A SCIENTIST

By simply watching a child playing in the sandbox or having fun on a swing set or monkey bars, we see the child making observations and generalizing about matter, momentum, energy transfer, and the properties of objects. The child may not realize it, but he or she is actually using science process skills and testing scientific ideas while playing. The child is acting like a young scientist!

Science process skills are the investigative tools for inquiry. The scientist uses process skills, such as observing, measuring, predicting, inferring, classifying, experimenting, and communicating, to make sense of a new experience, collect evidence to form an explanation, and connect that new explanation to previously held knowledge, conceptions, and models. Other science process skills include controlling variables, collecting data, interpreting data, graphing, model building, using numbers and time-space relationships, estimating, and sequencing. Although we generally describe science process skills as separate skills, they rarely function individually. For example, when scientists make inferences, those inferences are based on observations. In other words, scientists use observations to draw conclusions and make inferences.

All children are scientists. They use the same process skills as scientists do, but on a simpler level. When children observe, they use their five senses—seeing, hearing, smelling, tasting, and touching—to collect data about the things around them. Scientists also make observations as part of their work; however, they use more sophisticated instruments and equipment to extend their senses to gather data, read X-rays, or view microscopic organisms. Both the child and the scientist make observations to collect significant information about objects and phenomena surrounding them.

In the same way, we also use observations for other critical thinking skills, such as comparing and contrasting and finding patterns in nature. We use observations and data to make predictions about future events. The better our observations are, the more confidence we have in our predictions. Teachers also know that when a young child makes a new observation in class, communication soon follows. The child wants to tell everyone in the class about the discovery!

We have now seen that learning science is an ongoing process of conceptual change and modifying our understanding. Similar to the way scientists continue to modify their models and theories, learning is a continuous, active process. For many of us, inquiry is the perfect vehicle for facilitating a cognitive-based, constructivist approach to learning. In an inquiry/constructivist approach, the learner is engaged in a hands-on, science-related question, problem, or investigation. During an inquiry investigation, the child observes, questions, and gathers evidence to test his or her present understanding, forming a concrete or mental model that explains and justifies the phenomenon. As the child constructs meaning for new scientific knowledge, he or she builds an identity as a scientist.

QUESTIONS FOR REFLECTION AND DISCUSSION

1. Consider a topic in elementary or middle school science about which students may hold misconceptions. What three questions could you pose during a misconception interview to uncover the possible misconceptions?

2. In their book *Understanding Models in Earth and Space Science*, Gilbert and Watt Ireton (2003) state, "When we conceive of our thoughts as models, we can better understand and accept the limits of learning. In fact, our ability to distance ourselves from conceptual creations is the heart of critical thinking and scientific skepticism" (p. 99). Apply this statement to a child's learning through inquiry.

3. In what ways is constructivism the "moral compass" to inquiry-based teaching?

4. Often we hear teachers describe a bright student as one "whose brain is like a sponge, sucking up everything I say." How is the sponge statement contrary to constructivist learning principles?

Creating a Culture of Inquiry

The pebble that drops into a pond is like an idea that sparks inquiry. The concentric ripples represent new questions that emerge from the first germ of the idea. The ever-enlarging pattern of ripples refers to the integrated knowledge that is acquired as each question is explored, limited only by the force of the inquirer's enthusiasm for the search. The greater the interest and the more probing the questions, the more encompassing the study, the bigger the ideas that it develops, and the deeper and more meaningful the knowledge the inquirer constructs.

—Marian Martinello and Gillian Cook
Interdisciplinary Inquiry in Teaching and Learning

Anatole France, the Nobel Prize winner for literature in 1921, wrote more than 85 years ago that the art of teaching is awakening the natural curiosity of young minds. It is that natural curiosity and inquisitiveness that inquiry-based teachers so value and cultivate. However, in reality, most elementary school teachers do not foster interest in inquiry solely through the subject of science. For the quintessential inquiry teacher, constructivist principles pervade all academic areas, including mathematics, language arts, and social studies. In essence, these teachers create a culture of inquiry in their classrooms. For the middle school science teacher who teaches only science, the culture of the classroom still expresses the sum total of the rites and rituals in which the teacher and the pupils interact.

A classroom's culture plays a dominant role that weaves the fabric of values, beliefs, and assumptions as a community of learners transacts. It is the "instructional glue" that bonds meaning, purpose, and performance. A classroom's culture shapes hundreds of daily behaviors and interactions between the teacher and the students and among students themselves. Although each classroom has its own distinct culture, inquiry-based classrooms seem to have a noticeable embedded culture, a stream of raising and valuing questions that habitually coerces curiosity in the midst of skepticism and stimulates intellectual capacity. As Carl Sagan wrote in his book *The Demon-Haunted World* (1996) "both skepticism and wonder are skills that need honing and practice. Their harmonious marriage within the mind of every school-child ought to be a principal goal of public education" (p. 306).

In a culture of inquiry, teachers are not threatened by questions that children ask. When a teacher doesn't know the answer, he or she just says, "Let's find out the answer together." In a culture of inquiry, a community of learners is committed to continuous improvement in an atmosphere of collaboration. In a culture of inquiry, a classroom that students are proud to call their own, members respect the intellectual diversity of the individuals and are passionate about creating a caring relationship among its members. In a culture of inquiry, investigations and projects are designed and rooted to facilitate the understanding of scientific knowledge and principles.

TRADITIONAL AND INQUIRY-CENTERED CLASSROOMS

In understanding two contrasting classroom cultures, imagine a typical Thursday morning in a conventional American school. Let's call it John Glenn Middle School. As you walk down the hall and peer into a classroom, how would you know if you were just about to enter an inquiry-centered room? What would the students be doing? What would the teacher be doing? What would the physical arrangement of the classroom look like? What would you see on the classroom walls and on the bulletin boards? Most inquiry- or student-centered classrooms look and feel different from traditional, teacher-centered classrooms.

To help us understand what inquiry classrooms are like, we will contrast a teacher-centered and a student-centered setting. However, before we begin, a disclaimer is warranted. For the sole purpose of distinguishing between "so-called" traditional and inquiry classroom settings, once again I will take the liberty of providing a somewhat overexaggerated and overgeneralized look at two dissimilar classroom settings. The following descriptions do not imply that one setting is always more advantageous than another; in reality, teachers select characteristics of each setting based on the nature of the curriculum topic or the needs and readiness levels of their students. Granted, there are times when we need to provide instruction that is direct and explicit, while other times a more implicit approach is appropriate. A prudent methodology includes a balance of both subsets.

Imagine yourself entering a science class in that typical school. Mr. Fenwick (the teacher name is fictitious) has been teaching at the school since 1978. Today, his lesson is "Heat as a Source of Energy." His desk and an overhead projector are centered in the front of the room. The day's topic is projected on the screen from the overhead. The students' desks are lined up in straight rows. Mr. Fenwick believes that knowing science means knowing the terms and vocabulary that define science. His responsibility in teaching is to impart knowledge to the students. This martinet presents a well-structured, teacher-centered lecture with notes for students to copy from the overhead projector. During this particular class, one at a time, students are reading paragraphs from the textbook aloud as Mr. Fenwick stands alongside his desk.

Following the individual reading assignment, Mr. Fenwick instructs the students to turn to the back of the chapter and answer the review questions on a separate sheet of paper, which is to be handed in by the end of the period. Quietly, the students open their textbooks to the proper page and begin the assignment, searching for the correct answers within the chapter. Mr. Fenwick announces that tomorrow the class will have a quiz on the chapter notes and, on the board, provides a list of terms students need to memorize for Friday's paper-and-pencil test.

Ms. Jackson's room is down the hall. She is in her sixth year of teaching science at John Glenn. She has just completed her master's degree and has substantial graduate-level coursework in inquiry-based teaching. In this classroom, Ms. Jackson's desk is at the side of the room. There is a portable worktable in a front corner that both the teacher and students share. The student desks are arranged in groups of four. There are six groups of students' desks. Ms. Jackson is also presenting a lesson on heat energy. In her lesson, students are working in collaborative groups, rotating from station to station, and completing an exploration at each station. As you walk around the room, you hear students analyzing the task and formulating plans to solve each station task. Students are predicting possible outcomes, sharing their strategies with other group members, and providing emotional and academic support for challenging aspects of the task. Ms. Jackson moves about from group to group listening to their responses and assisting and encouraging students to work as independent learners. As she circulates about the room, she assesses how students sense the difficulty of each task and gauges each student's level of understanding. She stimulates their thinking skills by posing additional questions that encourage them to analyze and make judgments about their investigations. Ms. Jackson knows that there are no right or wrong answers to her questions, just opportunities for students to reflect on their work, negotiate their prior experiences, construct meaning from their previously held knowledge, and make sense of their natural world. Next week, she will give the students an opened-ended lab to apply what they learned during the station experiences.

CONSTRUCTING A DEFINITION OF AN INQUIRY-CENTERED CLASSROOM

Keeping the contrasting classrooms in mind, visualize an inquiry-centered classroom for your grade level. Visualize what you, the teacher, would be doing. Also visualize what the students would be doing and how the classroom is arranged. Use a graphic organizer similar to Figure 5.1 at the end of this chapter to begin to identify the characteristics of an inquiry classroom. On your graphic organizer, describe the students' role in this classroom. You may list statements such as "asking questions," "making observations," "working in cooperative groups," "designing procedures to test a prediction," or "sharing ideas with others." When characterizing your role, typical statements might include "posing questions to students," "acting as a facilitator of learning," or "exploring interests of the students." You may have depicted the classroom environment as "interactive and engaging" with indicators such as "students' desks arranged in groups" or "students' work is displayed on walls and bulletin boards."

The following sections provide a background for observing each of these three aspects of the classroom: the students, the teacher, and the physical environment. At the end of this chapter, go back to your graphic organizer and make additions and changes to your understanding of an inquiry-centered classroom.

STUDENTS IN INQUIRY-CENTERED CLASSROOMS

Because students are at the center of inquiry-based learning, it is appropriate to begin our discussion with student behaviors that characterize inquiry. When observing students doing inquiry, we generally observe the following:

1. Students acting as researchers

2. Students working in groups

3. Students using critical thinking skills

4. Students showing an interest in science

The next sections will highlight each of the four observations.

STUDENTS ACTING AS RESEARCHERS

Curiosity is the heart of inquiry. Curiosity pumps questions throughout the learner. When students act as researchers in inquiry classrooms, they take on new roles and responsibilities. Acting as researchers leads students to using integrated process skills such as identifying variables, making predictions, designing experiments and investigations, constructing data tables and graphs, and analyzing the relationships between variables.

Having students act as researchers is a challenging endeavor for both students and teachers. For students to take on new roles, teachers must assume new roles as well. In a culture of inquiry, teachers must believe that students have the abilities and interest to carry out their own investigations and generate their particular, and sometimes peculiar, ideas. When students act as researchers, they commence taking responsibility for their own learning. Most students prefer to answer their own questions and solve their own problems rather than respond to someone else's. As researchers, students can make decisions about their own work, such as how they will collect and organize data and how they will communicate their findings to the rest of the class. By planning and designing their inquiries, students begin to use higher-level, critical thinking skills, such as analyzing and evaluating, to guide the design and course of their investigations. Teachers will begin to find that they need to provide fewer answers and more support to students. A teacher's support may include (a) guiding the students to a location to search the Internet for a particular topic, (b) suggesting that they consult an expert on the topic, or (c) recommending primary sources for the students to review.

According to the *National Science Education Standards* (NSES) (NRC, 1996), in challenging students to accept and share responsibility for their work,

> teachers [should] make it clear that each student must take responsibility for his or her work. Teachers also create opportunities for their own learning, individually and as members of groups. Teachers do so by supporting student ideas and questions and by encouraging students to pursue them. Teachers give individual students active roles in the design and implementation of investigations, in the work with their peers, and in student assessment of their own work. (p. 36)

STUDENTS WORKING IN GROUPS

According to the American Association for the Advancement of Science (1990),

> The collaborative nature of science and technological work should be strongly reinforced by frequent group activity in the classroom. Scientists and engineers work mostly in groups and less often as isolated investigators. Similarly, students should gain experience sharing responsibility for learning with each other. (p. 202)

In many instances, students should work individually; at other times, collaborative group work is more appropriate. This decision is often made at the teacher's discretion, depending on the objective and nature of the lesson being studied. Group work can allow students to learn from one another, share and challenge their ideas, and distribute the work in an equitable fashion. Students learn to construct knowledge together and build positive peer relationships. Group work also allows students to build self-confidence while working collaboratively in a group to complete a common goal. Having students work in groups, however, always requires consideration of gender and cultural equity, as well as the interests, needs, and abilities of the group members.

According to Adams and Hamm (1998),

> cooperative learning is more than having students cooperate in a group activity or project. There is a set of strategies that encourage student cooperation while learning in a variety of settings, disciplines, and different grade levels. The process involves promoting positive interdependence by dividing the workload, providing joint rewards, holding individuals accountable, and getting students actively involved in helping each other master the topic being studied. Creative social engagement is paramount. (p. 2)

In both elementary and middle school settings, group work often becomes louder than traditional seat-time work. Because students are expected to communicate, debate, and move about the room while working in groups, the teacher's classroom management techniques become essential. Students need and want rules of conduct to be established. They want to know the limits of classroom behavior.

Problems often occur in inquiry classrooms when the teacher fails to effectively communicate the expectations for group work. The teacher can enhance expectations and rules for appropriate behavior by having students participate in deciding what rules need to be enforced while doing a scientific investigation. The students can agree to the rules and post them in the classroom. Classes can consider adopting rules of conduct by citing the positive behaviors that are expected (starting with the word *Do*) rather than rules written in a negative tone (starting with the word *Don't*).

STUDENTS USING CRITICAL THINKING SKILLS

In a *community of inquirers*, using exploration and discourse strategies stimulates students to think critically about the data and evidence accumulated during their inquiry. This motivates students to analyze and synthesize the data and to make judgments and evaluations about the results and conclusions. These types of higher thinking skills are far superior in developing scientific literacy than the skills involved in answering the kinds of questions repeatedly posed to students in classrooms where recall and memorization of science fact are valued. In contrast, as students experience inquiry investigations, they use critical thinking skills that cause them to reflect about their work and pose logical arguments to defend their conclusions.

In grades K–2, thinking skills in inquiry involve students generating questions and making sense of their ideas. In Grades 3–5, students are beginning to make the transition into higher-level concrete operations and are more likely to understand the relationships between their prior knowledge and their new experiences. In middle school, students in Grades 6–8 are better equipped to see cause-and-effect relationships, formulate hypotheses, interpret and draw conclusions, evaluate relationships between variables, and use two- and three-dimensional models to explain their conclusions (Hester, 1994). Throughout the middle school years, many students begin to make the transition from concrete operations to formal levels of operations and thinking more abstractly.

STUDENTS SHOWING INTEREST IN SCIENCE

"Why do we have to learn this stuff anyway?" one eighth-grade girl asked. "Because," the teacher responded, "you have to know it when you get to high school." Have you been asked that question? It seems that every experienced teacher has been asked it a hundred times in his or her career. From the point of view of the student, what does the question mean? Does it mean she doesn't like science? Does it mean she doesn't like this particular lesson? Or does it mean she doesn't understand what she is expected to do? All we know at this point is that the student might not see the relevance of the content she is expected to learn.

Posing problems of importance and relevance to students is an integral aspect of inquiry and constructivist teaching (Brooks & Brooks, 1999). That does not mean that in inquiry classrooms the students decide what and when they want to learn. Nor does it mean that teachers must wait until the students want to learn about

Newtonian physics before the subject can be presented. It does mean, however, that in inquiry classrooms the teacher mediates relevance by engaging students in meaningful problem-solving investigations. According to Brooks and Brooks (1999), "The inquiring teacher mediates the classroom environment in accordance with both the primary concept she has chosen for the class's inquiry and her growing understanding of students' emerging interests and cognitive abilities within the concept" (p. 38). Making learning meaningful is another central theme in a culture of inquiry. Brooks and Brooks go on to say

> It's unfortunate that much of what we seek to teach our students is of little interest to them at that particular point in their lives. Curriculums and syllabi developed by publishers or state-level specialists are based on adult notions of what students of different ages need to know. Even when the topics are of interest to students, the recommended methodologies for teaching the topics sometimes are not. Little wonder, then, why more of those magnificent moments don't occur. (p. 106)

In inquiry classrooms, students are engaged in investigations that interest them through prompting and mediation from the teacher. As a result, students demonstrate open-mindedness and furthermore gain an appreciation for science. Acting as researchers promotes interest in science as well as a positive attitude that encourages students to pursue more rigorous science courses in the years ahead.

In the 1990s, NETWORK, Inc. (Andover, Massachusetts) received a grant from the National Science Foundation to support inquiry-based learning. The project, titled Vermont Elementary Science Project (VESP), was located at Trinity College in Burlington, Vermont. Participants in VESP discussed the actions of students engaged in inquiry science. As a result of that discussion, they created the *On the Run Reference Guide to the Nature of Elementary Science for the Student*. According to VESP,[1] "the intent is not to use the guide as a checklist, but as a statement of what we value in the area of science processes, science dispositions, and science development. We urge you to capture evidence of your own students engaging in these indicators." VESP suggests that "when students are doing inquiry-based science, an observer will see" the following:

Students View Themselves as Scientists in the Process of Learning

1. They look forward to doing science.

2. They demonstrate a desire to know more.

3. They seek to collaborate and work in cooperative groups with their peers.

4. They are confident in doing science; they demonstrate a willingness to modify ideas, take risks, and display healthy skepticism.

5. They respect individuals and differing points of view.

Students Accept an "Invitation to Learn" and Readily Engage in the Exploration Process

1. Students exhibit curiosity and ponder observations.

2. They take the opportunity and time to try out and persevere with their own ideas.

Students Plan and Carry Out Investigations

1. Students design a fair test as a way to try out their ideas, not expecting to be told what to do.

2. They plan ways to verify, extend, or discard ideas.

3. They carry out investigations by handling materials with care, observing, measuring, and recording data.

Students Communicate Using a Variety of Methods

1. Children express ideas in a variety of ways: journals, reporting about, drawing, graphing, charting, etc.

2. They listen, speak, and write about science with parents, teachers, and peers.

3. They use the language of the processes of science.

4. They communicate their level of understanding of concepts that they have developed to date.

Students Propose Explanations and Solutions and Build a Store of Concepts

1. Students offer explanations from a "store" of previous experience and from knowledge gained as a result of ongoing investigation.

2. They use investigations to satisfy their own questions.

3. They sort out information and decide what is important (what does and doesn't work).

4. They are willing to revise explanations and consider new ideas as they gain new knowledge (build understanding).

Students Raise Questions

1. Students ask questions (verbally or through actions).

2. They use questions to lead them to investigations that generate or refine further questions and ideas.

3. Students value and enjoy asking questions as an important part of science.

Students Use Observations

1. Students observe carefully, as opposed to just looking.

2. They see details, seek patterns, detect sequences and events; they notice change, similarities, and differences.

3. They make connections to previously held ideas.

Students Critique Their Science Practices

1. They create and use indicators to assess their own work.

2. They report and celebrate their strengths and identify what they'd like to improve upon.

3. They reflect with adults and their peers.

TEACHERS IN AN INQUIRY-CENTERED CLASSROOM

The teacher's competency is paramount in inquiry classrooms. It sets the stage for teaching and learning. When observing inquiry-based teachers, we often see a different style of presentation, organization, questioning skills, and even body language from what is seen in conventional settings. The following is a laundry list that often accompanies good teaching as well as inquiry-based learning. In inquiry classrooms, we often see teachers:

1. Choosing topics to study on the basis of national standards

2. Limiting the use of lecture and direct instruction to times when the lesson cannot be taught through hands-on or inquiry-based instruction

3. Being focused yet flexible by having preplanned lessons and questions while mediating the lesson to follow the direction of the students' questions

4. Assessing prior knowledge before starting a lesson or unit of study and using students' prior knowledge as a basis for introducing new concepts

5. Listening to students' responses and becoming aware of their misconceptions

6. Making learning meaningful by exploring student interests, taking student interests into account, and basing lessons on students' prior suppositions

7. Using investigations to anchor new information to previous knowledge

8. Initiating classroom discussion and discourse by asking starter questions, giving prompts, and posing reflection questions throughout the lesson

9. Asking questions that necessitate critical thinking skills

10. Using *wait-time* appropriately rather than interrupting students in the middle of their questions and answers

11. Posing prompts and clarifying and rephrasing student questions and responses rather than divulging answers, so that students can begin to answer their own questions

12. Saying "Thank you" for student contributions and giving positive reinforcement for their contributions and good work in cooperative groups

13. Asking follow-up questions to student answers rather than saying "Okay" or repeating the student's answer

14. Maintaining appropriate classroom management during hands-on investigations by displaying rules in a positive way, providing expectations, giving structure, and creating a safe and well-organized room

15. Establishing everyday routines for group interaction and for getting and returning materials

16. Arranging students' seats to work in groups

17. Focusing the lesson on engaging, relevant, and problem-solving situations

18. Moving about the classroom and rotating to each small group

19. Kneeling to make on-level, eye-to-eye contact when speaking to students seated in small group settings

20. Valuing student responses

21. Keeping students on task by having them support their findings by debating, challenging, and questioning their conclusions

22. Using instructional time efficiently

23. Integrating science content with process skills and problem-solving strategies as well as mathematics, technology, and other subjects

24. Acting as a facilitator, mediator, initiator, and coach while modeling the behaviors of inquiry, curiosity, and wonder

25. Using primary sources of information rather than textbooks

26. Using resources from inside and outside the school setting

27. Encouraging communication skills such as speaking and listening

28. Encouraging students to use concept mapping and drawing models to explain and demonstrate newly acquired knowledge

29. Assessing student performance in a variety of forms and monitoring student progress continuously on a day-to-day basis

30. Assisting students in monitoring their own progress

As stated before, good teaching involves a balance between allowing students to discover for themselves and providing explicit instruction (Holliday, 2006). The exact proportion of the continuum is usually determined by the capability of the teacher, the readiness level of the students, the topic being studied, and the physical environment.

AN INQUIRY-CENTERED CLASSROOM

As we begin to see, the inquiry classroom environment is somewhat different from traditional settings. To begin, inquiry classrooms are often described as learner-centered and interactive. That doesn't mean traditional classrooms are not child- or learner-centered. For the purpose of constructing a definition of an inquiry classroom, ask yourself, How would I know if I walked into a classroom where the students learn through inquiry? What would the classroom look like? How would it be arranged? Would I expect to see the desks arranged in straight rows? Where would the teacher's desk be located? How would the classroom be different from a conventional classroom?

You may want to begin to answer those questions by designing an inquiry-based classroom of your own. On a separate sheet of paper, design a room for the number of students in your classroom. Place the teacher desk, the student desks, and *learning centers* in any way that complements a culture of inquiry.

Although not all inquiry classrooms appear to be the same, there are some common features to look for. In inquiry-based classrooms, we often see the following:

1. "What if" and "I wonder" questions posted throughout the room

2. Concept maps displayed on the walls

3. Evidence of student work throughout the room

4. Students' desks arranged in groups of two, three, or four

5. Expectations for student behavior posted

6. Learning centers for individual and small-group work

7. Fiction and nonfiction books, magazines, and resources on the shelves

8. The teacher's desk at the side or back of the room rather than front and center

9. A box or crate for student portfolios and journals

10. Materials and supplies readily available in bins or containers

11. Areas set aside for storing projects and investigations in progress

12. Videotaping equipment available for recording student presentations and reflecting on and analyzing performances

13. Computers available for accessing information beyond the school building

How were these descriptors similar to what you described in your inquiry-based classroom? Because of the increased student movement, teachers must pay specific attention to traffic patterns. Making the room accessible, safe, and organized is an important consideration when designing an inquiry classroom.

At the beginning of the school year, when students arrive for the first time, the room traditionally is set up for them in advance by the teacher. A month into the school year, the teacher may offer students the opportunity to rearrange the room according to their own design. This makes the room truly "their room" and adds a personal touch to the environment. To support this notion, the *NSES* (NRC, 1996) says:

> The arrangement of available space and furnishings in the classroom or laboratory influences the nature of the learning that takes place . . . [and] schools must restructure schedules so that teachers can use blocks of time, interdisciplinary strategies, and field experiences to give students opportunities to engage in serious scientific investigation as an integral part of their science learning. (p. 44)

Now that we have completed the first five chapters, go back to the statements or concept maps you made in Chapters 2, 3, and 4. Make any modifications or additions. Figure 5.1 is an example of one teacher using a graphic organizer to separate

Figure 5.1 Scientific Inquiry

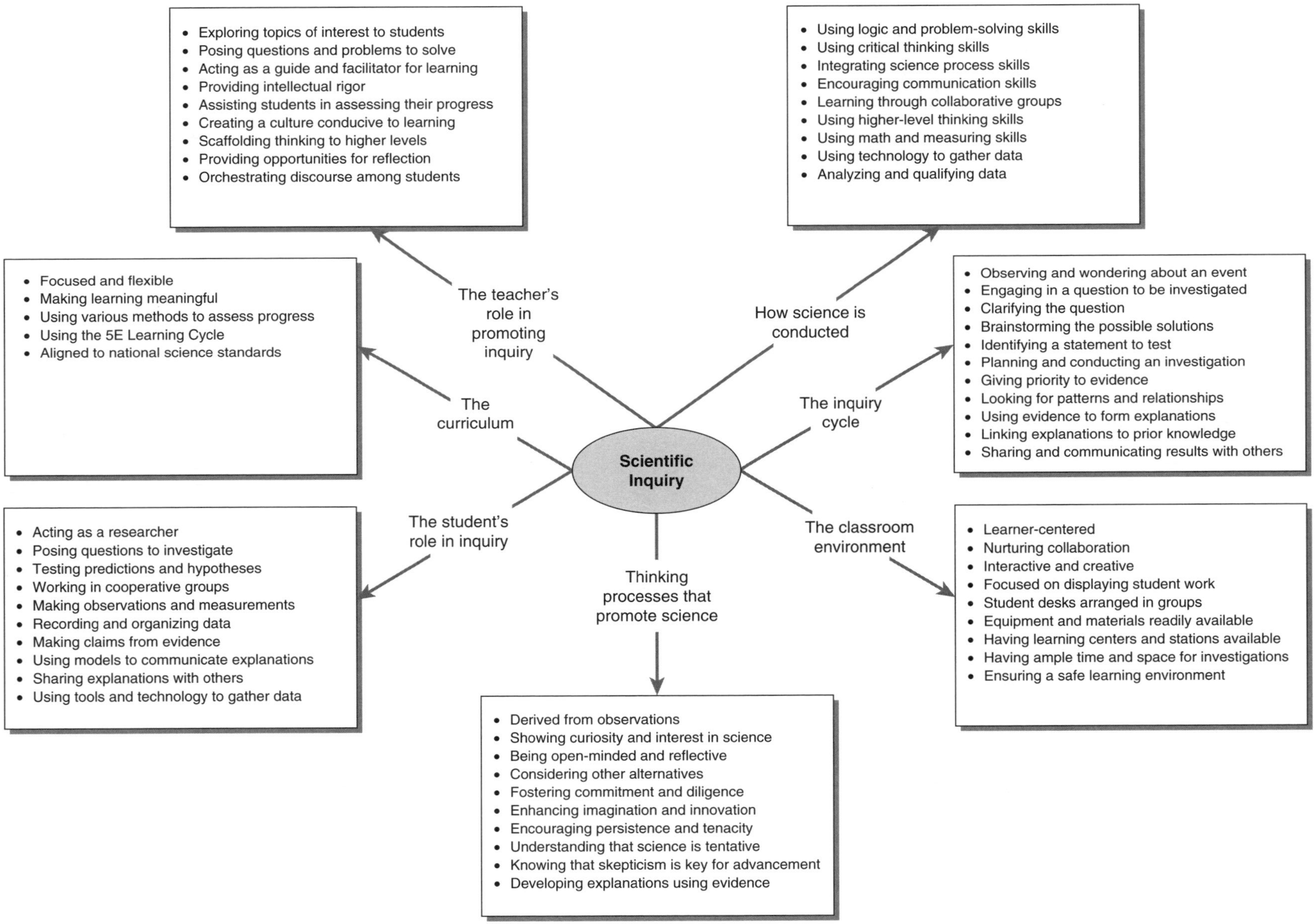

- Using logic and problem-solving skills
- Using critical thinking skills
- Integrating science process skills
- Encouraging communication skills
- Learning through collaborative groups
- Using higher-level thinking skills
- Using math and measuring skills
- Using technology to gather data
- Analyzing and qualifying data

How science is conducted

- Observing and wondering about an event
- Engaging in a question to be investigated
- Clarifying the question
- Brainstorming the possible solutions
- Identifying a statement to test
- Planning and conducting an investigation
- Giving priority to evidence
- Looking for patterns and relationships
- Using evidence to form explanations
- Linking explanations to prior knowledge
- Sharing and communicating results with others

The inquiry cycle

The classroom environment

- Learner-centered
- Nurturing collaboration
- Interactive and creative
- Focused on displaying student work
- Student desks arranged in groups
- Equipment and materials readily available
- Having learning centers and stations available
- Having ample time and space for investigations
- Ensuring a safe learning environment

Scientific Inquiry

- Exploring topics of interest to students
- Posing questions and problems to solve
- Acting as a guide and facilitator for learning
- Providing intellectual rigor
- Assisting students in assessing their progress
- Creating a culture conducive to learning
- Scaffolding thinking to higher levels
- Providing opportunities for reflection
- Orchestrating discourse among students

The teacher's role in promoting inquiry

The curriculum

- Focused and flexible
- Making learning meaningful
- Using various methods to assess progress
- Using the 5E Learning Cycle
- Aligned to national science standards

The student's role in inquiry

- Acting as a researcher
- Posing questions to investigate
- Testing predictions and hypotheses
- Working in cooperative groups
- Making observations and measurements
- Recording and organizing data
- Making claims from evidence
- Using models to communicate explanations
- Sharing explanations with others
- Using tools and technology to gather data

Thinking processes that promote science

- Derived from observations
- Showing curiosity and interest in science
- Being open-minded and reflective
- Considering other alternatives
- Fostering commitment and diligence
- Enhancing imagination and innovation
- Encouraging persistence and tenacity
- Understanding that science is tentative
- Knowing that skepticism is key for advancement
- Developing explanations using evidence

her statements on inquiry into seven different subtopics: the curriculum, the classroom environment, the student's role, teacher's role, how science is conducted, the inquiry cycle, and thinking skills that promote science.

QUESTIONS FOR REFLECTION AND DISCUSSION

1. There has been some debate recently about direct instruction versus inquiry-based instruction. What is a reasonable proportion of these two approaches for your students?

2. Why is it important for teachers to foster curiosity and inquisitiveness for a scientifically literate society?

3. How could you instill elements of inquiry in mathematics? In language arts? In social studies?

4. How would you deal with an incoming class of students who were not curious and were reluctant to raise questions?

NOTE

1. The following material is from the Vermont Elementary Science Project, *On the Run Reference Guide to the Nature of Elementary Science for the Student* (p. 13). Burlington, VT: Trinity College. © 1991 by the Vermont Elementary Science Project, Trinity College, McAuley Hall, Burlington, VT 05401. Phone (802) 658-3664. Used with permission.

6

What Are the Different Levels of Inquiry?

If all children are to have opportunities to learn then activities are needed which engage their different interests and methods of teaching used which enable equal participation for all children in their own learning.

—Wynne Harlen, *Teaching and Learning Primary Science*

WHY JOHNNY CAN'T INQUIRE

Although research has cited many benefits to inquiry-based instruction, for years now, we have heard elementary and middle school teachers say that their students lack the ability to raise thoughtful questions and the skills to think critically, lamenting students' lack of ability to inquire. When asking why Johnny can't inquire, some point their finger toward the student sitting behind the desk, while others blame the adult standing in front of the class. The stance taken here is not to reproach either the student or the teacher, but rather to examine the realities that face elementary and middle school science teachers every day in implementing inquiry-based instruction. By understanding the *barriers* to inquiry, we can better empower teachers to seek solutions to confront those obstacles.

The literature (Barell, 2003; Colburn, 2004; Costenson & Lawson, 1986; Songer, Lee, & Kam, 2001; Trautmann, McKinster, & Avery, 2004) has well identified the barriers that preclude, or at least discourage, teachers from using inquiry in their classrooms. We will now address the external and internal (and sometimes self-imposed) obstacles that teachers encounter when implementing inquiry-based instruction. However, for the sake of our discussion, we will use the term *challenges* rather than barriers. Like a barricade, roadblock, or obstacle, a barrier is something that bars, restrains, or obstructs our access or passage. It's difficult, or nearly impossible, to get around a barrier. Challenges, on the other hand, are tests of our creativity and endurance; they can be seemingly overwhelming and yet surmountable.

At a recent workshop on inquiry-based learning, K–8 novice and expert teachers were asked about the obstacles they face in teaching science through inquiry. Each participant wrote his or her responses on 3×5 cards that provided a laundry list of well-intended reasons (and excuses) why it's difficult to teach through inquiry. As you read through the teachers' responses, consider how many of them you have heard before. How many reasons do you feel are valid? How many reasons do you feel are excuses? Here's a sample of the reactions:

- I have a mandated, fact-driven curriculum to cover.
- I need to prepare students for a high-stakes, end-of-the-year assessment.
- It's too difficult to grade inquiry assignments and labs. Plus it takes too long.
- We don't have the money to purchase inquiry kits.
- I don't have enough preparation time and classroom time for inquiry.
- I could do inquiry if I had a smaller class size.
- Inquiry is too slow and takes too much instructional time.
- My kids can't do inquiry. They don't have the background.
- I rely on the textbook for teaching science.
- Students need to be told how to do a science experiment.
- I don't have the materials or the equipment to do inquiry.
- Students are accustomed to getting the answer.
- I feel more comfortable teaching guided labs. That's the way I was taught.
- I've always taught in an expository way. I can't change now.
- Factual knowledge is the most important student outcome in science.
- I don't have flat tables for group work or even a sink in my room.
- I feel threatened by science. I feel I have to know the answers to all the questions the students ask.
- With inquiry, the classroom gets too loud and you can lose control.
- Most of the K–6 teachers in my school have "science phobia."
- I don't have a background in science.
- My administrator wants the classroom to be orderly, not chaotic.
- At the elementary school level we feel the pressure to focus on the basics: reading and math. There's little time for science, much less inquiry.
- The yearly state assessment tests just science facts, not inquiry.

As you work as an individual, in a study group, a summer seminar, or a college course, discuss each reason listed above. Classify each reason (and add those not listed here) into groups: (a) those external to the teacher's influence and over which the teacher has no control; (b) those over which the teacher has influence and control; (c) those that are more generic to the elementary school grades; and (d) those that are more generic to the middle school grades. Your discussion leader may choose to use four colors of sticker dots for participants to classify the responses, knowing that each response may fall into more than one category. Consider and discuss which ones can be overcome through the three R's: those that can be overcome by *restructuring* the curriculum, those that can be overcome through professional development and *retooling* the knowledge and skills of the teacher, and those that are a result of the teacher's individual bias and beliefs concerning how children learn and can be overcome through *reculturing* classroom standards and expectations. At the end of your discussion, you can expect to arrive at the understanding that, as with anything else, there are hurdles to leap in any new pedagogy of teaching and learning. However, exemplary teachers persistently find ways to triumph over the challenges of inquiry instruction, balance optimism with reality, and learn ways to help Johnny to inquire.

Let's now turn our attention from the challenges in inquiry-based instruction and toward building a positive culture for enhancing student inquiries.

PROMOTING STUDENT INQUIRIES

Now that you are developing a first-rate perception of what inquiry-based science classrooms look like, we can direct our focus to describing the activities that take place in those classrooms. This chapter will help you distinguish between typical science activities from those that provoke students' curiosity and encourage them to resolve their own questions.

On the dawn of most inquiry journeys, teachers usually raise two questions: What are inquiry activities? and How do I get my students started with inquiry? Answering these two fundamental questions is an essential first step for any teacher interested in creating an inquiry-centered classroom. This chapter will answer both of them.

Starting in the primary grades, children display a natural curiosity about science. Edwards (1998) says:

> Young children seem to have a never-ending supply of questions. Older children, on the other hand, rarely ask questions, preferring instead to let their teachers perform this duty. They are accustomed to providing memorized answers to questions asked by the teachers. It can be safely said that this behavior is shaped by the educational system. The consequence of this conditioning process is well established in most learners once they have spent a few years in school and can significantly interfere with their ability to formulate questions and conduct self-directed investigations. Teachers interested in promoting inquiry have a challenging task to overcome the tendency of many older students to become passive. (pp. 18-20)

At the middle school level, teachers daily face prepubescent and budding adolescents whose bodies are filled with roller-coaster hormones and emotions. Students in Grades 5–8 are often self-conscious about raising questions and appearing to stand out in the class. For this reason, middle school science teachers who have students with little prior experience in inquiry should gradually introduce their classes to student-initiated investigations. The "Invitation to Inquiry Grid" (Figure 6.1) serves as a means to identify varying levels of inquiry-based investigations and help guide teachers in purposely shifting instruction toward inquiry.

INVITATION TO INQUIRY

The activities, experiments, and investigations we do in science can be divided into three discrete sections:

1. Posing the question

2. Planning the procedure

3. Formulating the results

Picture a teacher, in this first scenario, posing a question to his or her students. Imagine that same teacher describing how the procedure of the "experiment" will take place and actually performing the steps of the experiment. Also imagine the teacher orally providing the results of the experiment and then formulating the conclusions to the class. We will call this first scenario a demonstration. In the second situation, a teacher poses the question to the students and provides a procedure for answering the question. The students follow the procedure and formulate their own results. We will call this an activity. In the third situation, the teacher poses the question to the students and invites the students to plan and carry out the procedure to answer the question and finally formulate the results. We will call this a teacher-initiated inquiry. In our final situation, the teacher provides an initial exploration or experience from which the students pose a question. The students then plan a procedure for answering their question, carry out the designed procedure, collect data, and finally formulate their results. We will call this a student-initiated inquiry.

We have just categorized (see Figure 6.1) four levels of "inquiry" instruction, each as a means to initiate student-led questions, procedures, and results. Now let's delve into each in greater detail.

DEMONSTRATIONS

According to the "Invitation to Inquiry Grid" (Figure 6.1), demonstrations focus the attention on a particular phenomenon. The instructional sequence is "controlled" by the teacher. Said another way, demonstrations are very teacher-centered. We are very familiar with doing demonstrations; they grab hold of the attention of the audience while "showing" science at work. Demonstrations also make the teacher the center of attention. Many of us like playing "Bill Nye the Science Guy" or "Wilhelmina the Science Gal." When done well, demonstrations are captivating and interesting to watch.

Many scientific concepts are best presented through demonstrations. When is it best for teachers to perform demonstrations? There are several excellent reasons. We usually do demonstrations when

- All students need to observe a particular phenomenon or event.
- The procedure is complicated for students to follow.
- The results of the situation need to be controlled.

Figure 6.1   Invitation to Inquiry Grid

Invitation to Inquiry Grid				
	Demonstration	*Activity*	*Teacher-Initiated Inquiry*	*Student-Initiated Inquiry*
Posing the question	Teacher	Teacher	Teacher	Student
Planning the procedure	Teacher	Teacher	Student	Student
Formulating the results	Teacher	Student	Student	Student

- Dangerous, toxic, or flammable materials are used.
- An explosion may (or will) result.
- Safety is a concern.
- Materials or equipment are limited.
- Expensive chemicals or supplies are being used.
- Time is of the essence.

You can probably think of ten other reasons when it is appropriate to perform a demonstration. Although conventional demonstrations usually are presented to exhibit or prove a particular concept, when a demonstration results in an observation or conclusion that is counterintuitive to a student's normal experience, it often evokes "What if" or "I wonder" questions. Demonstrations that invite further questions and inquiries are called discrepant events.

DISCREPANT EVENTS

Discrepant events are mind-engaging demonstrations or activities where students observe unexpected results that are contradictory to their normal experience or anticipation. Wondering why these unexpected things happen provides students with the motivation and interest to formulate questions to pursue. Discrepant events are especially effective in the beginning of a lesson or a unit because they capture the students' interest and promote curiosity.

Teachers often use discrepant events, using low-cost, everyday household items, to introduce scientific concepts.

Observing a discrepant event can serve as a springboard to science inquiry. Rather than introducing a new topic or concept and later providing a demonstration to prove that the concept is correct, a teacher should use a discrepant event in the beginning of the lesson to capture the students' attention and sense of wonder. Discrepant events initiate a *wanting to know*. Several steps are recommended in integrating discrepant events into a lesson:

1. Demonstrate the event. Present students with an opportunity to observe results that contradict their normal expectancy. Provide students with an opportunity to confront the discrepancy being raised.

2. Prompt students to investigate the event. Students should be encouraged to test the event or discrepancy by using science process skills such as observing, inferring, recording data, formulating hypotheses, and generalizing. Allow sufficient time to test the event and form hypotheses or questions. Encourage students to raise "What if" and "I wonder" questions about the discrepancy. Provide guidance while introducing inquiry strategies without giving away the answer or explanation.

3. Allow time for students to test their "What if" and "I wonder" questions and share the results of their inquiries.

4. Discuss the causes of the discrepancy while introducing the topic being studied (density, pressure, heat, etc.). During the discussion, refer back to the demonstration to *personalize* the concept being presented.

5. Apply the concept being studied to an application level beyond the classroom. Provide a culminating activity or laboratory experience that extends the learning rather than proving that what was already said is correct.

For a comprehensive resource on discrepant events, see *Invitations to Science Inquiry* in Resource A.

ACTIVITIES

With our time-honored, hands-on activities, the teacher provides the question to be studied or tested, usually at the top of the activity or lab sheet. The students are told what materials to use and what procedures to follow to generate expected and predictable data. These activities are sometimes called *cookbook* science because, like a cook following a recipe in a book, students are expected to follow prescribed directions and procedures that produce results that are predictably similar. Many teachers subscribe to this type of *confirmation activity* because it provides structure for students, directs them how to carry out the experiment, and confirms the existence of a scientific concept or phenomenon. Colburn (2004) refers to this as the *verification approach*. In this approach, the lab manual provides the question and introduces the activity to the student with background information as to the lab's purpose. In some cases, the introduction even discloses the expected outcome for the "experiment" by telling the student the answer to the lab! Many of the run-of-the-mill "experiments" found in noninquiry science textbooks for elementary and middle schools fall into this category.

Teachers often "stick to what's in the textbook" and rely on prescribed activities or labs as their resource for hands-on science. They feel that such activities are easy to follow and provide students with focus and direction in carrying out the activity.

Although activities do provide students with an opportunity to do manipulative-based science, cookbook activities confirm the expected. It is the teacher's role to promote and encourage further questions and pursue self-directed investigations, the goal of inquiry-based learning.

Activities can become a means of inviting inquiry—a catalyst for inquiry. Like discrepant events, they can provide, when properly planned, opportunities for students to make observations or discoveries that are unexpected and unpredicted. In the "Inquiring With Fruit" activity cited in Chapter 2, Mr. Roberts provided the question to study. He also provided the procedures for directing students to make their own predictions. Whether a particular fruit floated or sank spurred the students to raise "What if" or "I wonder" questions.

Providing *extension* or *going further* questions at the end of an activity is an ideal way to engage students. Let's say, for example, that in a straightforward activity, a teacher poses the question, How do the dissolving rates differ between a sugar cube and granulated sugar?

Then, the teacher provides the following materials to be used:

- Two empty 250-ml beakers
- One 500-ml beaker of room temperature water
- One sugar cube
- One packet of granulated sugar
- One stopwatch

Next, the teacher provides the following procedures for the students:

1. Fill one 250-ml beaker with 125 ml of water.

2. Place the sugar cube in the 250-ml beaker with water.

3. Use the stopwatch to record the time it takes for the tablet to dissolve.

4. Record the time in the data table.

5. Fill the second 250-ml beaker with 125 ml of water.

6. Pour the granulated sugar from the packet into the second 250-ml beaker.

7. Use the stopwatch to record the time it takes for the sugar to dissolve.

8. Record the time in the data table provided.

Although this is a relatively simple and straightforward activity that most elementary or middle school students can complete, you can see how teacher-directed it is. The original question and procedures are provided by the teacher to the students. All the students have to do is follow the step-by-step procedure and record the time in the appropriate column in the data table. You can see that this activity can be thought of as a type of cookbook activity, and although it is hands-on, it is not inquiry-based. These cookbook-type activities are sometimes referred to as structured inquiry.

One step toward incorporating inquiry into the lesson would be to have several prearranged extension questions for students to investigate on their own. The teacher could pose several questions to investigate, but on the basis of their knowledge from the original activity, the students would be expected to write their own procedures and carry out their own investigations. Several preplanned or extension questions could include the following:

- How does stirring the water affect the dissolving rate?
- How does the temperature of the water affect the dissolving rate?
- How does the amount of water in the beaker affect the dissolving rate?
- Does granulated brown sugar dissolve slower or faster than white sugar?
- Does artificial sugar or sweetener from the pink or blue packets dissolve faster or slower than regular sugar in the white packets?
- Does a solid antacid tablet dissolve faster or slower than a powdered antacid?
- Does adding food coloring to the water affect the dissolving rate?
- How can you make a sugar cube dissolve in the shortest amount of time?

In this way, a simple, basic activity can be extended into an inquiry lesson.

TEACHER-INITIATED INQUIRIES

In teacher-initiated inquiries, sometimes called *guided inquiry*, the teacher poses the original question or problem and then allows time for the students to (a) consider possible solutions, (b) plan an investigation, and (c) go about answering the question or problem posed to them. When students are not accustomed to initiating questions on their own (this is especially true at the beginning of the school year), teacher-initiated inquiries work especially well. Teacher-initiated inquiries also are appropriate when encouraging *problem solving*.

A teacher-initiated inquiry that is especially enjoyable for third and fourth grade students is called "Pumpkin Math & Science" and aligns with the *National Science Education Standards* (NSES) (NRC, 1996) for Grades K–4:

Science as Inquiry Standard

Students will

- Employ simple equipment and tools to gather data and extend the senses (p. 122 of the NSES)

Physical Science Standard

- Objects have many observable properties, including size, weight, shape, [and] color (p. 127)

Life Science Standard

- Each plant has different structures that serve different functions in growth, survival, and reproduction (p. 129)

Students are given the starter question, How can you find the volume of a pumpkin? They begin by *brainstorming* ways to measure the pumpkin. The teacher may prompt some students to measure the height by cutting a hole in the center of a piece of cardboard and placing the cardboard over the stem of the pumpkin. While holding the cardboard parallel to the surface of the tabletop, students could use a ruler to measure the height of the pumpkin and determine who has the tallest pumpkin. Others may want to measure the "fatness" or circumference of the pumpkin, using a string or belt from their pants to measure the distance around the pumpkin. Students may also be prompted that a water displacement method is really the best means of determining the pumpkin's volume. To accomplish this, a student might suggest using the classroom wastebasket filled to the top with water. Another might suggest using a dishpan to catch the water that spilled over as the pumpkin was pushed completely down into the water. By measuring the water overflow, the students can easily determine the volume of the pumpkin!

After exploring and observing pumpkins firsthand, students can then make a list of what they want to know about pumpkins. Here are several questions a teacher can provide to students:

- How thick is the shell of the pumpkin? Do bigger pumpkins have bigger shells? How does the shell protect and store the seeds inside?
- Do all pumpkins have the same number of "grooves" on the outside? How are the grooves like the longitude lines of a globe?
- How many seeds are in a pumpkin? How do the seeds enable the plant to reproduce? Do all pumpkins have the same number of seeds? Do bigger pumpkins have more seeds than smaller pumpkins?
- How heavy is a pumpkin seed? Do pumpkin seeds float? What's inside a pumpkin seed?
- Do all pumpkins float?
- How can you tell by the color of the shell which side of the pumpkin grew down on the ground, and which side was facing up toward the sky? Which way does the stem of the pumpkin grow?
- Is a pumpkin a vegetable or a fruit? What's the small round circle at the bottom of the pumpkin for?
- Using the Internet or other resources, what is the size and weight of the largest pumpkin ever grown?
- Are pumpkin pies really made from pumpkins?

Pumpkin investigations can last well into mid-November. In fact, you may prefer to start your pumpkin investigations after Halloween. The market value of pumpkins drops significantly after October 31. If you wait until then to ask a store-owner or a farmer for their pumpkins, you will probably get all you'll need for free!

STUDENT-INITIATED INQUIRIES

The highest level of inquiry occurs when students raise and initiate their own questions. According to the "Invitation to Inquiry Grid" (Figure 6.1), in student-initiated inquiries, sometimes called *full inquiry*, *true inquiry*, or *open*

Figure 6.2   Teacher and Student Participation Modes

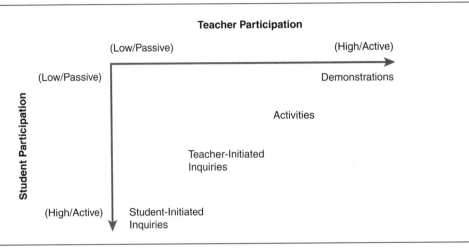

inquiry, students raise their own questions, formulate their own procedures, and determine their own results. In some cases, students may need prompting or an open-ended exploration to gingerly "seek" questions out of them. The ice hand investigation was one example of a student-initiated inquiry. The ice hands provided the exploration phase for students to make observations and raise questions to investigate. Students generally raise questions on the basis of their prior experiences and from observing discrepancies; therefore, it would have been more difficult for them to think of ice questions to investigate without the ice hand exploration. In their investigations, students raised and investigated their own questions. This characterizes the student-initiated inquiry category because the questions originated from the students, not the teacher. In other situations, students may raise questions without being prompted or persuaded; however, getting them to develop their own questions may take many guided experiences, especially when dealing with students who have not had prior experience in inquiry-based lessons.

We now see that the degree of self-directed participation and involvement on the part of the teacher and the students varies significantly for each learning level described. During a demonstration, the teacher play an active role, while the students play a more passive role. In contrast, during the student-initiated inquiry, the students are fully engaged, and the teacher appears to play a less active role. In actuality, the teacher is very involved as a coach and facilitator. The illustration in Figure 6.2 summarizes the participation level of each level of inquiry.

GUIDING STUDENTS INTO INQUIRY

Most students (and teachers as well) are not ready to begin with full student inquiries at the beginning of the school year. During the first few weeks of school, teachers need to set expectations for classroom management, discipline, classroom routines, grading procedures, and so on. Establishing and maintaining a healthy and safe classroom is a prerequisite for an inquiry lesson. Without rules, inquiry lessons become unruly and unmanageable.

It is normal for teachers to wait until they grow accustomed to their classes before starting a full inquiry-based unit. This is especially true for teachers who have students coming to them without prior experience in inquiry instruction.

For these reasons, the "Invitation to Inquiry Grid" also serves as a means to plan instructional units so that students are gradually, but continually, encouraged to take on more responsibility for their own learning. During the early months of the school year or when students are unfamiliar with inquiry learning, the teacher may choose to begin with the demonstration mode, focusing on having students observe and experience discrepant events. During the next several months, the teacher can then move into the activity stage, concentrating on providing sound hands-on activities that create the opportunity for extension investigations. By mid-year, a reasonable expectation would be to have students involved in one or more teacher-initiated inquiries, with the goal of evolving the students' expertise into several fully student-initiated inquiries before the end of the school year (see Figure 6.3).

The "Invitation to Inquiry Grid" can also be used as a monitoring tool for teachers in designing their yearlong science plans. As the school year proceeds, teachers can ask themselves, Am I moving my students from teacher-dependent to more independent experiences? Am I providing opportunities for student-initiated inquiries as the year goes on?

Figure 6.3   Inquiry Grid Flowchart

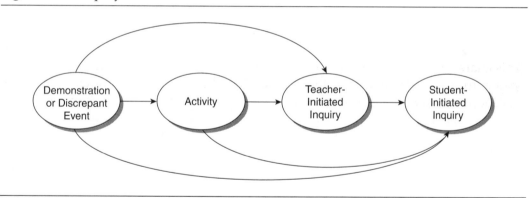

You now have a first-rate grasp of the distinctions between hands-on and inquiry-based science. You know that although true inquiry involves hands-on and minds-on learning, not all hands-on activities are inquiry-based. When a hands-on activity provides the question to be solved, what materials to use, how to go about finding the answer, and how to organize the data collected, it's probably *not* inquiry.

A lesson on momentum, using ramps and marbles, is presented in four different ways to further explain the differences between a demonstration, an activity, a teacher-initiated inquiry, and a student-initiated inquiry. Using the same concept, we can then see how each stage differs from one another. Let's suppose we want students to determine how the height of an inclined plane (the release point of the marble on a grooved 12-inch ruler) affects the distance a marble travels when allowed to roll down (see Figure 6.4).

Figure 6.4   Setup for Rolling Marble Investigation

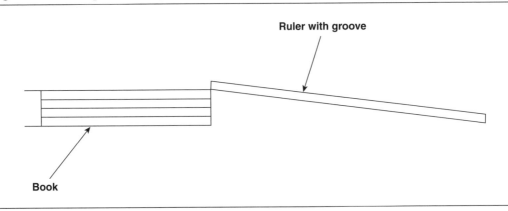

In a demonstration lesson, the teacher stands in the front of the class, behind a demonstration table. He or she poses a question such as How does the height of an inclined plane affect the distance a marble will travel? The teacher then shows and describes the supplies and materials to be used in the demonstration.

Following the steps of the procedure, the teacher sets up the materials so that one end of the ruler is elevated one inch. The teacher releases the marble at this point and the marble rolls down the groove of the ruler. One student is called on to measure the distance the marble traveled in each of three trials while the rest of the students record each distance for the three separate trials on their data sheets. The teacher then explains that the height of the top of the inclined plane (or release point) changes by adding more books to the end of the ruler.

Next, the height of the inclined plane increases to two inches, with the same procedure followed and data recorded for each trial. The procedure repeats for heights of three, four, and five inches. At the conclusion of the demonstration, the teacher summarizes the data, plots them on a graph, and describes to the students the relationship between the height of the ruler and the distance the marble had rolled.

Because this demonstration does not represent a discrepant event, the teacher may pose going-further or extension-type questions to the class or may end the demonstration without further discussion. The demonstration would probably take 10 to 20 minutes to complete.

In an activity-type lesson, the students are at tables in groups of threes or fours. A worksheet (see Form 6.1) is distributed to the groups. The teacher provides an overview of the activity and answers questions about the procedure. In this case, the question to be studied is provided by the teacher on the activity sheet along with supplies and materials and the step-by-step procedure. The students are expected to complete the steps and record the distance the marble rolled for each trial in the data table provided.

As the students work on the activity, the teacher circulates among the groups providing assistance in answering their questions. In this activity, the students are experiencing a hands-on science lesson with many opportunities to observe, make mathematical measurements, manipulate materials, collect and record data, and draw conclusions from the evidence. The activity takes 30 to 45 minutes to complete.

Form 6.1   Marble Activity Worksheet

Marble Activity Worksheet

Problem: How does the height of an inclined plane affect the distance a marble will travel?

Hypothesis: The higher the end of the inclined plane, the further the marble will roll.

Materials: One 12-inch ruler with groove   One marble

Five books, each 1 inch thick   One measuring stick

Procedure: 1. Using the diagram in Figure 6.4, place the ruler on the edge of a 1-inch book.

2. Place the marble in the groove as far up the ruler as possible.

3. Release the marble.

4. Using the measuring stick, measure the distance (in inches) the marble traveled.

5. Record the result in the data table.

6. Repeat the same procedure for trials 2 and 3.

7. Repeat the same procedure for 2 inches. Place a second 1-inch book on top of the first book. Place the ruler on the top of the second book so the height of the ruler is now 2 inches. Repeat the same procedure for 2 inches. Repeat the same procedure for 3 inches. Then repeat the same procedure for 4 inches and 5 inches.

8. Use the table below to calculate the average for each slot.

Data table:

Height	Distance marble traveled (in inches)			
	Trial #1	Trial #2	Trial #3	Average
1 inch	____	____	____	____
2 inches	____	____	____	____
3 inches	____	____	____	____
4 inches	____	____	____	____
5 inches	____	____	____	____

At the end of the activity, the questions posed by the students determine whether the activity leads into a teacher- or student-initiated inquiry. For example, suppose the teacher had two different rulers, 12 inches and 18 inches long, and posed the question How does the length of the inclined plane affect the distance the marble will roll? Students could then "move" from the activity level to the teacher-initiated level, assuming that the teacher prompts the students to formulate their own procedure to answer the question. The teacher could also ask, As the height of the incline plane continues to increase, does the distance the marble travels also continue to increase? What are the limiting factors of the investigation? Is there a maximum height for the one end of the incline plane given the length of the ruler? Why did students record the distance for three trials? Why not record just one or two trials?

On the other hand, suppose a student raises the question, How does the mass of the marble affect how far the marble will travel? Then, if the teacher hands the student small, medium, and large marbles and encourages the student to formulate his or her own procedure to answer the question, the student would "move" from an activity level to a student-initiated inquiry level.

At the teacher-initiated inquiry level, the teacher poses the question, How does the height of the inclined plane affect the distance the marble will roll? and challenges students to formulate a procedure to answer the question. The teacher has different sizes of rulers, some with grooves and some without, various sizes of marbles of different masses and colors, and measuring tapes available. Each student is encouraged to write a prediction, plan a procedure, and select the appropriate materials needed to investigate the question and put his or her supposition to the test. After the plan is completed, the students are free to carry out their plans and collect evidence to test their predictions.

During this time, the teacher (a) circulates from group to group and listens to their discussions, (b) becomes aware of comments made by the students that reveal any misconceptions about momentum, and (c) provides additional prompts to test their misconceptions. Depending on the class and the level of their investigations, this inquiry could take from 45 to 60 minutes to complete. During the investigation, the teacher poses further questions for the students to consider and has additional inquiries available for those groups who completed their investigations early. For example, one inquiry could involve a steel ball and a glass marble of the same size. The teacher could pose the question, Does the mass of the ball affect the distance the ball will roll?

In a student-initiated inquiry, the teacher can use the KWL approach (Ogle, 1986) to assess prior knowledge (K) and uncover misconceptions by asking students to share what they already know about ramps, balls, and inclined planes. The teacher would then record their prior knowledge by listing them under the "K" column on the board or poster sheet (see Form 6.2). Next, the teacher allows time for nondirected experience in which students engage in messing about at tables, exploring and observing momentum with balls and ramps. Following this engagement and exploration time, the teacher would encourage students to raise their own personal questions and inquiries about momentum, suggesting that they begin their inquiries with "What if," "I think," or "I wonder" (W). At this time the teacher or the students would record the questions in the "W" column of the KWL chart.

The teacher again asks the groups to share their questions, while making a list on poster sheets. Following this exercise, the teacher would identify each question as:

- One that is ready to be answered through an investigation (How does the mass of a marble affect the distance it will travel?)
- One that needs to be revised or rewritten before it can be investigated (Which ball will roll farther, a wooden or a glass ball?)
- One that requires an outside expert or resource to answer (Why does the marble roll farther when it is released from a higher point?) (see Figure 6.5)

It is important for students to classify their questions in these categories to further understand the direction their questions will take them. For example, questions starting with "why" do not make good questions to investigate. They usually require an outside "expert" (or resource) to answer. Take, for example, the quintessential, age-old science question young children always ask: Why is the sky blue? This question and other "why" questions like it are not easily answered through an investigation. These questions beckon an explanation from an outside resource and need to be revised into "What" or "What if" questions before they truly can be investigated by students.

With student-initiated inquiries, sufficient materials and supplies should be readily available at a supply center for groups to gather as needed. As the students brainstorm ways to solve their questions and go about carrying out their plans, the teacher rotates from group to group and encourages the groups to write down other questions that come up during the course of their investigations. At the end of the lesson, the teacher brings all the groups together so they can share their observations and conclusions and what they learned (L) from the experience by filling in the "L" column of the KWL chart.

Each of the four levels of inquiry has its own definite advantages and disadvantages, and of course, each teacher can plan and implement the lesson differently from what is described here. By using demonstrations, the time requirement is greatly reduced, and each student is ensured the same opportunity to observe the same phenomenon being studied in the identical manner. The activity level allows the teacher to guide all the students to arrive at the same conclusion. This approach may be practical when you are introducing a specific concept and want all students to acquire the same information. Activities usually are tightly structured and, except for any extension questions that may come about, are very straightforward, with limited creativity and ownership of the problem or the procedure. Teacher-initiated inquiries, however, are excellent instructional strategies for allowing students to plan and solve problems. Both teacher- and student-initiated inquiries take an extended amount of time. Often, the teacher may not know where the students' questions will take the discussion. These inquiries, however, provide a means for students to empower themselves by directing the course of their own work.

A summary of each stage is listed in Figure 6.6.

MODIFYING AN ACTIVITY INTO AN INQUIRY INVESTIGATION

Many science teachers prefer prescribed, confirmation-type activities and cookbook labs with their students. These teachers may be more comfortable with this variety of activity because it is probably the way they were taught. Moving toward inquiry

Form 6.2 KWL Chart

What do you **KNOW?**	What do you **WANT** to know?	What have you **LEARNED?**

Figure 6.5   Sorting Students' Questions

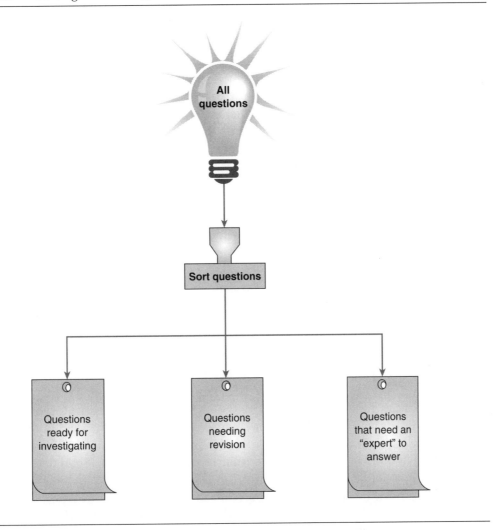

does not mean you have to give up your favorite time-honored science activities. Changing a step-by-step lab activity into an inquiry-based investigation can be relatively straightforward. There are ways to modify the long-established activities and labs that have been part of your instructional repertoire for years. So, as you realize that prescribed activities and cookbook labs no longer meet your new instructional goals, consider modifying your structural approach. Because experienced teachers assert that it's conveniently reasonable to redesign the labs "backward," the following suggestions start with the *end* of the activity and work their way to the *beginning* of the activity.

1. Add an Inquiry Investigation (or Question) to the End of the Activity. When you add extension and inquiry investigations after the activity, you use the activity as a launchpad into inquiry. To take the activity further, encourage students to raise "What if" and "I wonder" questions. You can also present questions as prompts to commence students thinking in ways to apply the activity in other situations.

In the momentum example, the following extension questions could be asked after the initial activity and lead students into more inquiry-based learning:

- How does the marble's mass affect the distance the marble will travel? (Compare the mass of a small marble with that of a large marble.)
- How does the ball's composition affect the distance it will travel? (Compare a 1-inch glass marble with those of a 1-inch steel, Styrofoam, or wooden ball.)
- How does the surface affect the distance the marble will travel? (Compare the surfaces by rolling a marble along a tabletop, a rug, a sandpaper surface, a tile floor, or a rubber surface.)
- How does the length of the ruler or ramp affect the distance the marble will travel? (Compare 6-inch, 12-inch, and 18-inch rulers. Will a 12-inch ruler cause the marble to travel twice as far as a 6-inch ruler?)
- How does the release point affect the distance the marble will travel? (With the "0" end of the ruler touching the floor, compare releasing the marble at the 4-inch mark of the ruler, the 8-inch mark, the 12-inch, etc.)

2. Look at the Results Section. If the textbook or activity provides a predetermined data table or graph, remove it. Let the students determine how they will collect and organize the data. Students will have to construct meaning for the data to organize and record them into a table. If they cannot formulate a data table, you probably can conclude that they do not understand the significance and correlation of the data to the activity or they have not mastered strategies for organizing data.

In the momentum example, the data table was provided. What would your students do if the table was not provided and they had to construct their own way to organize the data? Would they know how to organize the data? Some will be confused at first, others may record more data than necessary, and others may record data as expected and design a table similar to the one in the original activity.

3. Look at the Procedure Section. Meaningful learning does not occur when students are merely following the procedures identified in a prescribed activity (Shiland, 1999). If the textbook or activity provides a step-by-step list of procedures, remove it. Let the students brainstorm about designing an experiment or investigation to answer the original question or prediction. This makes the activity more like a teacher-initiated inquiry. You can also print the individual steps of the procedure on single strips of paper and give them to students. The students would have to read the steps and sequence them into a logical order.

In the momentum example, a step-by-step procedure was provided for the student to follow. By eliminating this section, students could design their own ways to test the prediction. Encourage students to work in groups and generate possible experimental designs. Have the group choose one (or several) set(s) of procedures to test. After designing the procedure, the students must decide how they will collect and record their data by designing a data table.

Also consider taking away the materials list. After the students design the procedure, have them generate their own list of the materials they will need. You can also provide a list of materials containing items not needed for the experiment. Students will have to determine which items are needed and which are unnecessary.

4. Look at the Question Section. If the textbook or activity provides a starter question to answer, as they usually do, remove it. Start by demonstrating a discrepant event

Figure 6.6 Invitation to Inquiry Grid Summary

Invitation to Inquiry Grid Summary				
	Demonstration	*Activity*	*Teacher-Initiated Inquiry*	*Student-Initiated Inquiry*
Posing the question	Teacher	Teacher	Teacher	Student
Planning the procedure	Teacher	Teacher	Student	Student
Formulating the results	Teacher	Student	Student	Student
Starter question	Predetermined	Predetermined	Posed by teacher	Generated by student
Plan or procedure	Predetermined	Predetermined	Designed by student	Designed by student
Outcome	Predetermined	Expected	Guided toward a concept	Open-ended
Time	5–30 minutes	30–60 minutes	45–60+ minutes	60–120+ minutes
Role of teacher	Active	Provides direction	Guide/facilitator	Facilitator
Role of student	Observer	Direction follower	Problem solver	Investigator
Materials	Provided	Provided	Suggested	Suggested
Content	Focused	Focused	Needs some focusing	Requires focusing

to observe. Encourage the students to think of questions to investigate. Provide prompts and initial explorations to engage students in the original question of the activity. By encouraging students to come up with the question or problem, the investigation becomes more personal and meaningful, causing more ownership of the problem. This makes the activity more like a student-initiated inquiry.

In the momentum example, a starter question was provided for the students to test. Consider eliminating the starter question and beginning the lesson with a demonstration of momentum for students to observe. Following the demonstration, students should be provided time to develop "What if" and "I wonder" questions to investigate. The teacher can also provide prompts to guide students in choosing the question from the original activity. The teacher may choose to have students investigate one or several questions together. After the questions are decided, students can determine a set of procedures, a materials list, and a way to collect and record data.

PRINCIPLES OF EFFECTIVE INQUIRY

In this chapter, you learned ways to categorize science experiences, from demonstrations to student-initiated inquiries. As you design your yearlong science program, the "Invitation to Inquiry Grid" can serve as a guide to move students from teacher-centered activities toward more self-directed opportunities. If the goal of your science curriculum is to provide students with opportunities to engage in inquiry, then planning a gradual shift from "teacher-dependent" to "student-empowered" science explorations will become part of your professional development plan and a reason to start (or continue) the journey toward becoming an inquiry-based teacher. If your class is new to inquiry, present several demonstrations during the first month of the school year. During the middle of the second month, introduce several discrepant events as thought-provoking demonstrations. Plan to move into hands-on structured activities in October and November. Plan several guided teacher-initiated and problem-solving opportunities for December. Finally, move into a full, open inquiry in January and intend to engage students in three or four student-initiated inquiries later that school year.

Teaching through inquiry is not solely about modifying activities and planning investigations; it's also about the teacher valuing and respecting the student's point of view and providing the mechanism for unearthing innovation and creativity in a child's mind. It's also about finding time for reflection and discourse about what drives the student's interests in science.

Effective inquiry fosters the core ethical values of character education: caring, commitment, creativity, honesty, fairness, integrity, persistence, responsibility, and respect for others' work. These are habits that reach beyond the science curriculum; they extend into all aspects of the child's life. Combining inquiry with character education helps to develop moral decision making and builds a *community of learners*. Together they help instill intrinsic motivation. The second half of this book will address the intrinsic nature of inquiry.

QUESTIONS FOR REFLECTION AND DISCUSSION

1. Look at the challenges to inquiry statements in the beginning of the chapter. Sort the challenges into categories. Identify the top five statements that most apply to you. Identify the middle five statements that sometimes apply to you and then the statements that do not usually apply to you. Discuss how you can, if possible, eliminate, reduce, or restrict the top five statements that challenge you to teach science through inquiry.

2. Take a favorite step-by-step activity or lab and follow the suggestions in the chapter on how to modify it to be more inquiry-based. Share your before and after activity or lab with a partner. If possible, teach the step-by-step lab to one class and the inquiry lab to another. Record notes on the ways students complete the labs and the types of questions they ask. Set aside time with your partner to reflect on the two approaches.

3. Consider your yearlong instructional plans for science. Use the Inquiry Grid to design opportunities for students to gradually experience and practice scientific inquiry throughout the year.

Designing Investigations

[The inquiry] standard should not be interpreted as advocating a "scientific method."
The conceptual and procedural abilities suggest a logical progression, but they do
not imply a rigid approach to scientific inquiry.

—*National Science Education Standards*

C hapter 2 offered several myths about inquiry. One of them stated that when students use the step-by-step scientific method they are also doing scientific inquiry. Although the scientific method, problem solving, and inquiry are somewhat related, many would propose that the three are definitely not the same. This chapter shows the similarities and differences among them.

THE MYTH OF THE SCIENTIFIC METHOD

As a society, we place confidence in a product that has been *scientifically tested.* The phrase "clinically proven" assures the consumer that a product has undergone rigorous testing and is approved by a renowned scientific testing company. We assume that these testing conditions follow a scientific process.

"The scientific method," as painted by some textbooks, is a commonly accepted set of sequential steps or procedures that begin with identifying a problem or question. The problem is stated as a *testable prediction*, and there is an identified gap between the information that exists and the question being posed. The hypothesis, based on some prior notion of the outcome of the problem (Macrina, 1995), undergoes rigorous testing through data collection and careful observation to determine the merit of the prediction. Carefully controlling which variable determines the outcome of the experiment, scientists use this time-honored tradition to guide their experiments and discoveries. Unfortunately, the notion of "the scientific method" sends mixed messages to teachers and students alike. Some, including the *National Science Education Standards* (NRC, 1996) and *Benchmarks for Science Literacy* (AAAS, 1993) suggest that a single method of science does not exist. As a result of teaching the scientific method in today's science classrooms, according to Lederman (2006), "a very narrow and distorted view of scientific inquiry is promoted in our K–12 students" (p. 310).

Authentic scientific research seldom follows these prescribed steps as closely as we would like to think. Often, scientific investigations, influenced by human endeavors and events, proceed with so many twists and turns that researchers may find it unrealistic to follow a single approach. In *The Double Helix: A Personal Account of the Discovery of the Structure of DNA*, Watson (1968) describes how science seldom proceeds in the straightforward and logical manner we might expect. Although students sometimes follow a sequential set of procedures in school-based science, these steps are not used to provide an unyielding structure for designing investigations. Rather, they guide students to think logically, explore all possibilities when studying given phenomena, and add credibility, reliability, and validity to the results and conclusions.

The steps of a controlled investigation generally include some or all of the following:

1. Making observations, comparisons, and speculations

2. Stating the question or problem to be solved

3. Identifying the variables within the question or problem

4. Constructing a statement to test

5. Identifying the manipulated variables, the responding variables, and the controlled variables

6. Designing the procedures for the investigation

7. Determining what supplies, materials, and equipment are necessary to perform the investigation

8. Carrying out the investigation and acquiring data and evidence

9. Organizing data on a chart or table or constructing a graph

10. Describing the relationship between the variables

11. Determine the validity of the evidence and drawing claims on the basis of the evidence

12. Communicating the results to others

When stating the problem to be solved, begin by asking yourself, What is the question you want to investigate? State the problem as a "What if" or "I wonder" question. Some explorations might begin with "what," "how," "which," or "will." Returning to the marble activity in Chapter 6, a student wanted to explore the relationship between the angle of an inclined plane (a grooved 12-inch ruler) and the distance a marble would travel when allowed to roll down it. In this investigation, the question was stated as, How does the height of an inclined plane (the release point) affect the distance a marble will travel?

To understand the importance of controlling variables and to identify all possible variables inherent in the problem, the student brainstorms different factors that could affect the outcome of the experiment by first making a list of the variables or factors. In the marble activity, these variables included the size of the marble, the length of the ruler, the height of the ruler, the surface the ball rolled on, the height (or position) of the marble when placed in the groove of the ruler, how the marble was released, and the density of the marble. Can you think of other factors that would affect the outcome of the experiment? The student later uses the list to control all variables except one, the *manipulated variable* or *independent variable.* This is the variable that affects the outcome. The student then makes a statement or prediction about the expected outcome of the experiment. In the marble activity, the statement could have been, As the height of the inclined plane increases, the distance the marble travels will also increase.

When identifying the variables of the investigation, the factor or variable that is deliberately changed in the situation is the manipulated variable. The variable that will change as a result of the manipulated variable is called the *responding variable* or *dependent variable.* In the marble activity, the student deliberately changed the height of one end of the inclined plane. This was the manipulated variable. The distance the marble rolled on the surface, which was measured to determine the result of changing the height of the ruler, was the responding variable. This way, only one variable, the manipulated variable (the height of the ruler/release point), affected the distance the marble rolled. In the investigation, the student used the same size of marble during all the trials, rolled the marble on the same surface throughout the experiment, and placed the marble in the same spot on the groove for each trial.

When we allow more than one variable to affect the responding variable or the outcome of the investigation, we don't have a fair experiment. Imagine our marble results if a student had given the marble a little push in some trials but not in others. Pushing the marble during some trials would provide additional energy to the marble and would affect how far the marble rolled. It would be equally unfair to use a small marble for some of the trials and a larger one for others. In short, it would not be a fair experiment.

Designing the procedures is often difficult for some children. It may be helpful for a student to first brainstorm the design and then draw an illustration or picture of what the setup will look like. The drawing can be used to identify and sequence the steps of the procedure. After the student designs the plan, the teacher should review it for any flaws. In some cases, the teacher can provide hints or prompts to revise the procedure without directly stating what needs to be changed. In other cases, the teacher, knowing the plan is flawed and will not work as planned, might want the student to do the procedure anyway. There may be some benefit in the child conducting the experiment as planned and discovering that the investigation needs a new or revised procedure. Too often, young people think of science as the way to search for the right answer. We need to assure them that making mistakes and learning from them is all part of the learning process in science (Sprung, Froschl, & Campbell, 1987).

While designing the procedure, the student should determine which supplies and equipment are necessary by revisiting the drawing and identifying the necessary materials. In the marble activity (see Figure 6.5), a list of materials was provided.

Students must also consider how to acquire and organize data. If a data table is not provided in the activity, it should be designed while planning the procedure. After the data are collected, the student can produce a visual representation of the data by graphing the results. Graphs are an excellent means of studying patterns and relationships among variables, reinforcing math skills, and providing evidence of student work, which can be posted in the classroom.

When asked to describe the relationship between the manipulated and the responding variables, students often have difficulty drawing reasonable conclusions. In Step 10 above—describing the relationship between variables—what may seem obvious to the teacher may not be so obvious to the child. Another reason for a student's difficulty may be that teachers sometimes neglect to emphasize this significant step in the data analysis. Before students can draw conclusions from their data, they must first analyze the relationship between the two variables. As the manipulated variable increases, what happens to the responding variable? Does the graph form a straight line? A curved line? Is there a direct proportion? In the marble activity, the student would have first examined the data table and then compared the distinction between the two columns representing the variables. As the height of the ruler increased, what happened to the distance the marble rolled? Only by describing the relationship between the two variables can students analyze their results and draw accurate conclusions from their data. The good news is that this is a skill that can be reinforced by showing students various data tables and graphs and having them describe the relationship between the manipulated and the responding variables. With a little practice, students will suddenly become analytical wizards in interpreting data.

After the results are analyzed, the student uses the data to determine the validity of the statement. Do the data support or refute the statement? Is the statement accurate? If not, how should the statement be restated, and what new follow-up investigations should occur?

The final step lies in communicating the results. This may be done in different ways. The results can be written up as a laboratory report identifying each step of the experiment, or the student could do an oral presentation in front of the class to share his or her findings. When students have been working in groups, the teacher may want to hold a *convention* in which each group makes a trifold poster board or PowerPoint presentation to present its findings and its results. At this point, the teacher or the instructional technology specialist in the building may also introduce how to use spreadsheets to construct appropriate graphs. The convention can be videotaped and shared with parents during an open house or other school event.

The communication phase allows the teacher and the students to reflect on the procedure followed, share their conclusions, and make recommendations on what could be changed if the experiment were to be repeated. By communicating and critiquing the procedure, students can assess how well they or their group functioned and evaluate the quantity and quality of their learning. During the communication phase, students who worked together in groups can process each group member's contribution to help maintain a collaborative atmosphere and effective working relationships (Johnson, Johnson, & Holubec, 1984). Through reflection and dialogue, the teacher can elaborate on the processes and understandings the students have gained about scientific inquiry. By providing closure to the investigation, the teacher and students celebrate the learning process and are rewarded for a job well done. This process also provides a time to record other new ideas and questions that arose during the investigation, ones that might lead to new inquiries and ways to improve methods, procedures, and data collection.

EXPLORING RAMPS AND BALLS

For children in primary grades, scientific inquiry can be reduced to a few simple steps. By taking the same momentum example, we can see how scientific inquiry can be applied with younger children. Once a question or problem is posed, the children are involved in four basic steps: (a) predicting (or guessing) the outcome, (b) conducting and observing the experiment, (c) documenting the results, and (d) discussing the outcome (Sprung et al., 1987).

The following inquiry investigation has been adapted for third and fourth graders from *What Will Happen If* (Sprung et al., 1987). "Exploring Ramps and Balls" aligns with the *National Science Education Standards* (NSES) (NRC, 1996) for Grades K–4:

Science as Inquiry Standards
Students will:

- Ask questions about objects, organisms, and events in the environment (p. 122)
- Plan and conduct a simple investigation (p. 122)
- Communicate investigations and explanations (p. 122)

Physical Science Standards

- The position of an object can be described by locating it relative to another object or the background (p. 127)
- An object's motion can be described by tracing and measuring its position over time (p. 127)

Pre-investigation activities for "Exploring Ramps and Balls" may include having the teacher set a purpose by gathering the children during circle time to explain that they will become young scientists and participate in a scientific "experiment." Children should be told that they will be predicting (or guessing) the outcome, conducting and observing the experiment, and documenting and discussing their results. Other pre-investigation preparations may include having the teacher ask the children what they know about ramps and rolling balls, which could help to assess their preconceptions and possible misconceptions about momentum. Their comments and questions can be written on a chalkboard, poster, or easel paper. Some class time may also be spent by setting expectations for individual behavior and group participation.

The children's comments on ramps and rolling balls can lead the teacher to pose the question, How will the height of the ramp affect the distance a tennis ball will roll?

Predicting an Outcome

Let's return to the children's predictions. They can be written as simple statements, such as: The higher the ramp, the farther a tennis ball will roll. For younger children, the teacher can write one prediction for the entire class. Older children or more experienced classes can have each group make its own prediction. In either case, the teacher should spend some time reviewing the prediction(s) to ensure that all children understand the purpose of the task. Often, having a student repeat the prediction or reword it for another student can provide the teacher with enough feedback to assess whether students actually understand the prediction to be tested.

Conducting and Observing the Investigation

During the first half of this step, the teacher should decide whether to have the entire class brainstorm about setting up the "experiment" or to have each group come up with its own procedures. Younger students may or may not have enough experience testing their scientific ideas to independently suggest their own procedures. The teacher's interaction with the class and the children's prior experience should determine which path the teacher follows.

First, the teacher will instruct the groups to place a strip of masking tape across the floor. This will mark the location and position for the bottom of the ramps and ensure that all the balls start rolling on the floor from the same place.

Given two 2 × 4-inch boards (each three feet long) and six smaller 2 × 4-inch blocks (about six inches long), one group will build a ramp using the two long boards propped up at one end by one smaller block. The bottom of the ramp should line up with the strip of masking tape. The two long boards should be separated by a two-inch gap to form a groove for the ball to roll down. Students can use the width of the smaller block to measure the gap between the two long boards. A second group will build a similar ramp using two blocks to prop up the boards, and a third group will use three blocks (see Figure 7.1).

Through class discussion, the teacher should point out that all ramps must be built and lined up the same way to make this a "fair experiment." The teacher may explain how variations in building the ramps could alter the results.

After the ramps are built, the teacher should restate the original question, How will the height of the ramps affect the distance the ball will roll? Students should understand the connection between the question to be studied, the materials, and the setup procedure being used. At this time, the teacher should have students pose their predictions and understand the correlation between the prediction made and the setup procedure. Students can then brainstorm about how they will measure the distance the ball rolls. The teacher may want to suggest that the children use small pieces of tape or adhesive dots to mark the spots where the balls stop rolling.

When the predictions are made, the teacher should hand each group a tennis ball to roll down the ramp. The teacher may point out the need to release the ball without pushing it down the ramp. Depending on the level of the class, students may want to devise a way to release the ball the same way in all cases. Some students may discover that using a stick to act as a gate to release the ball down the ramp is a good way to start the ball rolling.

Figure 7.1   Three Ramps

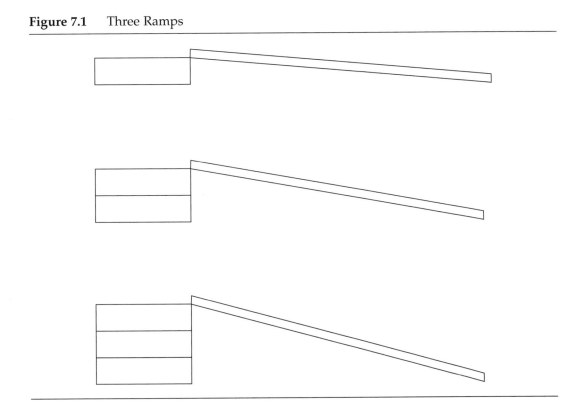

Documenting the Results

Children in primary grades may discover that they need to repeat the procedure several times. I have not yet seen a class of young scientists who were content to let the ball roll down the ramp just once! They can use the tape or dots to mark the locations of the farthest distance the ball traveled, or some classes may want to use measuring sticks. Each group can now write its results on the poster or easel paper.

Discussing the Results

When the procedure is completed, ask the class what they observed and learned. Several questions can guide their thinking:

- Which ramp made the ball roll the shortest distance?
- Which ramp made the ball roll the farthest distance?
- Did the ball roll as far as you predicted?
- How accurate were your predictions?
- Were some predictions more accurate than others?
- How can we show our results on a chart or graph?

At this point, the students should come to the understanding that the ramp with three blocks caused the ball to roll farther than the ramps with one or two blocks. Explaining the concept of potential energy may not be appropriate at this point.

Having individual members of the class summarize the investigation will help the teacher assess the students' understanding of ramps and rolling balls. By providing a discussion and summary, students can now pose any additional and related questions they have.

More "What Will Happen If . . ." Questions

The value of any good investigation lies in its ability to generate more questions in children's minds. The ramp and rolling ball investigation will surely invite other questions for students to investigate:

- What will happen if we use four blocks? Five blocks?
- What will happen if we place the ball on a flat ramp without any blocks?
- What will happen if we use a basketball instead of a tennis ball?
- What will happen if we use a bowling ball instead of a tennis ball?
- What will happen if we roll the ball on different surfaces such as a rug, or a tile or wooden floor?

The ramp and ball activity is one of several ways to investigate forces and momentum with younger children. Depending on the size and makeup of the class, the teacher may choose to demonstrate a ramp with one ball and pose questions such as, What would happen if we added one more block to the ramp? What would happen if we increased the height of the ramp? How does the height of the ramp affect how far a ball will roll? Any of these questions would provide a sufficient invitation to inquiry following the single-block demonstration. In this situation, the teacher uses a demonstration to introduce a teacher-initiated inquiry.

In the ramp activity, the class was divided into groups, with each group testing momentum for a different height of the ramp. Depending on the number of ramps, blocks, and balls available, an alternative strategy would be to have each group complete the procedures for one, two, and three blocks. This alternative maximizes the involvement of the groups. Another alternative could have the teacher demonstrate the ramp with one ball and then call on individuals or small groups to test the different number of blocks, one at a time, in front of the entire class.

SCIENTIFIC PROBLEM SOLVING

Albert Einstein is quoted as saying, "The formulation of a problem is often more essential than its solution." Problem solving, like inquiry, commonly is thought of as a path of thinking about and processing information that enables students to construct understanding through personally meaningful experiences as they become competent decision makers. Hunkins (1995) describes problem solving as a "heuristic organizer that allows us to contemplate ways in which we can and perhaps should organize and reorganize knowledge to solve a perceived difficulty" (p. 11).

In a problem-solving situation, one often uses one's abilities to analyze a situation and design a way to solve the problem. Problem solving is found in all subjects and disciplines. In this chapter, the way we describe and detail scientific problem solving is different from the way we would describe mathematical problem solving. Problem solving in the scientific sense is a systematic and orderly way to explore new situations and generate solutions to real problems and discrepancies that face us. Gagne (1970) suggests that problem solving can be viewed as a process through which the learner discovers a combination of previously learned rules that can be applied to achieve a solution for a novel situation. Hester (1994) describes problem solving as an activity that engages and stimulates the learner in the movement toward problem or conflict resolution. Hester also makes a primarily developmental differentiation between inquiry and problem solving. He believes that

> although inquiry processes resemble problem solving and include many of the same procedures as early reasoning, there is a fundamental difference—problem solving and formal reasoning require the ability to reason abstractly . . . and make logical deductions. On the other hand, inquiry is tied to concrete thinking, factual information and the use of sensory (discovery) learning. Inquiry is less formal, less structured, and partakes of hands-on learning in which fully developed scientific reasoning is not required. (p. 22)

Although inquiry and problem solving are closely related, in problem-solving situations the problem is often provided by the teacher, and the students use scientific reasoning skills to develop a solution to solve the problem. Referring to the inquiry grid in Figure 6.6, we can see that problem solving is similar to teacher-initiated inquiry. The central emphasis is on designing an outcome or product.

As an example, a problem-solving activity may involve students designing and building a container to keep a block of ice or an ice cube from melting over a 24-hour period. The teacher may place limitations on the task as to the maximum size or weight of the container. The students would then decide the design and the best materials to be used in constructing the container. To address the challenge posed to the students, they will need to

1. Devise a container by brainstorming and generating possible solutions,

2. Research the advantages and disadvantages of each design,

3. Select appropriate materials that represent good insulators of heat,

4. Make models and illustrations of their designs,

5. Choose which design to use as the model for their project,

6. Test the design to solve the challenge, and

7. Communicate their results.

Before testing the designs, the class would also need to brainstorm and determine a method to measure the percentage of melting after the period of time. Two possibilities include weighing the mass of the ice cube before and after, or measuring the volume of melted water after 24 hours.

SCIENTIFIC PROBLEM SOLVING VERSUS INQUIRY

In a problem-solving situation, students are faced with a dilemma and are expected to devise a solution to the problem. Generally, a problem-solving activity starts with a problem and results in a product that bridges the gap between a present condition and a desired condition. Over the years, hundreds of problem-solving activities for elementary and middle school children have been published in the National Science Teachers Association's (NSTA) *Science and Children* and *Science Scope*. Examples of problem-solving experiences include:

- Designing and making a container that will keep an ice cube from melting
- Designing and making a container that will keep a liquid hot as long as possible
- Designing a filtration system using cotton, gravel, sand, and charcoal to purify dirty water
- Designing and making a wallet for a visually impaired person
- Designing and making a bridge that will support the most weight possible

Inquiry, on the other hand, involves students in observing and exploring a particular phenomenon to raise questions worthy of investigating. In inquiry situations, the process of seeking answers to questions usually results in expanding students' understanding of a concept. For example, while exploring and observing the rate at which a small marble falls within a cylinder of a thick liquid, such as corn syrup, students will broach additional questions, such as

- How does the size of the marble affect the rate at which it falls through the liquid?
- What would happen if I dropped a marble in different liquids, such as detergent or oil?
- Do different grades of motor oil affect the rate of a falling marble?
- Does the density of a liquid affect the rate of fall?

A MODEL FOR SCIENTIFIC PROBLEM SOLVING

Although various models of scientific problem solving are available, they generally include the following components and guiding questions:

1. Recognizing that a problem exists and defining the problem to be solved
   a. What is the nature of the problem?
   b. How widespread is the problem?
   c. Who and what does the problem affect?

2. Collecting and analyzing information about the problem
   a. What alternatives may solve the problem?

3. Generating possible solutions to the problem
   a. What do you want to accomplish?
   b. What are the limitations of the solution?

4. Selecting and designing a strategy or plan
   a. What assistance or resources will be needed?

5. Implementing a plan
   a. How will the plan or the solution be implemented?

6. Evaluating and communicating the results
   a. How will the solution solve the problem?
   b. Is the solution working?
   c. Is the problem solved?

Often, the components of the problem-solving process are illustrated as a wheel or cycle rather than the linear progression of steps typical of the scientific method. This implies that problem solving is a systematic, cyclical process in which investigators sometimes return to steps and various stages of the cycle. A typical problem-solving wheel is shown in Figure 7.2.

As a middle school example, consider the following problem-solving task: As a laboratory technician, you are presented with the problem of determining the relative amounts of two compounds in a mixture. You have been given a 10-gram sample of a mixture of sugar and sand. Your task is to design a procedure for determining the percentage of the mass of sugar and the percentage of the mass of sand in the total mass of the sample. Once you have planned your procedure, follow it carefully and report your findings.

Figure 7.2   The Problem-Solving Wheel

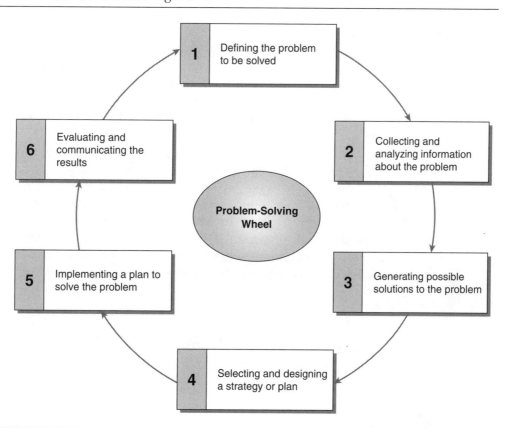

This task aligns with the *Physical Science Content Standards* for Grades 5–8:

Students should develop an understanding that "a substance has characteristic properties . . . such as solubility, all which are independent of the amount of the sample. A mixture of substances often can be separated into the original substances using one or more of the characteristic properties" (NRC, 1996, p. 154).

In Step 1 of the wheel, the student recognizes that a problem exists and defines the central problem to be studied. According to Hester (1994), recognizing that a problem exists usually is the first step in critical thinking. This usually is accomplished by identifying a discrepancy or uncertainty with the given phenomenon. The student should write a statement of the problem to be investigated so that all members of the group have a common understanding of the problem. The problem ideally should be something meaningful to the students and worth their time to solve. Often, in defining the problem, students consider the dilemma between the *present state* versus the *desired state.* This places the problem in concrete and understandable terms.

In Step 2, the student uses critical thinking and research skills to collect relevant information about the problem. The student uses resources to analyze the stated problem and raise possible solutions. In the sugar and sand problem, a student may rely on his or her prior knowledge about solubility, mass, evaporation, and filtration to solve the problem.

In Step 3, the student brainstorms possible solutions to the problem and weighs the value of each solution. In this step, each student in the group communicates his or her ideas and thoughts on the problem. Here, the student is encouraged to "think outside the box" and generate various possible solutions to the problem. Two- and three-dimensional models also can be designed to illustrate plausible solutions.

In Step 4, the student selects the best solution from those generated in Step 3 and plans a procedure to solve the problem. The procedure should be logical and sequential. A list of supplies, equipment, and resources needed to solve the problem usually is identified in this step. In the sugar and sand task, the student may choose to use a triple-beam balance, filter paper, a funnel, beakers, a heating source, an evaporating dish, a ring stand, and stirring rods. In some situations, the student may also identify measures to evaluate the success and effectiveness of their solution. In this step, the student should also determine which safety procedures need to be carried out.

In Step 5, the student implements the plan and procedures written in Step 4 to solve the problem and collects information from the procedures. In some cases, the student may organize the data collected on a graph or table.

Finally, in Step 6, the student reviews the data collected and evaluates the solution to the problem. The student usually communicates the results in an oral presentation to the entire class. The presentation may include a demonstration of the prototype design of the actual model constructed, a trifold poster board, or a PowerPoint presentation. In most cases, the results support the solution to the problem. In a few cases, new solutions must be generated, sending the student back to Step 2.

THE BENEFITS OF SCIENTIFIC PROBLEM-SOLVING ACTIVITIES

Engaging students in problem-solving situations in science opens the door for opportunities to integrate higher-order thinking skills across the curriculum, including analyzing, synthesizing, and making judgments. During Steps 1–3 of the problem-solving process, students usually are involved in sharing their commonly held theories, comparing and contrasting their ideas and understandings, justifying their positions and theories, analyzing relevant information, choosing avenues of action, and explaining and evaluating alternative solutions. During Steps 4 and 5, students put their collective reasoning skills into action by implementing a possible solution to the problem. In the final step, students evaluate their observations, analyze the success of the solution posed, and communicate their results to others.

Watts (1991) identifies eight reasons to provide students with problem-solving experience:

1. Problem solving enables youngsters to assume ownership of a task.

2. Problem solving encourages decision making and social skills.

3. Problem solving is a form of both active learning and discovery learning.

4. Problem solving is a vehicle for teaching many scientific skills and for reaching the content aspects of science.

5. Problem solving allows for cross-curricular and interdisciplinary activities.

6. Problem solving provides relevant and real-life contexts.

7. Problem solving is among the highest and most complex forms of human activity.

8. Problem solving enhances communication.

In this chapter, we have read about the similarities as well as the differences between scientific inquiry and problem-solving. Both serve parallel outcomes for students: a means for becoming scientifically literate. As elementary and middle school teachers create a culture of inquiry within their classrooms, they intertwine these two expressions of science, promoting openness, persistence, self-reliance, and responsibility on the part of the learner.

QUESTIONS FOR REFLECTION AND DISCUSSION

1. Having an aquarium in the classroom can spark student questions. How can you use an aquarium with fish and aquatic plants to have students learn about scientific inquiry? About problem solving?

2. Some teachers say they don't have time for inquiry and problem solving. They may also state that children learn best and perform better on standardized tests by memorizing information. How do you respond to these teachers?

3. Suppose a student wanted to investigate the question, Does bread mold grow better in dark areas than in lighted areas? Is this a good question to investigate? How should the question be revised? Would you suggest the student follow the inquiry cycle or the problem-solving cycle?

What Is the Learning Cycle?

Of one thing I am convinced, I have never seen anyone improve in the art and techniques of inquiry by any other means other than engaging in inquiry.

—Jerome Bruner, *The Process of Education*

Let's go back to John Glenn Middle School from Chapter 5 and drop in on Mr. Fenwick's class again. He's teaching an earth science unit on the different types of rocks. From Monday through Wednesday Mr. Fenwick talks about the various characteristics and examples of sedimentary, metamorphic, and igneous rocks. Each rock group is present on a different day. While Mr. Fenwick gives each lesson, students take notes from the board and take turns reading paragraphs aloud from the textbook. Toward the end of the 45-minute period, Mr. Fenwick assigns the students homework questions to answer from the back of the chapter. He allows the students to use the last five minutes of the class to start their homework assignment. On Thursday, students complete a lab sheet on the properties of rocks. The teacher passes out samples of limestone, marble, and basalt for students to observe. Working in groups of four, students make observations and identify each sample using a classification chart from the textbook. Mr. Fenwick tells the students that they are practicing real science process skills: observing and classifying. With five minutes left in the period, students are instructed to hand in their lab sheets and to expect a unit test tomorrow. On Friday, Mr. Fenwick uses the first 10 minutes to review the chapter material and the information he gave earlier in the week. He asks if the students have any more questions, and hearing none, passes out the unit test on rocks.

Down the hall, Ms. Jackson is also teaching a unit on rocks. On Monday, she starts the unit with a general discussion about rocks and solicits what students already know about various rocks. She writes their responses on the board and then posts a large laminated sign in the front of the room with two questions: What are the different types of rocks? and How are rocks classified according to their properties? Ms. Jackson explains that these are the two essential questions driving the class's rock unit. She then quickly moves into open-ended, hands-on experience in which students are given a bag of rock samples and are asked to describe the similarities and differences of the samples. Several triple-beam balances are available for students to measure the mass of a rock and a tub of water to test whether the rock will float or sink when placed in water. To their amazement, one porous, white-colored rock floats. Students make T-charts in their science journals to record their observations. Students note that some rocks are shiny, while others seem to have a dull luster. Some rocks seem "flaky," while others have pointed edges. At the end of the period, Ms. Jackson gathers the students together to allow them to share their observations with the entire class for each rock sample. Some students know the names of some rocks, while others use the rock identification books on the shelf to find the names of unknown rocks.

On Tuesday, Ms. Jackson provides a description of each sample and its name. She introduces the three types of rocks—sedimentary, metamorphic, and igneous—and assists students in classifying their samples into each type. On Wednesday, she provides a brief presentation on the rock cycle and how one rock type transforms into another by heat, erosion, or pressure. On Thursday, each student is given an individual rock to research. Students find the name and type of their rock using resources in the classroom, additional testing procedures, and the Internet. Each student is expected to produce a poster sheet on his or her rock including its name, where it's found, and its chemical and physical makeup.

In this chapter, we will see how Ms. Jackson's lesson complements the "Learning Cycle," a constructivist approach to lesson planning, and how this Learning Cycle can be used to structure inquiry-based lessons in science. When teachers apply Piaget's stages of cognitive development and the ideas about how children progress from concrete to formal operations, they realize the importance of introducing a concept by first providing concrete, motivational experiences *before* introducing new concepts and information. This, we will see, is the basis of the Learning Cycle.

THE 5E LEARNING CYCLE

The Learning Cycle is one of the most familiar and effective models for science instruction. It was originally proposed in the early 1960s by Atkin and Karplus (1962). The model was later used as the instructional basis for the Science Curriculum Improvement Study (SCIS) program, by Karplus and Thier (1967). It was further documented by Lawson, Abraham, and Renner (1989); Barman and Kotar (1989); Beisenherz and Dantonio (1996); Marek and Cavallo (1997); Bybee (1997); Abraham (1997); and Colburn and Clough (1997).

According to Beisenherz and Dantonio (1996), the Learning Cycle

> enables students themselves to construct discrete science concepts. It includes an Exploration Phase, in which students are exposed to hands-on activities; an Introduction Phase, in which a concept is formally introduced;

and an Application Phase, in which the concept is reinforced and expanded through additional experiences. All phases of the Learning Cycle use teacher questions to guide the learning experience. (p. vii)

Initially, the Learning Cycle was proposed as a three-stage model (Exploration, Concept Development, and Application). In another model, however, Martin, Sexton, and Gerlovich (1999) suggest 4 Es (Exploration, Explanation, Expansion, and Evaluation). With the recent emphasis on constructivism and assessing prior knowledge, the Engagement stage has been added (see Figure 8.1), making the Learning Cycle a 5E model.

- Engagement
- Exploration
- Explanation
- Elaboration or Extension
- Evaluation

We will see that when teachers plan lessons and units around the five stages of the Learning Cycle, students move from concrete experiences, to the development of understanding, to the application of principles.

During the *Engagement* stage, the teacher sets the stage for learning. This is accomplished by stating the purpose of the lesson. Often, the teacher introduces the topic of

Figure 8.1   The Learning Cycle

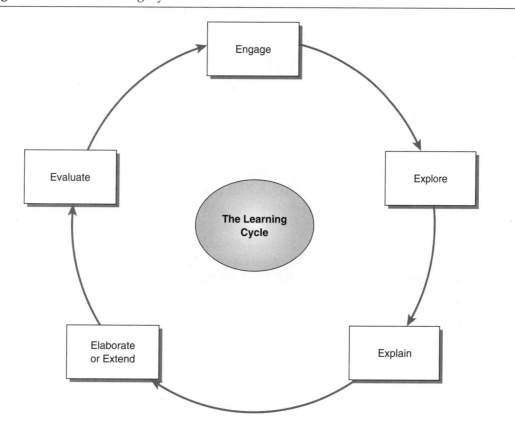

the lesson and states the expectations for learning by introducing an *essential question* and explaining what the students should know and be able to do by the end of the lesson or unit. The Engagement phase is also a means of channeling the students' attention and focus. By using attention-grabbing demonstrations and discrepant events (Liem, 1987), the teacher creates a *cognitive hook* to grasp students into learning. Discrepant events generate interest and curiosity, which sets the stage for inquiring about a particular phenomenon. Discrepant events serve to create cognitive dissonance, or in Piaget's phrasing, disequilibrium, because the observation of such events does not readily assimilate into the students' presently held understanding. Because the observations made from discrepant events run counterintuitive to the students' prior experience, they quickly activate students' attention and learning.

From a constructivist perspective, the Engagement phase also provides an opportunity for the teacher to assess prior knowledge and have students share their prior experiences about the topic. During the Engagement stage, the teacher can note possible naïve conceptions or misconceptions stated by the students. These misconceptions can be addressed while the students have an opportunity to work through the Exploration and Explanation stages. It should be noted that it is nearly impossible for any teacher to ascertain all misconceptions held by all students. However, the Learning Cycle—specifically the Engagement stage—does provide the teacher with a means of assessing students' current beliefs and understanding.

The *Exploration* stage is an opportunity to engage students in inquiry. During the Exploration stage, students explore, raise questions, develop statements to test, and work without direct instruction from the teacher. They go about collecting evidence and data, recording and organizing information, sharing observations, and working in cooperative groups. The Exploration stage enables students to build on a common experience as they go about their investigation. This common exploration is essential because students enter classrooms with different levels of experience and knowledge about the topic being studied. The Exploration stage enables all students to experience hands-on learning and helps to "level the playing field" within a culturally diverse classroom. For classroom management considerations, the teacher may choose to assign *responsibility roles* to the individual students working in a group or permit students to choose their roles according to their strengths or interests. Students may assume the role of recorder, materials collector, reader, or group manager.

During the *Explanation* stage, the teacher adopts a teacher-directed role and facilitates data- and evidence-processing strategies for the individual groups or entire class (depending on the nature of the investigation) from the information collected during the exploration. For some, the myth exists that inquiry teachers do not lecture. Quite to the contrary, they do, when appropriate. The Explanation stage is the appropriate time for teacher-led instruction. The information is discussed, and the teacher often explains the scientific concepts associated with the exploration by providing a common language for the class to use. This common (or scientific) language helps students articulate their thinking and describe their investigations and experiences in scientific terms. During the Explanation stage, the teacher continues to introduce details, vocabulary terms, and definitions to the lesson as students assimilate their understanding with scientific explanations. This can be accomplished by using guided instruction, short lectures, audiovisual resources, online sources, and computer software programs. Here, the teacher uses the students' prior experience to explain the concepts and addresses misconceptions uncovered during the Engagement or Exploration stages. The Explanation stage is sometimes called the *concept development* stage because evidence and newly developed concepts are assimilated into the cognitive structure of the student. During the Explanation stage, students may work to (a) assimilate or accommodate new information as they make sense of their understanding and (b) construct new meaning from their experience.

During the *Elaboration or Extension* stage, the teacher helps reinforce the concept by extending and applying the evidence to new and real-world situations outside the classroom. This stage also facilitates the construction of valid generalizations by the students, who may also modify their presently held understanding of the phenomena being studied. Whereas the Exploration stage can introduce a concept through a structured activity, the Elaboration stage can be an opportunity to investigate several of the questions generated from the Engagement stage or provide an opportunity to engage in an open-ended inquiry.

During the *Evaluation* stage, the teacher brings closure to the lesson or unit by (a) helping students summarize the relationships among the variables studied in the lesson, and (b) posing higher-order and critical thinking questions that support students in making appraisals and judgments about their work. Connections among the concepts just studied can be illustrated with a concept map. By using one color for the "pre" knowledge and another color for the "post" knowledge, the students can visually compare their prior understanding identified during the Engagement stage with the newly formed understanding gained from the lesson. The multicolor strategy demonstrates to students how they are constructing new knowledge. During the Evaluation stage, the teacher provides a means for students to assess their learning and make connections—from prior understanding to new situations that encourage the application of concepts and problem-solving skills. Assessment examples may include multiple choice items, extended-response questions, essays, authentic tasks, portfolios, rubrics, monitoring charts, concept maps, and student self-assessments.

INVESTIGATING MEALWORMS

Studying mealworms is an excellent way to introduce students to a life science unit on invertebrates, insects, life cycles, metamorphosis, and the needs of living things. "Mealworms to Go" involves students in learning about an invertebrate animal through inquiry and questioning. This two-week unit follows the 5E Learning Cycle format and is appropriate for Grades 5–8. The unit aligns to the *National Science Education Standards* (NSES) (NRC, 1996):

Life Science Content Standards

As a result of their activities in Grades 5–8, all students should develop (an) understanding that

- The characteristics of an organism can be described in terms of a combination of traits. Some traits are inherited and others result from interactions with the environment (p. 157)

Science and Technology Standards

As a result of their activities in Grades 5–8, all students should develop the ability to

- Design a solution or product (p. 165)
- Implement a proposed solution (p. 165)
- Evaluate completed technological design or products (p. 165)

Prior to the start of the unit, a sixth-grade teacher, Ms. McArdle, obtains a source for mealworms. Mealworms are readily available from pet stores and are quite inexpensive. Ms. McArdle has contacted a colleague, Mrs. Rivera, also a sixth-grade teacher, to participate in the task. With the two classrooms separated by 500 miles, the two have agreed to complete the unit simultaneously. The task involves both classes studying the life cycle of an invertebrate animal and designing a package that will allow the mealworms to be shipped successfully from one classroom to another. The purpose of the task is to design an effective package to ship 25 mealworms and to exchange the mealworm packages, comparing packing designs and the number of live mealworms reaching their destinations. Let's see how the task plays out.

The Engagement Stage

To start the unit, each teacher assesses her students' prior knowledge by showing them several mealworms and asking them what they already know about these little creatures. Some students have little or no experience with mealworms, while others say that they have used them as bait for fishing or as food for pet turtles. The students record their responses and experiences in their science journals and then pair and share that information with a partner. Ms. McArdle and Mrs. Rivera solicit responses in their individual classes from their students, encouraging them to communicate their prior experiences (and misconceptions) with mealworms. The teachers writes the comments on a blackboard or poster sheet by making a concept map or list of "What we know about mealworms." Both teachers are aware that many of their students may think that mealworms are really worms. The mealworm is actually the larval stage of the beetle, *Tenebrio molitor* (see Figure 7.2). With many students raising misconceptions about mealworms, Ms. McArdle decides it's best to wait until the end of the Explanation phase, when students have had an opportunity to learn more about mealworms, to challenge this common misconception.

Before beginning the investigation, in both classes students brainstorm a list of health and safety rules for handling the mealworms. They call this their "Mealworm Bill of Rights." This enables students to create their own self-imposed rules to follow while they handle the mealworms and identify the proper procedures for animal care and responsibility. Students need to be reminded to wash their hands before and after handling the mealworms to ensure proper safety and sanitary conditions.

The next step in students becoming "mealwormologists" is to encourage them to make firsthand observations about the mealworms to find out everything they can about these organisms. During this time, students use magnifying lenses and measuring rulers to observe and collect information about the mealworms. They record their observations about the mealworms' size, color, number of "legs," and movements in their science journals. Students are encouraged to use various sources of information both in the library and on the Internet to determine the scientific name of the mealworm and to gather more information about the life cycle of the beetle. The information they collect will help them during the Extension phase, when they design their "Mealworms to Go" containers.

As they observe and collect information, students also write questions about mealworms. Questions may include the following:

Figure 8.2   The Life Cycle of a Mealworm

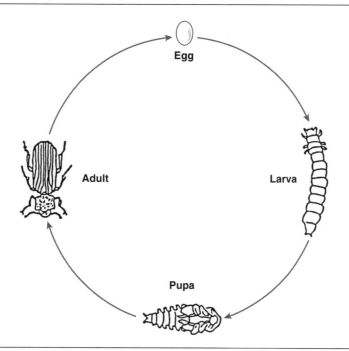

- What do mealworms prefer to eat?
- Where do mealworms live?
- Do mealworms prefer to stay in sunny or dark areas?
- Do mealworms prefer wet or dry surfaces?
- Do mealworms have eyes? How do they know where they are going?
- Are mealworms really worms?
- Are mealworms related to earthworms?
- What materials do mealworms like for bedding?
- Do all mealworms have the same number of segments?
- Do mealworms prefer hot or cold locations?
- How fast does a mealworm travel?
- Can a mealworm go through a maze to find its food?

In the final part of the Engagement phase, the teachers and students identify and classify the questions into three categories mentioned previously in Chapter 6: those that can be answered through experimentation, those that require revision before being answered through experimentation, and those that require library research and other expert sources to be answered.

The Exploration Stage

During the Exploration stage, students plan and carry out their inquiries. After the questions are stated clearly, the students plan a means to find answers to their questions and identify the materials they will need. At this point, students complete the "Mealworm Inquiry Plan" (see Form 8.1) to document the design phase of their investigations.

The Mealworm Inquiry Plan serves as a format for students to write and organize their ideas. Before beginning the actual investigation, students should critique one another's plans. Students can peer-review one another to determine whether the procedures are clear and understandable. After the Mealworm Inquiry Plans are completed and the teacher has approved the procedures, the students are ready to carry out their investigations.

The Explanation Stage

At the completion of their inquiries, students need time to organize their data into charts, tables, or graphs and look for patterns and relationships. During the Explanation stage, students use this data to communicate to the class what they found out about mealworm behavior during their inquiries. Each teacher organizes a "Mealworm Convention," where the mealwormologists present their findings during three-minute presentations. Students are encouraged to make posters, trifold display boards, or PowerPoint presentations to summarize their observations and results.

The Elaboration or Extension Stage

The Elaboration or Extension stage (sometimes referred to as the application phase) for this unit comprises "Mealworms to Go," a problem-solving and performance task. Here students use the information they gathered during their investigations to design a shipping container that will enable each class to send 25 mealworms to the cooperating science classroom. The container's design should ensure the maximum survival of the mealworms. The success of the container will be measured by counting and comparing the survival rates of the mealworms transported by the two classrooms.

The Extension stage begins by having Ms. McArdle and Mrs. Rivera introduce the students to the cooperating class. The classes share information about themselves by providing their names, school demographics, and other information. The classes also exchange photographs and letters either by postal service or by e-mail.

After being presented with the task, the students design containers that will ensure that the mealworms arrive alive and still in the larval stage. Students are given time to brainstorm concerns about designing an appropriate container. Ms. McArdle's and Mrs. Rivera's classes consider the issues:

- How will food and water be kept in the container?
- How long will it take for the package to arrive at the cooperating school?
- Does the U. S. Post Office have requirements for transporting live animals?
- How would the package be constructed differently if the package were sent in December rather than in May?
- What will be used to cushion and protect the mealworms?
- How many days does it take to complete the beetle's life cycle?
- How old do the mealworms have to be so that they arrive in the larval stage?
- What criteria will the two classes use to determine whether a mealworm arrives alive or dead?
- Should there be size and cost limitations for the containers?

Working in cooperative groups, several prototype containers are constructed. Each class votes to determine which design will represent their school.

Form 8.1   The Mealworm Inquiry Plan

Mealworm Inquiry Plan

I wonder [my question is] _____

_____

I predict [my hypothesis is] _____

_____

The manipulated variable is _____

The responding variable is _____

The controlled variables are _____

The steps I will follow are

1. _____

2. _____

3. _____

4. _____

5. _____

The observations I made are _____

_____

_____

The patterns or relationships I found are _____

_____

_____

The answer to my question [my conclusion] is _____

_____

After the two containers are completed, each class simultaneously packs and ships the mealworms to the students in the cooperating school. When the mealworm package from the cooperating school arrives, a videotape is made of the opening of the container. The teachers each decide to send their video to the cooperating class to view.

Following the opening of the package, the students count and record the number of living and dead mealworms. They calculate the survival rate with the previously determined criteria. Groups then send the videotape of the container opening and survival rates to the cooperating class, and it's time to move on to the final E, Evaluation.

The Evaluation Stage

Over the past 10 years, progressive changes have been made in science programs, instruction, and assessment measures to assess knowledge, skills, and attitudes. With the changing pedagogy in science education, assessment has also moved to emphasizing a combination of hands-on and minds-on skills (Hein & Price, 1994). Assessment procedures must align with the new goals and objectives of the NSES to ensure that students are moving toward levels of increasing academic achievement and becoming globally competitive, scientifically literate citizens.

According to the NSES (NRC, 1996):

> Assessment and learning are two sides of the same coin. The methods used to collect educational data should teach what students should learn. And when students engage in an assessment, they learn that it [assessment] is an effective tool for communicating the expectations of the science education system to all concerned with science education. (p. 76)

That is to say, when teachers provide students with low-level, recall questions, they communicate the notion that memorizing scientific facts is the essential outcome of learning science. If they provide students with writing and extended-response questions, they are saying that communication, especially in written form, is an important way to demonstrate their understanding of science. By providing students with performance tasks similar to "Mealworms to Go," teachers emphasize ways "to apply scientific knowledge and reasoning skills to situations similar to those they will encounter in the world outside the classroom, as well as to situations that approximate how scientists do their work" (NRC, 1996, p. 78).

Before beginning the final phase of the Learning Cycle, we first must distinguish assessment from evaluation. Assessment is the process of gathering information regarding students' learning, what they know and what they can do, for the purpose of making adjustments in the teaching process. Teachers make midcourse adjustments in their lesson plans and units of study when formal and informal assessments indicate that students are not acquiring the desired outcome(s) from the instruction. There are generally two types of assessment: formative and summative. Formative assessments occur throughout the lesson or unit of study, while summative assessments occur at the end of the lesson or unit. Evaluation refers to the process of interpreting and making judgments about tests and assessments for the purpose of grading, selection, or promotion.

Consider two teachers' approach to testing. Teacher X prepares a lesson by simply planning the instructional sequence, then teaching the lesson or unit, and finally writing a test at the end of the lesson or unit, most likely the night before the test is given. The day following the test, Teacher X returns the corrected tests and goes on to the next lesson. Sounds logical enough? Sure it does. Now consider Teacher Y. Teacher Y begins planning for a lesson or a unit by reflecting on what he or she wants the students to know and be able to do by the end of the instruction. The lesson's objectives are guided by district, state, or national standards and curricula. Teacher Y uses those outcomes to write the test, even before the lesson planning begins. On the basis of the learning outcome, Teacher Y then plans the instruction that will guide the students toward successfully meeting the stated outcomes. As the lesson or unit begins, Teacher Y assesses students' prior knowledge for any misconceptions they may have about the topic. Teacher Y uses that information to adjust the learning sequence. The instruction begins with Teacher Y periodically checking for understanding and again adjusting and modifying the instruction on the basis of students' different needs and progress. Teacher Y provides occasions for reteaching because he or she knows that some students may not construct similar meaning at the same pace as others. At the conclusion of the lesson or unit, Teacher Y administers the test that was written prior to planning the instruction. If students have significant problems with certain areas of the test, Teacher Y uses the next class to reinforce areas and provides a different teaching approach than was used previously. This "backward" approach to instructional planning was made popular by Wiggins and McTighe in their book *Understanding by Design Handbook* (1999).

As for the "Mealworms to Go" task, start by asking, What are the scientific concepts, skills, and competencies a student should know and be able to demonstrate by the end of this unit? Many will obviously say that acquisition of content and basic science knowledge is most important, and many of us will agree with that. Although expanding one's scientific models and conceptions about mealworm and invertebrate organisms is important, some could argue that other scientific, thinking, and social skills are equally important. For that reason, the assessment of an inquiry lesson or unit should model the tenets of inquiry as closely as possible. Would it be effective to design a unit test for "Mealworms to Go" based solely on multiple-choice, true-false, or objective-type questions that measure knowledge or recall-level understanding? Probably not. The assessment instrument(s) for "Mealworms to Go" should reflect the goals and objectives of the teacher's instructional plans and include aspects of

1. Scientific knowledge and information (the life cycle of an invertebrate organism)

2. Science process skills (observing, measuring, predicting, collecting, recording, and organizing data)

3. Problem-solving skills (designing solutions and choosing best alternatives)

4. Communication skills (oral presentations and written journal entries)

5. Cooperative learning (group work and responsibility)

6. Science and technology (constructing models)

ASSESSING INQUIRY-BASED SCIENCE

In an era of high-stakes national science tests, assessments are placing excessive pressure on elementary and middle school teachers, especially those who teach through inquiry-based approaches. For many teachers, science assessment is slowly turning into undue science "a-stressment"! However, there is an alternative: authentic assessments. Authentic assessments are defined as evaluation strategies that are unconventional, meaningful, interesting to perform, and relevant to the learner. When compared with objective-type questioning techniques, authentic assessments involve active participation and usually entail higher-level thinking skills. Although multiple-choice and true-false items serve a vital purpose for assessing specific facts and knowledge, authentic assessments paint a more realistic picture of what the students understand and are able to do. When properly used, authentic assessments also complement the various individual learning styles that students display.

When choosing assessments for science, the National Center for Improving Science Education (NCISE) (1992) recommends that inquiry-based teachers consider the following:

1. Assessments that match exemplary science instruction

2. Assessments that include hands-on performances

3. Assessments that probe the depth of the student's understanding

4. Assessments that emphasize the process used to obtain an answer as well as the product or the final answer itself

5. Assessments that include opportunities for reflection and self-evaluation

6. Assessments that include performances such as presentations, journals, and displays

7. Assessments that involve group work designed around tasks too complex for students to undertake individually

"Not everything that counts can be counted and not everything that can be counted counts." This saying was reportedly posted in the office of Albert Einstein (Herman, Aschbacher, & Winters, 1992) and summarizes the need for conventional and performance-based assessments in science education. To match the NCISE goals, the assessment instruments for inquiry instruction usually incorporate both objective and alternative forms of assessing academic achievement; for example, multiple-choice items and constructive response questions combined with portfolios, rubrics, monitoring charts, concept maps, journal entries, lab reports, oral presentations, performance assessments, and self-assessments. Each of these assessment tools serves a specific purpose to measure and monitor student achievement and progress over time. For example, multiple-choice and constructive response questions may be best suited for assessing fact and comprehension-level science content, whereas portfolios, rubrics, monitoring charts, concept maps, journal entries, lab reports, oral presentations, performances, and self-assessments may be best suited for assessing students' abilities to do inquiry, abilities about inquiry, and nature of science. Although there are full books devoted solely to assessing inquiry-based instruction, all these assessment tools will be briefly addressed in the next sections. For suggested books on assessment, see Resource A.

MULTIPLE-CHOICE QUESTIONS

Multiple-choice questions are probably the most familiar test items for students. They can be designed to assess concepts and understanding at various levels of cognitive thinking and are, best of all, easy to score. Multiple choice questions are generally written in two formats: one in which the stem poses a question followed by four possible answers, and another in which the stem contains the beginning of a statement and is followed by four possible answers that completes the statement correctly. When listing the possible answers, use a numerical sequence when appropriate, such as:

When a student uses a compound microscope with a 10X eyepiece and a 20X objective lens, the total magnification produced is

a. 30X

b. 100X

c. 200X

d. 300X

In addition to content, teachers can also use multiple-choice questions to assess science process skills. Here's one example:

Gayle received a present three days before her ninth birthday. The size of the box is 24 inches high by 24 inches wide by 24 inches long and is covered with brown paper. The person who sent her the present wrote on the box, "Do not open before your birthday!" Gayle shakes the box and listens for any sounds. She makes several comments to her mother who is standing behind her. Which one of the following statements is an inference?

a. The box is square.

b. The box is big so the gift must be expensive.

c. The box has brown wrapping paper on it.

d. The box was sent to Gayle.

Multiple-choice items are also very effective in assessing science inquiry investigations when combined with a data table, diagram, graph, or illustration to analyze and interpret. When using a table or graph in a test item, place it above the question.

Most teachers prefer to place the multiple-choice section upfront in the test, followed by the constructive response questions or alternative assessments. Plan your multiple-choice section by placing easier questions first and progressing to more difficult or higher-level questions later. To help instill confidence in students, begin with a question that most can likely answer correctly.

CONSTRUCTIVE RESPONSE QUESTIONS

Most inquiry science teachers are very familiar with constructive response-type questions. Examples include fill-in-the blank items, short-answer questions, and brief essays. As with multiple-choice items, constructive response questions allow teachers to assess science content, investigation protocols, and process skills at various levels of comprehension. Although they do take longer to grade, constructive response questions assess levels of thinking including: application, analysis, and synthesis; and where students respond by explaining, comparing, interpreting, summarizing, applying, examining, and developing.

Some of the "Going Further" questions from the investigations in this book can be classified as constructive response questions. For example, following the ice hand investigation, students may be asked to write a paragraph explaining how water exists in three different states and how one state may be changed into another. In the Ramps and Balls investigation, students may be asked to design an investigation using the mass of the marble as a manipulated variable. In the pumpkin activity, students may draw an illustration to describe the life cycle of a plant. Or from the mealworm investigation, students may be asked to identify and then describe the life stages of a beetle.

PORTFOLIOS

A portfolio is a folder or container holding evidence and representative examples of student work, accomplishments, and performances that are collected, reflected on, and saved over an extended period of time. With portfolios, the work of the student is reviewed against specific criteria to evaluate and judge the student's progress and improvement. Each entry in the portfolio is a selected piece of work that exemplifies significant student accomplishments. The entries may be works in progress or finished products. In the "Mealworms to Go" unit, a completed Mealworm Inquiry Plan would be evidence that students would add to their portfolios to demonstrate their ability to (a) pose a question, (b) plan an investigation, (c) gather data, and (d) draw reasonable conclusions. Other examples of possible portfolio entries are excerpts from science journals, illustrations or artwork of the mealworm life cycle, a summary of contributions to the container design task, or a writing assignment that describes what has been learned about mealworms and their life cycles.

By combining portfolios with traditional, objective-type assessments, teachers, students, and parents can collaborate to paint a realistic and more complete picture of a child's performance and academic growth over time. When evaluation of student progress involves portfolios and performance tasks, students are motivated to demonstrate what they can do in completing complex tasks. The portfolio is increasingly considered an effective tool for assessing inquiry-based learning.

RUBRICS

The word *rubric* comes from the Latin "ruber" meaning red. The word originally referred to notes and directions written in red (to distinguish them from the rest of the text) in the margins of liturgical books. Today, teachers and students use rubrics as guidelines for scoring, assessing, and evaluating student work and performance.

Rubrics provide assistance in (a) describing the performance of students at various standards or levels of proficiency, (b) scoring and assessing student work without bias and inconsistency, and (c) enabling students to compare and discuss their self-assessment with the teacher's assessments.

Instructional rubrics usually contain three features:

1. Dimensions to be assessed

2. A numerical scoring ranging from 1 (for a low score) to 4 or 5 (for a high score)

3. Statements, behaviors, or expectations for each dimension being assessed

Rubrics generally are divided into two types: analytical and holistic. Analytical rubrics generally are quantitative and address performances divided into individual tasks or parts. Holistic rubrics generally are qualitative and address the entire performance as a whole. An analytical rubric provides science teachers and students with a consistent standard for each level or stage identified. By using analytical rubrics, students not only can assess their present level but also can become aware of the standards or behaviors they must achieve to advance to the next performance level. By providing the rubric at the same time the task is given, coupled with samples of student work at three levels (above standard, at standard, and below standard), teachers can allow students to see, in advance, what exemplary work looks like and what they must do to perform at a proficient or an exceptional level. Teachers find that students strive for higher standards of achievement when they are provided with guidelines for success. The rubric, like the portfolio, serves as a starting point for discussing and evaluating the learner's progress.

Several science rubrics can be found using the Internet. A search using the terms *rubric*, *science*, and *inquiry* will yield a host of rubrics. Here are three excellent Web sites for sources of science inquiry rubrics:

http://www.stclair.k12.il.us/services/scilit/Invstrbr.htm

http://www.stclair.k12.il.us/services/scilit/hlsticrb.htm

http://www.nwrel.org/msec/science_inq/guides.html

MONITORING CHARTS

Monitoring charts pinpoint what students are expected to do during the course of a scientific inquiry. The chart enables the teacher to identify and monitor skills used by students as they investigate solutions to their questions. By observing a predetermined set of behaviors, the teacher can move about the room and observe individual behaviors. Performance of these behaviors is recorded on a sheet by using either a *check plus* (✓+) for "above standard performance," a *check* (✓) for "at standard performance," or a *check minus* (✓–) for "below standard performance." The teacher can also assign a letter grade for each behavior (E = excellent, G = good, F = fair, N = not observed). Hart (1994) suggests that the teacher, while making class observations, also make informal and anecdotal comments using the following guidelines:

- Observe and monitor all students equitably
- Observe often and regularly
- Record observations in writing
- Note typical as well as atypical behaviors
- Make multiple observations to ensure reliability
- Document the date, time, and stage of the lesson

Figure 8.3 shows a science inquiry monitoring chart.

CONCEPT MAPS

As we saw in Chapters 2 and 3, concept maps often are used prior to a lesson to assess the aggregate knowledge of an individual or an entire class. Concept maps are also used as postassessment tools to clarify the student's ability to connect prior knowledge to new knowledge gained. Concept maps are used by all levels of teachers, from kindergarten through high school (Hein & Price, 1994) and college. Figure 8.4 shows a concept map for the mealworm unit.

A concept map is one means for teachers to assess a student's understanding of a particular topic. In this case, the teacher provides the student with a set of words or statements written on strips of paper. The words or statements are vocabulary terms used during a lesson or unit of study. The student's task is to arrange the words to form a concept map. The teacher may require that the student add linking verbs to connect one strip to another. After the concept map is arranged, the student explains the sequence and uses the concept words to review the main topic and subtopics of the lesson.

Resource B contains 18 statements about the Learning Cycle. Cut the words and statements into individual strips and rearrange them to form a concept map. Add linking verbs to connect the words, using the map to describe the Learning Cycle. Share your concept map with a colleague or partner by reciting an explanation of the Learning Cycle using the concept map of the 18 statements.

JOURNAL ENTRIES

Reflection is an important part of doing science and developing healthy habits of mind. It allows the investigator to step back and assess the processes and procedures of the inquiry. It also serves as a vehicle for expressing emerging understanding of the abilities about scientific inquiry as well as the nature of science. Many teachers use journaling as a means for students to take a metacognitive perspective and think about their learning by completing the statement, "Three things I learned today were. . . ." or "By completing this investigation I now know. . . ." or "Connections I made during this inquiry include. . . ." While drawing conclusions and judgments

Figure 8.3   Science Inquiry Monitoring Chart

Stage/Behavior	\: Investigation # :				
	1	2	3	4	5
Exploring					
Makes observations					
Records observations in journal					
Takes careful notes					
Draws illustrations/sketches					
Records "What if" questions					
Stating a question					
Sorts and revises questions					
States an investigation question					
Brainstorms possible solutions					
Identifying a statement to test					
Makes a statement to test					
Records statement					
Designing a procedure					
Brainstorms possible steps					
Arranges steps in sequential order					
Identifies manipulated variable					
Identifies responding variable					
Identifies dependent variable					
Determines materials to use					
Carrying out a plan					
Obtains supplies and materials					
Follows written procedure					
Follows safety guidelines					
Shares/respects ideas with group members					
Assumes responsibility for group role					
Makes constructive contributions to group					
Collecting evidence					
Gathers data					
Makes accurate measurements					
Organizes data in tables or charts					
Plots data on a graph					
Describing relationship between variables					
Draws conclusion; analyzes results					
Determines validity of hypothesis					
Communicating results					
Prepares trifold poster					
Makes contribution to presentation					
Uses appropriate terminology					
Makes eye contact with audience					
Speaks clearly					
Answers questions from audience					
Reflects on investigation					

Figure 8.4   Concept Map of Mealworms

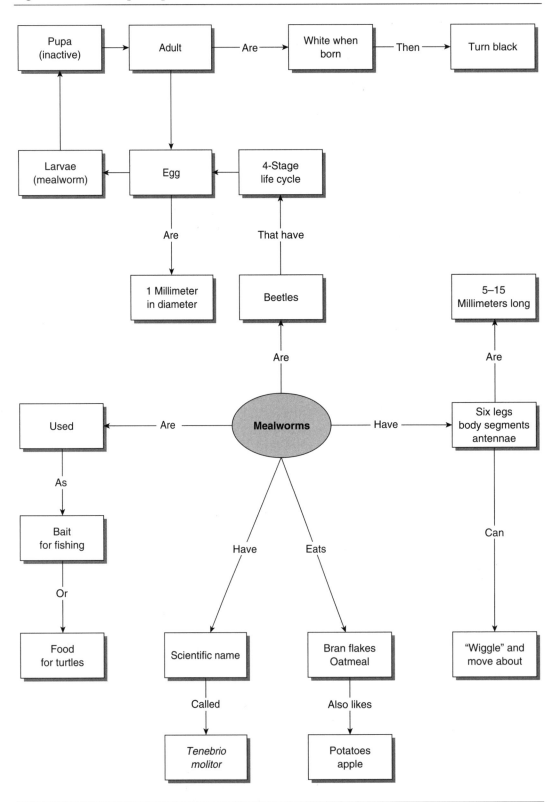

about their own work, students use science journals to promote their critical and higher level thinking skills. Whether you use speckled notebooks or three-ring binders, journaling also serves to integrate effective writing skills into the science curriculum.

LAB REPORTS

The Mealworm Inquiry Plan (see Form 8.1) is a good example of a planning document that can be revised into a lab report. To assess the lab report, place point values on each of the sections at the beginning of the inquiry. This will enable students to become aware of the grading procedures. For example, each section is assigned a specific number of points:

Question = 10 points

Prediction = 10 points

Identification of Variables = 10 points

Steps and Procedures = 20 points

Observations and Data = 20 points

Relationships and Claims Made = 15 points

Conclusions = 15 points

ORAL PRESENTATIONS

In Chapter 3, Camille Perlo's ice hands lesson provided an excellent example of students performing an oral presentation to demonstrate their skills and understanding. Oral presentations also develop speaking and listening skills, poise, and the use of visual aids to enhance the presentation.

PERFORMANCE ASSESSMENTS

Performance tasks are one of the most appropriate means to assess students' understanding of scientific inquiry and related science process skills. According to the National Research Council (2001), performance assessments are "assessments that allow students to demonstrate their understanding and skills (to a teacher or an outsider) as they perform a certain activity. They are evaluated by a teacher or an outsider on the quality of their ability to perform specific tasks and the products they create in the process" (p. 31).

Performance tasks are generally those tasks where students apply their knowledge to everyday settings. In some cases the task can be very prescriptive, while others are open-ended like problem-solving tasks. Consider this performance task based on a middle school unit entitled, "Estimating with the Metric System." In this unit, students have been learning measuring skills in metric measurements. As a hands-on performance for the end-of-the-unit test, the first task involves the student (given a ball of string and a pair of scissors) cutting a length of string 25 centimeters long. The student is directed to place the piece of string in a small labeled envelope. For the second task, the student is given a small pail of dried beans. The student's task is to place 100 grams of beans in a small, labeled bag and set it aside. For the third task, the student is given a beaker of water and a paper cup. The directions are to fill the cup with 100 milliliters of water. After all three tasks are completed, the student uses a meter stick, a graduated cylinder, and a triple beam balance to record the estimations. The student records the estimated values on a data sheet and determines the difference in the actual and estimated values. For each sample the student calculates a percentage of error by dividing the estimated value by the difference in values and multiplying by 100. For Jay, one seventh-grade student, the length of his cut string is 23 centimeters. Subtracting the estimated value (23) from the actual value (25) results in a difference of 2. Dividing 2 by 25 and multiplying by 100 results in an 8% error for Jay's first task. Here we can see how the performance assessment is an extension of classroom learning.

SELF-EVALUATIONS

Self-evaluations (which are actually self-assessments) are a means to collect feedback about how individuals perceive their abilities, attitudes, and performances. Although elementary and middle school students often rate their performances at exceedingly high levels, self-evaluations do provide a window into students' perceptions of how well they did on a science exploration. Self-evaluations also offer students the opportunity to reflect on how they might improve if they were to repeat their performance. Self-assessments also work well when used in conjunction with other traditional, objective-type test items. Form 8.2 is a self-evaluation for the mealworm unit. For primary level students in Grades 3 and 4, self-assessments and surveys can be modified to include responses with faces that express their feelings (I agree = happy smile, No opinion = no smile, and I disagree = frown).

In summary, inquiry-based science teachers use a variety of assessments to collect data about modifying instruction and determining the level of student achievement. According to the NSES, "assessment and learning are two sides of the same coin" (NRC, 1996, p. 76). By carefully aligning the curricular goals, the instructional program, and the assessment procedures, inquiry science teachers can focus on what is important for students to learn to become scientifically literate. These elements include:

- Being able to know science concepts and understanding,
- Being able to inquiry and reason scientifically,
- Being able to communicate about science effectively, and
- Being able to apply science principles to make decisions about everyday issues.

Form 8.2   Self-Evaluation Form for the Inquiry Unit "Mealworms to Go"

Self-Evaluation Form for the Inquiry Unit "Mealworms to Go"

Name:_____

	Almost Always	Often	Sometimes	Rarely
Engagement				
I handled the mealworms properly.	O	O	O	O
I washed my hands after handling the mealworms.	O	O	O	O
I made good observations and measurements.	O	O	O	O
I made accurate drawings of the mealworms.	O	O	O	O
Exploration				
I followed the procedures in my inquiry plan.	O	O	O	O
I productively participated in the group discussions.	O	O	O	O
I did my share of the group work.	O	O	O	O
I used my journal to record my observations and measurements.	O	O	O	O
I used the supplies and materials appropriately.	O	O	O	O
Explanation				
I used many sources to collect information about mealworms.	O	O	O	O
I shared what I learned about mealworms with others in my class.	O	O	O	O
I listened to other members of my group and respected their ideas.	O	O	O	O
Extension				
I shared responsibility during the Mealworm Convention.	O	O	O	O
I made good eye contact during the Mealworm Convention.	O	O	O	O
I projected my voice during the Mealworm Convention.	O	O	O	O

CELEBRATING LEARNING

At the conclusion of the mealworm unit, it would be appropriate to celebrate the learning process by awarding students with a diploma certifying them, for example, as "Certified Mealwormologists." Figure 8.5 shows a sample diploma.

Figure 8.5 Mealworm Award

SUMMARY OF "MEALWORMS TO GO"

Using the 5E Learning Cycle, the steps of the "Mealworms to Go" inquiry may be summarized as follows:

Engagement

1. Introduce the concept to be learned
2. Assess prior knowledge
3. Have students share what they know about mealworms with a partner
4. Make a concept map from what the entire class knows about mealworms

5. Provide time for students to observe mealworms and record observations in their science journals

6. Encourage students to write questions to investigate

7. Sort questions according to whether they can be answered through an investigation

8. Assist students in researching information in the library and on the Internet

Exploration

9. Assist students in planning an investigation using the inquiry data sheet

10. Support students as they gather data, organize their evidence on a chart or graph, look for patterns and relationships, and draw conclusions

Explanation

11. Provide information through direct instruction or class discussion on the topic being studied

12. Encourage students to communicate the results of their investigations by holding a "Mealworm Convention"

Elaboration or Extension

13. Introduce the performance task, "Mealworms to Go"

14. Have students brainstorm ideas about the container designs

15. Have students choose the best design and produce the container

16. Ship the container to the cooperating class

17. Videotape the opening of the container

18. Evaluate results

Evaluation

19. Select one or several methods for assessing what students are expected to know and be able to do as a result of this unit

20. Award "Mealwormologist" diplomas

The Learning Cycle is a powerful instructional tool for constructivist and inquiry-based teachers. By integrating inquiry into the Exploration or Extension stages of the 5E Learning Cycle, teachers can provide opportunities for students to engage in inquiry-based instruction. Consider using the Learning Cycle approach for your next science lesson and integrating an inquiry investigation into the cycle. You'll see how easily the two complement each other!

We will now look at two more applications of the 5E Learning Cycle.

INVESTIGATING OOBLECK

Oobleck, a hands-on science activity, provides an excellent opportunity for teachers to combine inquiry about an unusual substance while messing about and enjoying a new, gooey experience. The following lesson follows the 5E format and can be adapted to a variety of grade levels.

Title of Lesson: *Oobleck*

Grade Levels: 3–5

Essential Questions:

- How can you describe the properties of Oobleck?

Estimated Time: 60 to 75 minutes

Correlation to the NSES:

Science as Inquiry Standards

- Students will ask questions about objects, organisms, and events in the environment (NRC, 1996, p. 122)
- Students will use data to construct a reasonable explanation (p. 122)

Physical Science Standards

- Objects have many observable properties (p. 127)

Science Skills: Observing, communicating, testing ideas, formulating explanations, constructing models

Background for the Teacher: Scientists aren't exactly sure how to explain the phenomenon of Oobleck. Some think that under pressure, the smaller water molecules are "forced" in between the larger starch molecules to form a temporary semisolid property. Without pressure, the water molecules are free to slide over the starch molecules, giving it a slippery, liquid-like appearance. Substances like Oobleck are often called non-Newtonian because they take on the properties of both a liquid and a solid depending on the amount of pressure exerted on them.

Materials:

3-4 squeeze bottles of green-colored water

3-4 boxes of cornstarch

1 plastic tumbler or cup for each student

1 plastic spoon for each student

1 Styrofoam plate

A pile of newspapers

A science journal or a T-chart

1 wizard hat for each student (optional)

Preparation: Have students work at flat tables. Place newspapers over the table-top. In preparing the Oobleck, be sure to add water to the cornstarch and not cornstarch to the water. Have a bucket of water or sink available to rinse off the Oobleck from the students' hands. Do not allow students to pour the Oobleck down a sink. Throw the used Oobleck into a wastepaper basket.

5E Learning Cycle Stages

Engage: Assess prior knowledge and misconceptions about the properties of matter. Pose the question, "What are the properties of matter?" Read the book *Bartholomew and the Oobleck* by Dr. Seuss. After the story, pose these questions:

Why did the king finally admit to saying, "I'm sorry?"

Did you ever do something wrong and had to say you were sorry?

Why was it so hard for King Derwin to say he was sorry?

Explore: Have students make Oobleck by combining water (containing green food coloring) and cornstarch. Fill each cup half full with cornstarch. Add a "squirt" of water to the cornstarch. Use the spoon to mix a small amount of water into a half full cup of cornstarch. Continue adding water until a thick, pancake-like consistency is produced. Pour the Oobleck into your hands. Roll the Oobleck in your hands to form a ball. Allow it to "melt" into your hand. Observe and record the properties of Oobleck on a separate sheet of paper. Use a T-chart (Figure 8.6) to record observations and questions.

Explore the following questions:

- What happens when you place pressure on Oobleck?
- What happens when you push the plastic spoon with pressure into the cup of Oobleck? What happens when you push the plastic spoon gently into the cup of Oobleck?
- Can you make the Oobleck into a solid by squeezing it in your hands?
- What happens when you release the pressure from your hands?
- Pour the Oobleck onto a Styrofoam plate. Notice how liquid-like the Oobleck pours. Smash the palms of your hand onto the plate of Oobleck. Repeat with slight pressure. Observe the difference.
- Roll a glob of Oobleck in the palm of your hands. Describe how it feels.

Explain: Describe what happens when you hold Oobleck in your hand or you hit it with your fist. How is it like a liquid? How is it like a solid? What are the properties of Oobleck?

Extend: How is Oobleck like our personalities? (Just like putting pressure on Oobleck, when pressure is placed on us, we usually push back or "harden." Without pressure, we are often "softer." When you are hard on people, they often are hard on you. When you are soft on people, they are often soft on you.

Questions to Consider:

- Does the temperature of the water affect the property of Oobleck?
- What if you used potato starch instead of cornstarch?

Figure 8.6 T-Chart

Observations	Questions

- How can you test for the presence of Oobleck? (Test with iodine for starch.)
- Imagine you are traveling to the planet Oobleck. Design a spaceship so it can land on the surface without sinking into the planet's surface. Construct a model of the spaceship and test the landing in a bowl of Oobleck.

Evaluate: Compare Oobleck with a liquid and a solid. Review the essential questions and make a concept map to list the properties of Oobleck. What lesson did you learn from the Dr. Seuss story?

Accommodations for Special Needs: Students with physical disabilities may need assistance with mixing the cornstarch and water.

Resources/Literature Connections:

Geisel, Theodor. (1949). *Bartholomew and the Oobleck.* New York: Random House.

Sneider, Cary. (1985). *Oobleck: What Do Scientists Do?* Berkeley, CA: GEMS.

INVESTIGATING RAMPS AND BALLS

In Chapter 6, the marble activity worksheet provided a superb opportunity for students to explore the concepts of force and motion. In this section, we will see how a follow-up investigation can serve as the elaboration or extension to the initial exploration. Let's assume for the moment that Ms. Clark, an eighth-grade teacher, is using the 5E Learning Cycle to plan a unit of study on forces. For the Engagement stage of the lesson, she asks the students, "What do you know about rolling balls?" The students respond by placing their answers on a separate sheet of paper. After a few minutes, Ms. Clark tells the students to turn to a person next to them and pair and share their answers with that partner. She then walks between the groups listening for possible misconceptions from their conversations. Ms. Clark then has students share the responses from their sheets with the entire class as she makes a list of their ideas and experiences on the board. Ms. Clark follows up the pair and share activity with a brief demonstration showing a marble rolling down a ramp. She uses this brief demonstration to transition into the Exploration stage, where students determine how the height of the ramp affects the distance the marble will travel.

For the Exploration stage, Ms. Clark distributes the "Marble Activity Worksheet" (see Form 6.1). After a brief introduction to the activity, students read the lab and get materials. With the exploration activity taking a half hour to complete, the period is almost over. Ms. Clark has students review the results of their marble activity and poses several questions to them. She reminds them that tomorrow they will be taking notes on forces and motion and to read the *Forces and Motion* section in their textbook as homework.

The next day, she gives a brief presentation (the Explanation stage) on forces and reinforces many of the concepts the students discovered during the marble exploration. Ms. Clark introduces vocabulary terms including potential energy, kinetic energy, momentum, force, incline plane, and acceleration, and she relates all the new terms to yesterday's marble activity. She then leads into a teacher-initiated inquiry (the Extension stage) for the class: finding the effect the angle of the ramp has on the distance the marble will travel. She tells the students that tomorrow they will have an opportunity to investigate this question and design a procedure to test their hypotheses.

The next day, Ms. Clark presents the class with this question: How does the angle of a ramp affect the distance a marble will travel? She has the students assemble in groups of threes and shows that the supplies for the investigation are located at the materials table. The table has various sized marbles (small, medium, and large), 12-inch rulers (some with a groove and some without), 1-inch wooden cube blocks, measuring tapes (some in inches and others in centimeters), an assortment of balls (rubber balls, golf balls, and wooden balls), and protractors. She purposely placed both essential and nonessential materials on the table. This way the groups will have to decide which of the supplies are necessary to complete the inquiry and which are not.

As they are busily working on their investigations, Ms. Clark rotates from one group to another listening to their discussions and providing prompts, not answers, to their questions. Marcie's group thinks that "As the angle increases, so will the distance the marble will travel." Marcie explains that they are using blocks of wood to increase the angle. They plan to use the protractor to measure the angle formed by the different blocks and use the measuring tapes to measure the distance the marble travels. Marcie says, "This is easy. It's just like we did the other day with the marble activity." Her group predicts that as the angle increases, the data will show a graph in a straight, ascending line.

Carlo's group predicts that as the angle increases, so will the distance; however, there is a point where the angle maximizes the distance the marble travels. Carlo states that his group is trying to determine the optimum angle because when the angle of the ramp is 90 degrees, theoretically the distance the marble will travel is zero. He further states that the group thinks the data will produce a graph that first increases, but then decreases.

When Ms. Clark gets to Julie's group, they are still debating how to set up the procedure. Some members of the group want to increase the number of blocks forming the angle, while others want to use the same number of blocks for each trial. They are still uncertain, however, as to how the angle will affect the distance.

The groups continue to work on their investigations for the entire period. Some are still collecting data and others are moving on to displaying their results on a poster board. Ms. Clark tells the groups that if they need more time, they can come into the room after school and finish their projects. Tomorrow the groups will have the first half of the period to finish their posters and the second half to make a five-minute presentation to the class on their procedure and results. Ms. Clark distributes a rubric for an oral presentation that shows how they will be graded on their oral reports.

The next day, all the groups are excited to show their posters. Marcie's group has a poster that shows, as they predicted, the marble's distance increasing as the angle increased (see Figure 8.7). Carlo's group explains that their graph increases and then decreases (see Figure 8.8). Finally, Julie's group has a graph unlike any of the others (see Figure 8.9). Their graph curves down.

Ms. Clark now explains a misconception arising from the "angle" activity. During the angle activity, many of the groups used the ruler to make different angles of incline—10, 20, 30, and 40 degrees. They varied the angle of the ruler or ramp by lifting the end of the ruler or resting it on a stack of blocks. With the edge of the ruler leaning on a stack of blocks, they ultimately increased the height, or release point, of

Figure 8.7 Marcie's Group's Graph

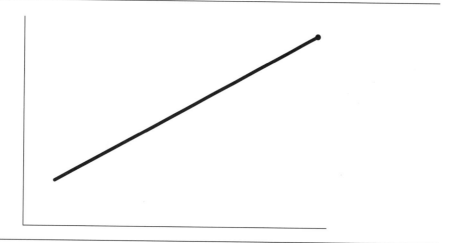

Figure 8.8 Carlo's Group's Graph

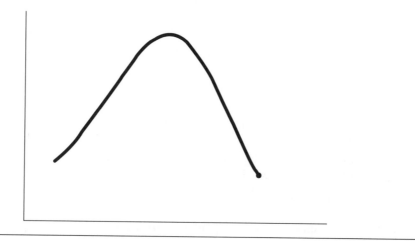

Figure 8.9 Julie's Group's Graph

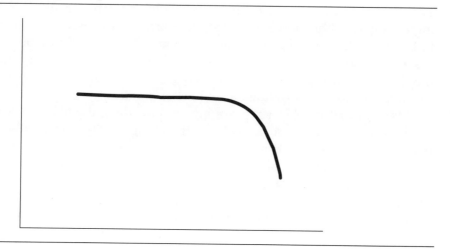

the marble. After releasing the marble at different angles and different heights at the top of the ruler, the participants concluded that as the angle increased, the distance the marble traveled also increased.

Marcie's group measured angles for 10, 20, and 30 degrees. When their data were graphed, the curve increased proportionally. Carlo's group measured angles for 10, 20, 30, 40, 50, 60, and 70 degrees. When their data were graphed, the curve increased up to 40 degrees and then suddenly decreased. They declared that the optimum angle was about 40 degrees.

When they analyzed the cause of the different distances the marble traveled, they needed to note that in the first two designs, as the angle increased, so did the height of the ruler and ultimately the potential energy of the marble. A misconception was developing!

Julie's group realized that the height of the release point (or the potential energy) had to be held constant in the investigation. They hypothesized that the height of the release point or the potential energy determines how far the marble travels, not the angle. They soon discovered that to test the effect of the angle, they needed to keep the height of the release point (or potential energy) the same for all the angles.

Julie's group placed the ruler on the edge of two one-inch square blocks of wood for a constant; keeping the potential energy the same for all three trials, and used the ruler to create different angles of the ramp.

Using the edge of the blocks of wood for a constant elevation, when the 12-inch end of the ruler rested on the two-inch block, the ruler formed a ramp with a 10-degree angle. When the eight-inch mark of the ruler rested on the edge of the book, the ruler formed a 15-degree angle. Here are the other positions and angles:

The six-inch mark formed a 20-degree angle.

The five-inch mark formed a 25-degree angle.

The four-inch mark formed a 30-degree angle.

The three-inch mark formed a 45-degree angle.

The two-inch mark formed a 90-degree angle.

Julie's group soon discovered that regardless of the angle, the marble should be positioned and released from the same height, which equaled the top of the blocks. This way, the height of the drop point is held constant for all trials. When measuring the distance the marble traveled, the participants discovered that the angle had little or no effect on the distance, assuming there is little or no friction between the grooved ruler and the marble. After school that day, Julie's group came back to the classroom to test a golf ball instead of a marble. Surprisingly, using a larger mass, the investigation still provided a similar set of data.

Ms. Clark added, "When graphing the new data, the line is nearly horizontal—until we get from 60 to 90 degrees. At these angles, the surface absorbs most of the marble's kinetic energy due to it hitting the surface of the floor or rug." Ms. Clark noted the investigations are two different questions with two very different results. Testing the effect of the angle is an excellent inquiry and may uncover students' misconceptions about controlling variables and experimental design!

Ms. Clark concluded the lesson by elaborating on how the students' prior conceptions guided their inquiries and how skepticism is an essential aspect of science.

Her students began to understand that science advances through analysis and sharing different approaches to solving problems. Marcie and Carlo's group members were astonished when they realized how their procedures and results compared with Julie's group. They reflected on how one group differed on their approach to the investigation than the other two. One member of Carlo's group even laughed at their faulty reasoning and commented how important it is to learn from others. They concluded that they certainly learned a lot about the nature of science.

For the final stage, Evaluation, students are given a two-part test. Part 1 includes multiple-choice and constructive response questions about the content of the "forces and motion" unit. Part 2 is a performance assessment in which students are given a golf ball, various sizes of grooved-ruler ramps, and several wooden blocks and asked to design a ramp system such that when the golf ball is released from any point on the ramp, it will stop within a target lying 10 feet away on the carpeted floor of the classroom. Students have 20 minutes to design and test their apparatus so the ball will stop the closest to the "bull's-eye" of the target.

QUESTIONS FOR REFLECTION AND DISCUSSION

1. While designing and completing experiments and investigations, students may have difficulty identifying the manipulated (independent) and the responding (dependent) variables. Discuss ways to help students distinguish between these two types of variables.

2. Suggest ways to help students decide if they need a control in a particular experiment.

3. Choose one of your favorite science activities or lab. Redesign the activity or lab to fit the 5E Learning Cycle format. Share your redesign with a partner.

4. Sometimes a simple activity may be the Engage, Explore, or Extend stage of the 5E cycle. Think of an activity or investigation that could fit into more than just one E.

5. Discuss ways the 5E Learning Cycle complements a constructivist learning philosophy. If they were alive today, what would John Dewey and Jean Piaget say about the 5E Learning Cycle? How do the 5Es support their ideas on how children learn?

Knowledge, Skills, and Attitudes of Inquiry-Based Teachers

Shall I teach you what knowledge is? When you know a thing, to recognize that you know it, and when you do not know a thing, to recognize that you do not know it. That is knowledge.

—The Analects of Confucius, Book II.17

A THREE-LEGGED STOOL

Understanding inquiry is like understanding a three-legged stool. Each leg represents a particular, discernable attribute. As inquiry teachers perfect their instructional strategies, they develop the essential *knowledge*, *skills*, and *attitudes* about inquiry. As for the well-balanced stool, each leg or attribute must be equally and equitably built to fulfill the intended task: in this case, a formidable transaction from teacher-centeredness to student-centeredness. It can be summarized with simple arithmetic: Knowledgeable Teachers + Innovated Pedagogy + Positive Attitudes = Engaged Learners. The purpose of this chapter is to consider several essential attributes in becoming an inquiry-based teacher and assess your present and desired capacity for teaching through inquiry. As we continue the journey of becoming an inquiry-based teacher, we begin to bring into alignment the knowledge, skills, and attitudes necessary for inquiry. As we continue to align these three attributes, we also align our head, our hands, and our heart into a commitment and continuous improvement through reflection and self-renewal.

THE IMPORTANCE OF MODELING INQUIRY

Teachers new to inquiry often ask, How do I become an inquiry-based teacher? One way to start is by finding someone who is recognized as an exemplary inquiry teacher and observe what he or she does. Take a notepad with you, record what the teacher says, how the teacher moves about the classroom, and how he or she values what students say. Observe the kinds of learning opportunities the teacher provides to the students. Observe the layout of the classroom. Listen to the interaction between the teacher and the students, the types of questions posed, and what the teacher says after a student gives an answer. Ask how the teacher uses national, state, and district standards to plan the lesson. Take notes on the types of assessments the teacher uses.

Many of us work with exemplary, creative, and inspiring teachers. They are the ones who are truly respected for their ability to engage students in the learning process. Excellent teachers are eager to open their classrooms for preservice and novice teachers to observe. When a new teacher observes a model teacher, he or she often comes away saying, "I want to be able to teach like that someday." The situation is analogous to an art student going to a museum and seeing the work of a great artist. A student must observe and appreciate great works of art to be inspired to set goals and keep striving toward excellence.

Never underestimate the power of modeling. Observing a role model is one way to begin. Unfortunately, there's no secret formula, no secret potion for becoming an inquiry-based teacher. The bottom line is that becoming an inquiry teacher takes time and a lot of practice, persistence, reading, and reflection. The good news is that practically everyone goes through the same process as they start to develop and hone their teaching skills.

YOUR FIRST TRY AT INQUIRY

Your first try at inquiry usually is not your best, but there is no need to dwell on how bad your first inquiry lesson might have been. You won't die, your students will survive, and best of all, you'll get another day to try again. If the first try goes badly, find a quiet place to sit and write down what you think went well and what you would do differently the next time. Make notes about revising your lesson. Make revisions and suggestions for the next time you do that lesson. You'll have another chance to do that same lesson again, only better. That is what second tries are for. Concentrate on what you'll plan to do differently tomorrow. Can you do better at anticipating students' questions? Can you make certain the proper materials and equipment are available? Should you move two students who can't work well in a group to a different setting? How can you make your directions more explicit? Did you remember to save enough time for cleanup and closure? During the second try, have a colleague whom you trust and respect observe your lesson. Ask this person for feedback and to act as a *reflective friend*. Tell your friend that you are trying to change your instructional style and that you want feedback on specific areas.

Teachers exploring new instructional strategies in inquiry can form a support group and meet each month over coffee to discuss and share their ideas. Use the time to critique and reflect on one another's lessons and examples of student work. Learn from your mistakes. Strive for improvement every time you do the lesson again. Perfection does not come on the first try.

Here's a story about a first-year middle school science teacher, Lisa, who presented an inquiry lesson on pulleys to 25 sixth graders on a Friday afternoon. Although Lisa had some college experience with inquiry-based activities, the lesson failed miserably. To add to the disaster, Lisa's mentor, Judy, was observing her performance. After the lesson, Judy shared her impressions of the class. Lisa sat listening to the comments and feeling completely dejected. Later that night, still distraught, Lisa considered starting a new career. About then, a little voice whispered in her head and planted the seed of self-doubt: "Is all this really worth it? Why don't you quit all this nonsense and just teach like everybody else does in this school? After all, just what are the kids learning anyway? Remember what happened during third period? Boy, was *that* a disaster!"

Refusing to give in to the voice, the next day Lisa began to rearrange parts of her lesson as Judy's suggestions rushed through her mind. She rewrote the sequence of the directions and redesigned the lesson from the students' point of view. The lesson now was in a language students could understand. Three hours later, she had a new lesson that she couldn't wait to teach again.

Self-doubt is a natural part of the change process. Don't listen to the negative inner voices, and don't listen to the cynics down the hall. Find that reflective friend, have lunch together, and gain the assurance that you are on the right track. After all, it's your classroom. You can either give in to the voices and go back to your old ways, or move ahead toward continuous progress. It's your call.

COMMITMENT

John Maxwell, author of *The 21 Irrefutable Laws of Leadership* (1998), says commitment separates the doers from the dreamers. Becoming an inquiry-oriented teacher starts with committing to doing three or four inquiry units a year. Consider videotaping one of your lessons and analyzing it on your own. Afterward, as your confidence grows, show it to someone also committed to inquiry learning and ask for an honest response. Save your videotaped lessons, and as you progress, view them over and over. As you become more comfortable with inquiry teaching strategies, you will also be able to do a better job analyzing your performance. Saving your prior lessons will also demonstrate how you have been able to progress over the years. You will be able to compare one of your earlier lessons with one you give after three or four years of implementing inquiry in your classroom. The commitment to inquiry teaching is a reward in itself. Once you start on a journey to become an inquiry teacher and appreciate the importance of inquiry in student learning, you probably will never go back to the previous ways of teaching.

Part of the commitment to adapting any new instructional strategy is to become conscious of your competencies. The consciousness/competence learning matrix is one way to illustrate this concept. The four areas of the consciousness/competence model include being

Unconsciously Incompetent

Consciously Incompetent

Consciously Competent

Unconsciously Competent

Figure 9.1 The Consciousness/Competence Learning Model

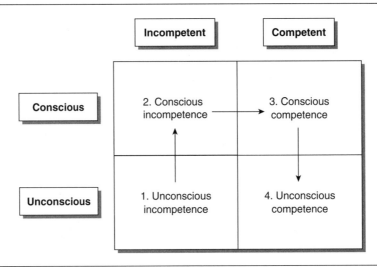

Although the original author or source of the matrix is unknown, many draw similarities to Ingham and Luft's *Johari Window*.

In the interest of our inquiry discussion, the consciousness/competence model will be illustrated as a sequence of steps.

When we speak of *consciousness*, we refer to one's sensibility of factors in our behaviors or decision making. Experiences enhance our consciousness and allow us to diagnose each situation on the basis of its uniqueness. Consciousness is considered the first step in learning, meaning that we need to be conscious of what we know and what we don't know to learn effectively.

When we speak of *competence*, we refer to our capability to perform a task. Like consciousness, competence is also enhanced through experience.

A person who is *unconsciously incompetent* stands at the first step. That person is not aware of the existence or relevance of inquiry or even might reject the relevance or usefulness of inquiry as a useful instructional strategy. The person at this step may not even be aware that he or she has a particular deficiency in inquiry learning. It's like saying "I don't know what I don't know." It is difficult for many of us to recognize and acknowledge what we do not know. Therefore, before developing a new instructional skill, such as inquiry, the person must accept the notion of admitting "blissful ignorance" and be willing to move to the next step of becoming conscious of his or her incompetence.

Figure 9.2   The Consciousness/Competence Ladder

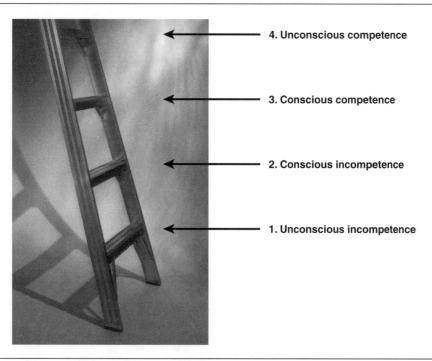

4. Unconscious competence

3. Conscious competence

2. Conscious incompetence

1. Unconscious incompetence

A person who is *consciously incompetent* stands at the second step. That teacher is aware of the existence and relevance of inquiry but also is aware of his or her own deficiency in this area and is attempting to use inquiry to broaden one's instructional repertoire. This person at this step says, "I don't know anything about inquiry, but I'd like to learn." The consciously incompetent person has an awareness of his or her present limitations and the degree of understanding required for developing competence. This teacher makes the commitment to learn and practice the skill of inquiry to move to the next step of being consciously competent.

A person who is *consciously competent* stands at the third step. This teacher becomes consciously competent in inquiry-based instruction when he or she can reliably perform it on demand when appropriate. At this step, teaching through inquiry requires little or no mentoring but necessitates calculated concentration and deliberation. Teaching through inquiry at this step is successful but has not yet become routine or "second nature" to the teacher. This person says, "I am mastering the skill of inquiry, but I still have to carefully plan and concentrate all the time while teaching it." The teacher at this step is able to demonstrate the skill to another teacher but is unlikely to be regarded as an expert. As the person continues practice inquiry, he or she escalates to the unconsciously competent level.

A person who is *unconsciously competent* stands at the top step. The inquiry teacher at this level becomes so proficient that he or she says, "At this point, inquiry has becomes so natural it's almost second-nature." This teacher is now able to coach others, model effective methodology, and present workshops at science education conferences. At the unconsciously competent step, the teacher not only can perform the skill but also can articulate its meaning and method. In short, inquiry moves from gut intuitions to cerebral intuitions, from acquired performances to instinctive performances.

The progression of the steps is sequential. It takes practice, coupled with collaboration, confidence, and coaching, to move from one level to another. As you continue your journey and proceed in advancing your inquiry skills, the instructional change will be predicated on three essential aspects: having a vision for change, having the knowledge of the change process, and having an inherent desire to improve. A wise teacher once asked, "What makes the difference between wishing and realizing our wishes? Lots of things, and it may take months or years for a wish to come true, but it's far more likely to happen when you care about a wish so much that you'll do all you can to make it happen." The teacher was Fred Rogers, from the children's show, *Mr. Rogers' Neighborhood*. In the next section, an inquiry rubric will help you proceed up each step of that wish.

AN INQUIRY RUBRIC

As introduced in Chapter 8, a rubric is a set of guidelines used to provide an assessment of a particular performance or task. Rubrics are commonly used when you want to identify performance at various levels of proficiency and identify areas for improvement. In this chapter, we use a rubric to assess and monitor your present level and progress in becoming an inquiry-based teacher.

Like other rubrics, the inquiry rubric in this chapter contains three features: (1) the subsets or dimensions to be assessed, (2) a rating scale, and (3) statements, behaviors, or expectations for each of the criteria at each level being assessed. By using the inquiry rubric, you can assess your present level of teaching through inquiry and become aware of the standards or behaviors necessary for advancing to the next level of performance.

To assess your performance, begin by asking a colleague familiar with inquiry or someone in your support group to observe you teaching an inquiry-based lesson or unit. If possible, videotape the lesson so you and your partner can view it together and discuss particular points of the lesson in comparison with the rubric. The use of the video will serve as a point of departure for a discussion and provide specific evidence in analyzing your lesson. You may choose to schedule a preconference with your observer before your lesson. The purpose of the preconference is to make the observer aware of your lesson or unit objectives. Your observer may prefer not to know ahead of time what the unit is about. He or she may prefer to observe the lesson knowing what the students know. If the observer is confused about the focus of the lesson in the first few minutes, chances are the students are too.

During the lesson, your partner should circle the behaviors listed on the inquiry rubric that he or she notes during the lesson. At the end of the observation, don't be surprised to see behaviors at various stages on the grid. Teachers often demonstrate different skills at different levels. During the postconference meeting, discuss the behaviors that were noted and find a pattern to the responses. Are some areas at a different stage than others? How would this demonstrate your strengths and weaknesses for each area?

As you use the inquiry rubric, you will find that not all the areas are observable during a classroom lesson but may be assessed through reflection and discussion. Areas such as curriculum and professional development are good examples. In any event, the rubric serves as a starting point for you to assess your level of performance and to identify what behaviors you need to improve to move to the next level.

It is important to remember that the use of rubrics is still very subjective and open to judgment. The purpose of the inquiry rubric is not solely to say that you are at the transitioning level or at the practicing level. Rather, it serves as a springboard to initiate engaging discussion on the components of an inquiry lesson and to reflect on your ability to analyze an inquiry-based lesson.

Table 9.1 (at the end of this chapter) shows a rubric for becoming an inquiry-based teacher. Because of the length and detail of the inquiry rubric, the first time you may choose to focus on two or three subsets in one observation. Then, gradually increase the number of subsets to focus on in subsequent observations.

AN INQUIRY SELF-ASSESSMENT SURVEY

You can also gain an understanding of your level of competency of inquiry through a self-assessment survey. The Inquiry Self-Assessment Survey was adapted from the National Science Teachers Association's (NSTA) *Guidelines for Self-Assessment* (1978). The survey lists statements about inquiry-based instruction that align with the inquiry rubric. You will identify responses for two dimensions: desirability and achievement (see Figure 9.3). For each of the statements in the survey, identify a rating for each dimension as follows:

Desirability

4 = Very good desirability, of high interest or need

3 = Good desirability

2 = Fair desirability

1 = Unimportant or undesirable

Achievement

4 = Very good achievement, of high accomplishment or practice

3 = Good achievement

2 = Fair achievement

1 = No achievement

Using the matrix corresponding to a numbered statement, circle the levels (1–4) on the vertical axis (desirability) and the horizontal axis (achievement) that best match your response to the statement. Then, place an X in the appropriate box that corresponds to or matches the intersection of the levels for that statement, as shown in Figure 9.4.

For example, 1.1: I provide lessons where students explore their ideas around questions that interest them.

Now, turn to Resource C. You will find the set of matrices for each category. Follow the same procedure for each statement in the following eight categories by placing an X in the appropriate box that corresponds to your answer for that statement.

Figure 9.3 Sample Survey Grid

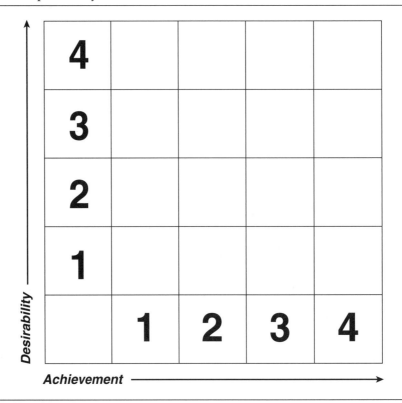

Figure 9.4 Marked Sample Survey Grid

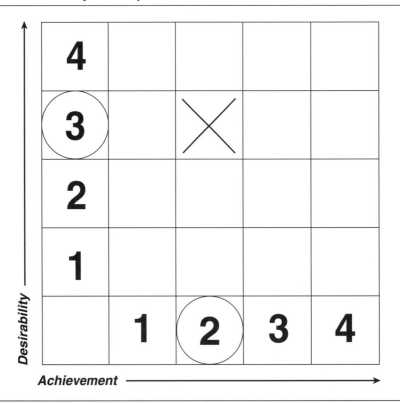

1. Curriculum
   1.1. I provide lessons in which students explore their ideas around questions that interest them.
   1.2. I provide resources and manipulatives to students to stimulate students' curiosity and thinking skills.
   1.3. I emphasize process skill development as part of my lessons.
   1.4. I plan and design my curriculum according to *National Science Education Standards* (NSES).
   1.5. I design my curriculum with student-centered lessons in which students plan their own investigations.
   1.6. Problem solving plays a major role in my curriculum planning.
   1.7. My curriculum uses various primary sources of information.
   1.8. The content of my curriculum is structured around learning concepts that are relevant and based on students' personal experiences.

2. Lesson Presentation
   2.1. My role as a teacher is that of a facilitator.
   2.2. My lessons provide opportunities for students to solve problems.
   2.3. I provide opportunities for students to design the procedures and data tables for their own investigations.
   2.4. My units begin with a highly motivating problem, question, or demonstration.
   2.5. I use the 5E Learning Cycle to prepare lessons.
   2.6. I prepare lessons in which science is integrated with other subject areas.
   2.7. My lessons begin with assessing students' prior knowledge.

3. Communication
   3.1. I provide opportunities for students to share their ideas and points of view in class.
   3.2. During a lesson, I move throughout the room, speaking from different areas of the room.
   3.3. When speaking to students in small groups, I usually kneel down or sit at a student desk to make eye-to-eye contact with them.
   3.4. I consistently provide praise and positive reinforcement when students give correct answers or make contributions to class discussions.
   3.5. I provide opportunities for students to reflect and share their ideas with one another.

4. Engagement of Students
   4.1. In my room, students are engaged in investigations, discourse, and reflection.
   4.2. I encourage students to be self-directed learners.
   4.3. I frequently plan lessons that are both hands-on and minds-on.
   4.4. I consistently solicit information, explanations, and thoughts from students.
   4.5. I encourage cooperative learning relationships among students.
   4.6. Before beginning an activity, I have students review and repeat the purpose and procedures to ensure that each student knows what is expected of him or her.

5. Classroom Organization
   5.1. Many supplies and materials are readily available for students to access on their own.

5.2. I allocate classroom time for scientific investigations.

5.3. I promote dialogue among my students.

5.4. I encourage students to make decisions about their own work.

5.5. I use constructivist teaching strategies in my classroom.

5.6. I encourage students to make decisions about the arrangement of the classroom.

5.7. My lessons frequently are designed around cooperative learning groups.

6. Questioning Skills

6.1. I pose various levels of questions to students.

6.2. I consistently ask open-ended questions to encourage students to think at higher levels.

6.3. I often follow up students' responses to questions with extension questions.

6.4. I consistently value students' opinions and responses.

6.5. I consistently use wait-time strategies.

6.6. I use probing statements, prompts, and redirectioning questions to solicit students' understanding.

7. Assessment Procedures

7.1. I use multiple assessments to evaluate student progress.

7.2. I have students use journals to record and organize their notes from class discussions and their scientific investigations.

7.3. I have students keep their science work in portfolios for reflection and discussion.

7.4. I regularly observe and assess students' attitudes in science as part of my evaluation of their progress.

7.5. I regularly observe and assess critical thinking skills in science as part of my evaluation of the students' progress.

8. Professional Development

8.1. I share my inquiry-based units with other interested teachers.

8.2. I am part of a support group to share ideas on teaching through inquiry.

8.3. I use *NSES* as part of my professional development plans.

8.4. I regularly read periodicals and books on inquiry and constructivism.

8.5. I have attended a workshop or seminar on inquiry or constructivism in the past two years.

EVALUATING YOUR RESPONSES

After filling out a matrix for each statement in the survey, you are ready to compile your responses for each of the eight categories. Each category has its own summary matrix (see Resource D). For the "Curriculum" category, for example, place the number of that statement in the corresponding box in the summary matrix (see Figure 9.5).

Repeat the procedure for each of the other seven categories.

Each matrix is made up of four areas (see Figure 9.6). Look at the number of statements in each of the four areas of the matrix.

Figure 9.5   Completed Sample Survey Grid

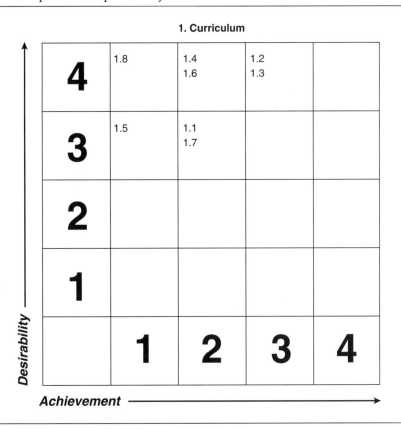

Figure 9.6   Sample Survey Grid Showing Four Areas

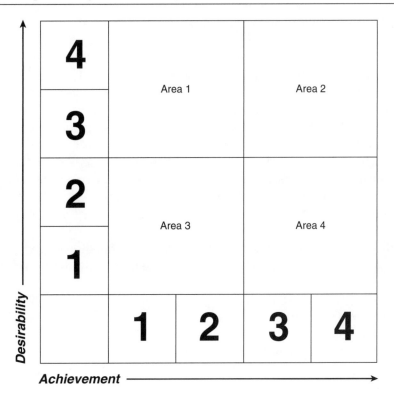

Area 1. Responses in this area indicate high desirability and low achievement. Statements in this quadrant are areas you indicate a need to improve on. These statements will become the focus of your professional development in the months and years ahead.

Area 2. Responses in this area indicate high desirability and high achievement. Statements in this quadrant are areas of your perceived strengths. These areas will require your continued maintenance.

Area 3. Responses in this area indicate low desirability and low achievement. Statements in this quadrant are areas of nonimportance for you. Center your efforts on improving in Area 1. If you take the survey again a year from now, see if any statements that were previously in Area 3 have now moved to Area 1. If so, that will be the time to focus on them. It is better to focus on one or two areas rather than to take on too much.

Area 4. Responses in this area indicate low desirability and high achievement. Statements in this quadrant are not applicable because they may indicate that you have skills you don't care about.

You now can use the self-assessment survey to plan your professional development needs by identifying the responses listed in Area 1. Brainstorm possible actions and solutions to improve your knowledge and skills in Area 1 for one or two of the eight categories.

BUILDING CAPACITY THROUGH BUGS-O-COPTERS

In becoming an inquiry-based teacher, a central focus is your ability to raise your own personal capacity to do inquiry. Building the capacity and ability for teachers to do inquiry is an essential goal of this book. Consider an analogy of four beakers, each having a different volume or capacity. Beaker 1 holds 100 mL of liquid, beaker 2 hold 250 mL, beaker 3 holds 500 mL, and beaker 4 holds 1,000 mL. What is the present capacity of your level of inquiry? Are you like beaker 1, 2, or 3? What is your desired level a year from now? Three years from now? Five years from now? When you reach the level of beaker 4, you have a full *liter* capacity and are poised to become a *leader* of other teachers. You can take a leadership role and act as a model and mentor for those at levels 1, 2, and 3.

Many teachers may already be familiar with *Bugs-o-Copters*. If that's so, it just enhances your prior knowledge. The Bugs-o-Copter inquiry is one means to assess (and raise) the capacity to see questions in an exploration. A detailed lesson plan for Bugs-o-Copters with an *NSES* correlation and background information can be found in Chapter 11.

Begin the exploration by making photocopies of the short-eared and the long-eared Bugs-o-Copters found in Resource E (if possible, copy them on heavier, 24-lb weight paper).

Cut out the short-eared Bugs-o-Copter as shown in Figure 9.7. Bend one ear forward at the crease (dotted line) and bend one ear back. The ears should be perpendicular to the body. Attach a paper clip at the "feet," or bottom of your Bugs-o-Copter, and hold it as high as possible with an outstretched arm. For added height, you might want to stand on a chair. Release the short-eared Bugs-o-Copter and

Figure 9.7 How to Cut Out a Bugs-o-Copter

Directions:

1. Cut along the outside solid lines.

2. Cut straight down between the two ears to the dotted line.

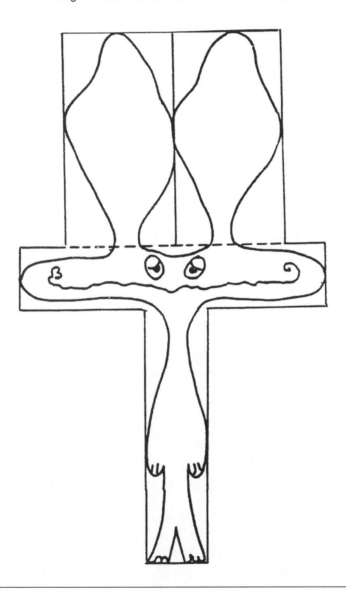

observe what happens. Try it several times. What did you observe? Did the Bugs-o-Copter react the same time for each trial? Record your observations on a separate sheet of paper.

Next, cut out the long-eared Bugs-o-Copter. Compare the two Bugs-o-Copters. What do you observe? You may notice that the two Bugs-o-Copters are similar except for ear length. Fold the ears along the crease as you did with the short-eared one. Make a prediction. How will the length of the ears affect the rate of falling? Will the long-eared Bugs-o-Copter fall faster or slower? How does the length of the ears affect the rate of spinning? Will the long-eared Bugs-o-Copter spin faster or more slowly than the short-eared Bugs-o-Copter? Choose a question to investigate, and record your prediction on a sheet of paper. Because you are going to test your prediction, the statement can be written as a hypothesis.

Before testing your hypothesis, think of how you will design your investigation. This is an important part of any inquiry. Students often go directly into testing before identifying the procedure. The procedure may easily come to mind, but this time we want to first write it down on paper.

Which variable will you test in your investigation? Which variables will stay the same? Which variable will be used to measure your results? After you have thought about all these questions, you are ready to test your hypothesis.

By investigating the effect of the ear length on the rate of falling, you probably identified ear length as the independent variable—in other words, what you manipulated on purpose. You should have "controlled" all other variables, such as dropping the Bugs-o-Copter from the same height, the same way, under the same conditions, and placing only one paper clip on each Bugs-o-Copter at the same location. These variables will stay the same with both Bugs-o-Copters.

This way only one variable, the length of the ears, will affect the outcome of the investigation. In the first question, the time it took the Bugs-o-Copter to hit the floor is the dependent variable. That is what we look for or measure to see whether the ear length made a difference. In the second question, the number of spins the Bugs-o-Copter makes is the dependent variable.

Drop both the short-eared and the long-eared Bugs-o-Copters at the same time. What happened? Record your observations.

YOUR IQ: INQUIRY QUOTIENT

On the basis of that initial Bugs-o-Copter exploration, what other questions come to mind that you can investigate? Think of several "What if" or "I wonder" questions. How many questions can you come up with? Take a few minutes and write all of them down. Write as many questions as come to mind.

How many questions were you able to think about that you could test using the Bugs-o-Copter? One? Five? More than five? This is actually a test of your *IQ*—your *Inquiry Quotient.* The more questions you are able to raise (including designing and carrying out the procedures), the higher your IQ. During professional development workshops for teachers, some participants will explore Bugs-o-Copter yet can't think of any more than one or two questions to test. Others will think of five to ten possible questions to investigate. Your questions may have included the some of the following:

- Does the number of paper clips affect the falling rate?
- What would happen if I place a paper clip on each ear of the Bugs-o-Copter?
- Does the thickness of the paper affect how the Bugs-o-Copter will spin?
- What would happen if I made a Bugs-o-Copter out of poster board instead of paper?

- What if I cut along the outline (shape) of the ears?
- Does the shape of the ears affect how the Bugs-o-Copter falls?
- What if I put the paper clip in a different location?
- How can I get the short-eared Bugs-o-Copter and the long-eared Bugs-o-Copter to hit the floor at the same time?
- What if I change the direction the ears are folded?
- How would cutting slits in the ears affect the spinning?
- Will the way the ears are folded affect how the Bugs-o-Copter will spin?
- How can I make the Bugs-o-Copter spin in the opposite direction?
- Which Bugs-o-Copter, the short-eared or long-eared, makes more spins before hitting the floor?
- Would the Bugs-o-Copter spin in the opposite direction in the Southern Hemisphere from the way it spins in the Northern Hemisphere?

Now that you have lots of questions to investigate, your next step is to design a procedure, carry out a test, gather and organize data, and draw a conclusion on the basis of the evidence or as many questions as possible.

TEACHING INQUIRY TO SECOND LANGUAGE LEARNERS AND STUDENTS WITH SPECIAL NEEDS

In the early 1900s, immigrants came across the Atlantic to this country from Italy, Ireland, and Germany with hardly a dollar in their pocket yet with dreams of new opportunities. As tens of thousands passed through Ellis Island in New York harbor, schools labored to provide basic education to the children of immigrant parents. As schools struggled to cope with an expanding student population, many immigrant children faced a "sink or swim" approach to learning a new culture and language at such an early age.

Today in the United States, non–English-speaking populations continue to increase at a significant rate. Some estimates (Riley, 1999) suggest that by 2050, nearly one quarter of our country's population will be of Hispanic origin. Many of these students will enter our classrooms with a language other than English as their native language. Teachers and school administrators are facing demographic changes in the school population and diversity in students, from second language learners as well as from students with other learning and physical challenges.

Although some schools react to the challenges of the test by reinventing "de facto" segregation of students in the form of tracking and ability grouping, teaching high-need students challenges science leaders to create classrooms in which all students achieve at high levels of academic success regardless of their race, culture, neighborhood, native language, or socioeconomic status. Teachers also are challenged to eliminate any persistent patterns or gaps of achievement among groups of students. In *Leadership for Equity and Excellence*, Scheurich and Skrla (2003) suggest that in the next 20 years, our success as teachers will depend directly on our ability to be successful with children of all colors and nationalities.

Bennett (2001) suggests that in culturally responsive classrooms, teachers strive for equity as opposed to equality. Whereas equality implies providing all students with the identical curriculum, textbooks, instructional strategies, and assessments, equity entails affording differentiated instruction and resources on the basis of the student's language, experience, and abilities. Gonzalez-Espada (2004) offers an interesting analogy to the equality-equity debate. In the past, airlines often offered only a single, fixed-meal selection. Although well intended, these decisions are concerned with equality, and ignore the fact that passengers have different cultural and dietetic needs and requirements.

Some airlines demonstrate an equity mind-set by offering gluten-free, low calorie, low fat, vegetarian, vegan, or even Hindu, Muslim, or kosher choices.

Scores of experts have decried how ill-prepared many classroom teachers are in meeting the demands of teaching children with a primary language other than English. Many teachers, according to Gonzalez-Espada, "are not used to thinking in terms of pluralism and cannot respond effectively to a situation if they cannot be 'in the shoes' of the other person" (2004, p. 5). We might imagine how difficult it would be to hone our inquiry skills if this book were in Japanese or Swahili. Thus, teaching inquiry in multilinguistic and multicultural classrooms is predicated on compassion, empathy, and patience.

Inquiry fits suitably into science classrooms where English language learners are acquiring language skills and proficiencies, and where they are developing socially acceptable group behaviors and interactions. The research is clear: Inquiry has been found to provide an excellent venue for learning a second language and learning science content. As teachers help students in becoming more conversant with both English and the language of science, oral and written language strategies become embedded in the lesson. Chamot and O'Malley (1994), in the Cognitive Academic Language Learning Approach (CALLA), group learning strategies for science into three categories: metacognitive strategies, cognitive strategies, and social or affective strategies.

In metacognitive strategies, students plan, monitor, and evaluate their science learning of concepts by using

1. Advance organizers (What's the question and the purpose for this experiment?)

2. Selective attention (What information requires my close attention?)

3. Organizational planning (What steps do I need to design or follow?)

4. Self-monitoring (Is my plan working?)

5. Self-assessment (How well did I solve the problem?)

In cognitive strategies, students interact with the information to be learned, changing or reorganizing it either mentally or physically by

1. Elaborating prior knowledge (What do I already know about the problem?)

2. Resourcing (What information can I find about the topic or problem?)

3. Taking notes, organizing data (How will I record and organize my data, observations, and questions?)

4. Using images and models (How will I communicate my understanding of the concept through illustrations or models?)

In social or affective strategies, students interact with others to assist their learning and apply positive attitudes in solving a problem by

1. Questioning for clarification (What help do I need? Who should I ask?)

2. Cooperation (How should I work with others to answer the question or solve the problem?)

3. Self-talk (What knowledge, skills, and attitudes do I need to complete the task?) (Adapted from Chamot & O'Malley, 1994, p. 204)

Fortunately, some experts suggest that many strategies that work well for second language learners should also work well for students with learning disabilities who are mainstreamed into regular English-speaking classrooms.

We know that students engaged in inquiry learning use language to make meaning from hands-on experiences. They use these experiences to bridge prior experience with new concepts and terminology. Furthermore, science lessons that integrate cooperative learning, the use of manipulatives, and group interaction provide social settings that foster language acquisition along with content development (Thomas & Collier, 1995). Learning through inquiry is inclusive, not exclusive. The opportunities for doing inquiries can never be limited to one's age or gender, cultural or ethnic background, abilities or disabilities, hopes and aspirations, or interests or motivation. Therefore, inquiry is the standard that encourages and promotes equity and excellence for all students in becoming scientifically literate.

As teachers are faced with more challenges and differences in students' abilities, inquiry becomes an instructional equalizer, the factor that levels the playing field between proficient and developing language learners. Inquiry and hands-on activities provide the opportunity for students to express their ideas about scientific phenomena. In any classroom discussion, however, limited English proficient (LEP) students often provide false indicators that they are acquiring and understanding scientific language. Indicators include head nodding, smiles, and short answers. It takes a savvy teacher to differentiate accurate body language from false indicators.

Strategies for Integrating Language Instruction and Science

One strategy that proves successful with LEP students is scaling terminology—providing both English- and native-language terms on diagrams, illustrations, and maps. As an example in a bilingual classroom of English- and Spanish-speaking students studying forces, a teacher writes three variations of a concept on the board: "*precione y jale*" ("push and pull"), the common, everyday phrase in the Spanish-speaking students' primary language; *push and pull*, the common, everyday phrase in English; and *force*, the scientific term. As the teacher explains the progression of the terms from the customary language to the scientific language, students can gradually modify their language and gain new vocabulary on the basis of prior usage and familiarity. In developing science vocabulary, Amaral, Garrison, and Duron-Flores (2006) suggest that

initially, students may refer to common items by the name used in everyday language (i.e., "measuring cup"). Doing a materials inventory [author's note: a preteaching strategy that introduces material identification] provides an opportunity for the teacher to introduce the scientific name ("beaker") of the item for the benefit of all the students. (p. 31)

A second strategy is scaffolding instruction. Scaffolding for English learners can occur in three steps: guided learning, semiguided learning, and independent learning. In guided learning, the teacher begins the lesson by assessing students' prior knowledge of the topic. English language learners can express their previous experiences using both languages if necessary. The teacher then visually models the steps of the upcoming activity and shows students how to complete the task. To assess their understanding of the activity, the teachers asks students to summarize the demonstration. In semiguided learning, the students work in small cooperative groups to replicate the procedure or steps of the activity demonstrated previously and to complete the activity. Finally, the student work independently to continue the activity individually.

As an example of scaffolding in a third-grade magnet lesson, the teacher would begin by demonstrating how to use a bar magnet to determine which objects are magnetic and which are not. By showing objects attracted to a magnet, the teacher supports the visual demonstration with an oral explanation and appropriate use of scientific terms. Next, given a bar magnet and a container of various objects (some that will be attracted to a magnet and some that will not), the students work in pairs to determine which objects are attracted to the magnet and which are not. The students then write the name of or draw the object under the appropriate column of a T-chart (see Figure 9.8). Finally, the students individually go around the classroom and find five objects that will be attracted to a magnet and five objects that will not. Again, the students complete the T-chart by writing the name or drawing a picture of the object under the correct column.

In a similar example of scaffolding in a fifth-grade electricity lesson, the teacher would begin by demonstrating how to use a circuit tester (a dry cell battery, a light bulb in a bulb holder, and four wires) (see Figure 9.9) to determine which objects were insulators and which were conductors. By showing objects that complete the circuit and light the bulb, the teacher, as in the previous example, supports the visual demonstration with an oral explanation and appropriate use of scientific terms. Next, given a circuit tester and a container of various objects (some that will conduct electricity and some that will not), the students work in pairs to determine which objects can be identified as conductors and which as insulators by writing the object's name or by drawing a picture of the object in the appropriate column of a T-chart (see Figure 9.10). Finally, students individually go around the classroom and find five objects that are conductors and five objects that are insulators. Again, each student completes the T-chart by writing the name or drawing a picture of the object in the correct column.

Inquiry activities also serve to bridge concrete experiences. Students use auditory, kinesthetic, and visual clues to make sense and meaning of the experiences, which facilitates understanding, and use these concrete experiences as a bridge to more formal (abstract) concepts while developing mental constructs and schemata of a new phenomenon. In inquiry, teachers encourage oral and written language to express scientific procedures, findings, and generalizations. Clues embedded in concepts maps, graphic organizers, diagrams, illustrations, and manipulatives also enable LEP students to think critically, analyze data and evidence, draw conclusions and create logical explanations, and communicate their ideas.

Another strategy involves modifying materials used as examples. Because some students may be unfamiliar with certain materials and equipment used in demonstrations, the teacher may have to modify the science materials used in a lesson. In a

Figure 9.8   T-Chart for Magnetism

Objects attracted to a magnet	Objects not attracted to a magnet

Figure 9.9   Photo of a Circuit Tester

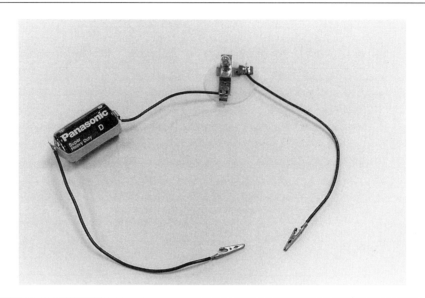

lesson on simple machines, some students may lack prior experience with such implements as can openers, nutcrackers, and egg slicers. Whenever possible, first show real objects when discussing a concept. If real objects are unavailable or inappropriate, use pictures or illustrations. If real objects or pictures are unavailable, use simple oral descriptions. In best practice, sequence the *level of abstraction* by showing the real object, followed by a picture or an illustration, followed by an oral description of the object. This provides a rich visual and verbal explanation of an object or concept.

Cooperative grouping is another strategy teachers frequently use with diverse student populations. By placing two (rather than one) LEP students within a diverse group, LEP students can collaborate with one another. Normally, when one LEP student is assigned to a group of English speakers, the LEP student often is assigned low status by other group members and thus has difficulty sharing his or her experience. This in turn results in the LEP student making little or no contribution to the task.

Modifying language and limiting the introduction of new terms (usually to six to ten new terms within any one lesson) is another strategy that works well for LEP students. Explaining the inquiry process terms in both the native language and English also can be helpful in acquiring and developing scientific terminology.

Whenever feasible, consider listing critical thinking and inquiry-related terms in English and the native language on a poster board. The teacher can refer to the terms throughout the inquiry investigation to ensure that all students understand the thinking and processing skill being used. The following is a list of 63 thinking skill and process terms associated with inquiry teaching. Note that many of the terms do not have a direct translation from one language to another and that some terms are more appropriate to elementary, middle, or high school levels.

Analyze	Calculate	Communicate	Constant
Apply	Classify	Conclude	Construct
Assess	Collect	Confirm	Contrast

Control	Evidence	List	Read
Copy	Experiment	Measure	Recognize
Data	Explain	Model	Record
Define	Explore	Name	Report
Demonstrate	Formulate	Observe	Separate
Describe	Hypothesize	Outline	Sequence
Design	Identify	Persuade	Show
Develop	Illustrate	Plan	Solve
Differentiate	Infer	Predict	State
Discuss	Inquire	Problem solve	Summarize
Draw	Interpret	Propose	Support
Estimate	Investigate	Provide	Variable
Evaluate	Justify	Question	

Concrete learners, especially English language learners and students with special needs, require the interaction and manipulation of materials to truly understand the concept or phenomenon. Memorizing the formula for photosynthesis or the three laws of motion does not mean students have assimilated the meaning of the food-making process in plants or the momentum of rolling objects. To illustrate how inquiries can stem from students' observations, let's look into Mr. Ramos' bilingual sixth-grade classroom.

Arturo, one of Mr. Ramos' brightest students, has just complained about the taste of the water from the drinking fountain outside the second-floor classroom. Elena jumps into the conversation by saying that she thinks the water on the first floor is just as bad. Using this as an opportunity to explore science and develop language skills, Mr. Ramos suggests the class take a blindfolded "taste test" to determine their preferences in school water from various locations. Mr. Ramos obtains water sources from the first and second floors' drinking fountains to determine whether students have a preference in taste. After the class's taste testing is complete, the next day Mr. Ramos suggests that the class design a taste test on their own, where students are blindfolded and given samples of various bottled and purified water. This allows them to compare the school water with other sources. In the third phase of the inquiry, Edgar, another class member, suggests they put students from the entire school to the test. The class then designs a taste test in which students are blindfolded and given water samples from various drinking fountains in the school, as well as bottled and purified water.

As the students conduct the investigation, Mr. Ramos makes a list of the terms, both in English and in the students' native languages, which they use in their discussions and must understand as they complete their investigation. In the end, the students post the results of their surveys on the bulletin board outside the classroom. Although the taste test inquiry is simple, it provides one more example of how scaffolding instruction, coupled with language instruction, builds confidence and use of scientific terms and vocabulary.

Figure 9.10 T-Chart for Conductors and Insulators

Objects that conduct electricity (conductors)	Objects that do not conduct electricity (insulators)

In the words of Mary Atwater (1994), an outspoken voice for science education and multicultural education issues, "diversity in the classroom is both a challenge and an opportunity. It is a challenge because our knowledge and skills in effectively teaching diverse student populations has not kept up with the influx of students we need to serve. It is an opportunity to teach about the joy of experiencing a variety of cultures, languages, and of respecting all people" (p. 560). In that same light, Hargreaves and Fink (2000) argue that "when learners are diverse and demanding, educators must be responsive to students' various cultures, inclusive of their own ideas in defining learning targets or sharing assessment criteria, and ready to involve families and communities to bring learning to higher levels" (p. 30).

For information about NSTA's stance on *Multicultural Science Education* and *Students With Disabilities*, visit www.nsta.org and click on Teacher Resources, then Position Statements. The NSTA Web site also provides *Libros de Ciencias en Español*, a list of recommended books in Spanish for science topics and units of study at the elementary and middle school levels.

For a more comprehensive and detailed set of strategies for LEP students, readers should acquire *Science for English Language Learners: K-12 Classroom Strategies*, an edited book by Ann Fathman and David Crowther (2006). The book is divided into four sections: Parallels in Language and Science Teaching; Strategies for Planning, Teaching, Assessing, and Extending Learning; Lessons for Science and Language Learning; and Contexts for Classroom Implementation. This is a must-have for elementary and middle school teachers integrating science standards, hands-on instruction, and inquiry-based teaching with LEP learners. Another resource, *Ladybugs, Tornadoes, and Swirling Galaxies: English Language Learners Discover Their World Through Inquiry*, by Brad Buhrow and Ann Upczak Garcia (2006), is especially suited for younger students.

INTEGRATING INQUIRY WITH TECHNOLOGY

The process of collecting, recording, organizing, and analyzing data is a central focus of inquiry. These process skills can be enhanced through handheld and computer applications. In this example, you will see how one sixth-grade teacher uses the Vernier Logger Lite GO! program to collect data from an inquiry investigation based on the 5E format.

In spring 2006, Mr. Martinez attended the National Science Teachers Association annual conference in Anaheim, California. During the conference, he attended one of Vernier's sessions on data-collection technology and learned how to use handheld probes in a physical science curriculum. After returning from the conference, he presented his principal, Dr. Maria-Torres, with a proposal and a request for five laptop computers along with Vernier software and probes to integrate technology into the students' laboratory activities. His proposal was built on the premise that using state-of-the-art technology would engage his students in the learning process, develop their computer data-collection skills, and ultimately improve their performance on district and standardized assessments. This was an offer Dr. Maria-Torres could not refuse.

In September of the next school year, Mr. Martinez presented his sixth-grade students with the following unit on the transfer of heat energy. In this unit, students investigated how heat moves from warmer to cooler objects and learned principles of heat energy, specifically conduction and insulation. The objective of the unit was to have students (a) determine how materials act as good or poor insulators of heat, (b) build a model for heat transfer, and (c) design a way to keep hot water in a glass container as hot as possible for as long as possible. This activity correlated with the NSES (NRC, 1996) by having students

- Design and conduct a scientific investigation (NSES, p. 145)
- Use appropriate tools and technology to gather, analyze, and interpret data (p. 145)
- Develop descriptions, explanations, predictions, and models using evidence (p. 145)
- Think critically and logically to make the relationships between evidence and explanations (p. 145)
- Recognize and analyze alternative explanations and predictions (p. 148)
- Communicate scientific procedures and explanations (p. 148)
- Understand heat moves in predictable ways, flowing from warmer objects to cooler ones, until both reach the same temperature (p. 155)

Day 1: Engagement

The unit started on a Thursday because Mr. Martinez knew that the extension and evaluation stages would last two days each and he did not want the final performance assessment to extend over the weekend. On the first day, he presented a demonstration involving three socks. "What would happen," he asked, "if I took three identical thermometers, all reading the same temperature, and wrapped each one in a different sock—one made of wool, one made of cotton, and one made of silk? Now let's say I left them in the classroom overnight. What do you think each thermometer would read the next day? Would they all be the same? Or would they be different? And why? Support your prediction with a reasonable answer."

"What I'd like you to do," he continued, "is to first make an individual prediction and record it in your science journal. In a while, you will share that prediction with a partner, and then later we'll see what the entire class thinks." From the class of 23, 19 students predicted the temperature in the wool sock would be the highest, that in the cotton sock would be in the middle, and that in the silk sock would be the lowest reading of the three. Two of the remaining four students predicted the temperature would be the same for all three socks, while two students thought it was a trick question and couldn't provide any answer. Mr. Martinez set up the three socks and thermometers and placed them aside until the next day. The children left the class eager to see what the results would be on Friday.

Day 2: Exploration

As the students entered the class on Friday, there was quite a buzz in the air. They quickly settled down so that they could find out whether their predictions were correct. Mr. Martinez removed the thermometers from the socks one at a time while a student, Juliana, volunteered to read each one and recorded the temperature on the board. Juliana read the temperature from the wool sock. "Seventy-two degrees," she read, then recorded the temperature on the board. Then she read the second temperature from the cotton sock. "Seventy-two degrees," she said, to the amazement of some students, and again recorded the reading on the board. "That can't be right!" shouted Jeremy. Juliana then read the temperature from the silk sock. Again, she read "72 degrees," visibly surprised, and she recorded the third and final temperature on the board.

"Mr. Martinez, is that a trick?" asked one student.

"No, it's not," he replied. Mr. Martinez asked the two students who predicted that the temperature would remain the same to explain what they thought happened. They explained that because the socks were not giving off any heat, and there was nothing inside the socks that would be expected to gain or lose heat (like an ice cube or a heated rock), the temperature would be the same for all three and that the temperature inside the three socks would reach room temperature regardless of the sock's material.

The next part of the day's lesson involved students using their experience from the sock activity to make a prediction about which of three containers made of different materials, each filled three quarters with hot water, would maintain the highest temperature for the longest time. Mr. Martinez explained that their misconception about heat may be cleared up with today's investigation. The socks, he explained, did not give off any heat. This day's investigation would provide new information with which to test and perhaps change their conception about heat and temperature.

Students in pairs were given three thermometers and three equal-sized and same-shaped containers: one plastic, one glass, and one Styrofoam. Mr. Martinez challenged students to design a method to collect and record data on the temperature change after the students added 100 mL of water heated to 100 degrees to each of the containers. At this point of the inquiry, students designed their own data tables for recording the appropriate information. Once all the data tables were proposed, Mr. Martinez reviewed each group's table design, and the students were ready to begin.

Each group worked conscientiously, making regularly timed measurements from each of the three containers. As they recorded the data on their tables, students began to see the effect the container's material had on the temperature change of the water. The class ended with a review of the data and a discussion of which container held the temperature the longest.

Day 3: Explanation

When the class resumed on Monday, Mr. Martinez led a discussion on the earlier misconception from the initial sock demonstration. As did the socks, the three containers had insulation properties. This time, however, the containers held the water's heat energy. Mr. Martinez used the previous two experiences to introduce concepts including heat energy, insulators, conductors, and the distinction between heat and temperature. Mr. Martinez also reinforced the need from Friday's experiment for controlling variables, such as the amount and temperature of the water, as well as the sizes and shapes of the three containers. Mr. Martinez also reintroduced the terms manipulated or independent variable, responding or dependent variable, and constants.

Days 4 and 5: Extension

On Day 4, Mr. Martinez introduced his class to a new technology: data-collection software and probes. For the first activity, students learned to use the Vernier's

Go!Temp temperature probe and Logger Lite software. With the Logger Lite software installed in the laptop computers, Mr. Martinez instructed students how to use the Go!Temp probe to measure the temperature of their clenched palms. Following the directions from the lab sheet provided by the Vernier *Let's Go! Investigating Temperature* manual, students clicked on the appropriate desktop folder to open the program. Each group was given a temperature probe. One at a time, each member took turns holding the tip of the probe in the palm of his or her closed hand while watching the temperature plotted on the graph on the computer screen (see Figure 9.11).

Mr. Martinez then suggested that students think of ways they could change the temperature of the palms of their hands. Some students suggested that put their hands in the cold water from the faucet, while others suggested they rub their hands together to heat their palms, or rub them on the classroom rug. After writing a prediction in their journal, students recorded the starting and ending temperature for each test. Later, they calculated the increase or decrease and found which methods caused the greatest temperature changes.

After students had gained an initial understanding of the data collection probe, Mr. Martinez transitioned the class into the next day's activity by introducing how to use the technology to collect data from an actual experiment. In this inquiry, students used their prior knowledge from the demonstrations and investigations to design an investigation to test the insulation quality of the three sock materials. In this investigation, students placed equal amounts of 100-degree water in each of three test tubes. They sealed each test tube with a single-hole rubber stopper to allow the probe to extend into the test tube and measure the temperature of the water inside (see Figure 9.12). Using the Go!Temp temperature probes, students set up a procedure to cover one test tube with the wool sock, the second with the cotton sock, and the third with the silk sock. Now students could actually determine the precise insulation quality of each of the three materials.

Figure 9.11   Graph of Temperature

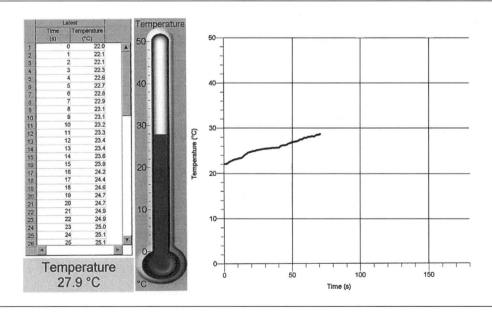

Figure 9.12   Photograph of a Temperature Probe in a Test Tube

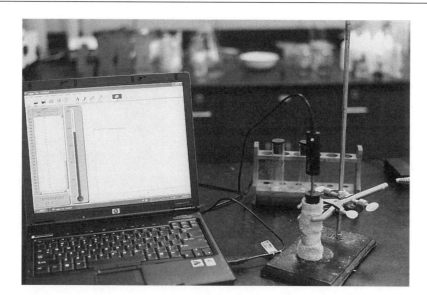

Days 6 and 7: Evaluation

The energy transfer unit culminated with a group performance task in which Mr. Martinez gave students a glass jar with a screw-top lid (with a hole punched through the lid so the temperature probe would fit into the jar—see Figure 9.13) and several insulating materials: scrap pieces of cloth and wool, bubble wrap, Styrofoam peanuts, newspapers, paper towels, wood chips, home insulation batting, and others. In the task, students chose insulation materials that would be placed in a shoebox to surround and keep hot water in an enclosed jar as hot as possible for as long as possible. Students again used the Go!Temp temperature probes to monitor the change in temperature of the water and ultimately the insulation quality of the chosen materials. On Day 6, students used their selected insulation materials (or combination of materials) to set up their experiments. Leaving the setup and the monitoring probes over night, data were collected over a 24-hour period to assess the insulation designs.

On Day 7, the students analyzed their data and graph to make a comparison among the various designs. The unit ended with a brief, five-minute presentation by each of the groups, describing their experiment and results. For the presentations, students printed paper copies of their graph from the software program; identified the manipulated, responding, and control variables in their experiment; and explained the results of their investigation. During the final presentation, each group explained a model for heat transfer and used appropriate terms, vocabulary, and concepts acquired throughout the unit.

This is just one example of how elementary and middle school teachers can integrate data-collection probes into inquiry investigations. For more information on Vernier's Go! products (such as gas pressure sensors, motion detectors, force detectors, and light probes) plus Vernier's elementary and middle school science manuals, go to www.vernier.com.

Figure 9.13 Photograph of a Temperature Probe on a Jar

QUESTIONS FOR REFLECTION AND DISCUSSION

1. Using the consciousness/competence learning model, where would you place yourself on the matrix or ladder?

2. Using the Inquiry Rubric, where would you place yourself on the matrix? What professional development would you need to progress to the next level?

3. Ideas are often summarized by quotations or phrases. One quotation on equity and inquiry is "Curious people are not bounded by their birthplace or the color of their skin, but merely by the extent of their intuitiveness." Write a phrase or catchy statement that captures the connection of inquiry with high-need students.

4. What other instructional strategies can you suggest to accommodate high-need or LEP students in an inquiry classroom? For physically disabled students? For students with learning disabilities? For visually impaired students?

Table 9.1   Rubric for Becoming an Inquiry-Based Teacher

Curriculum			
Noninquiry Approach	*Exploring Inquiry*	*Transitioning to Inquiry*	*Practicing Inquiry*
Student knowledge is based on acquisition and mastery of facts and information; based on broad coverage of topics.	Student knowledge is based on mastery of facts and science process skills; allows for flexibility for in-depth units.	Student knowledge is based on ability to apply facts and science process skills to solve problems and make connections to new situations; allows for flexibility for in-depth units.	Student knowledge is based on in-depth content and abilities to do and understand scientific inquiry; allows for flexibility to understand the nature of science.
Curriculum is teacher-centered and based on prescribed activities with anticipated results.	Curriculum allows for some flexibility for investigations according to the interests of the students.	Curriculum allows for flexibility of investigations and units of study according to the interests of the students.	Curriculum is student-centered and provides flexibility for students to design and carry out their own investigations.
Teacher does not use NSES to plan yearlong curriculum and daily lessons.	Teacher is aware of NSES and occasionally uses national standards to plan curriculum and daily lessons.	Teacher is aware of NSES and frequently uses national standards to plan curriculum and daily lessons.	Teacher is aware of NSES and consistently uses national standards to plan curriculum and daily lessons.
Curriculum based on a single textbook, lecture-driven approach.	Curriculum uses multiple textbooks and inquiry resources.	Curriculum uses multiple textbooks, Internet, and other software and inquiry resources.	Curriculum uses multiple textbooks, Internet, and other software and primary sources for planning science investigations.
When curriculum is not mandated, it is based on teacher's interests; rigidly follows textbook-driven approach.	When curriculum is not mandated, it is based on teacher's interests; allows for flexibility; students sometimes choose topics.	When curriculum is not mandated, it allows for flexibility; students often choose topics or relevancy.	When curriculum is not mandated, it is based on flexibility between teacher needs and student interests, abilities, and prior experiences.
Curriculum is based on science topics only.	Curriculum occasionally integrates relevant topics of science with math and technology.	Curriculum frequently integrates science with math and technology of relevance to students; also according to students' personal experiences.	Curriculum is theme-based and integrates science with math, technology, and other subjects of relevance to students; also according to students' personal and prior experiences.

(Continued)

Table 9.1 (Continued)

Lesson Presentation			
Noninquiry Approach	*Exploring Inquiry*	*Transitioning to Inquiry*	*Practicing Inquiry*
Teacher is center of lesson.	Teacher is center of lesson, occasionally acts as a facilitator.	Teacher is center of lesson, frequently acts as a facilitator.	Teacher consistently acts as an effective facilitator and coach.
Teacher frequently lectures and uses demonstrations and activities to verify science content.	Teacher lectures and does demonstrations and activities to explain science content.	Teacher occasionally lectures and uses demonstrations and activities to reinforce science content.	Teacher occasionally lectures and uses investigations to apply science content to settings outside the classroom.
Teacher lectures first and then provides students with activity or lab to complete.	Teacher makes initial attempts to use 5E Learning Cycle approach.	Teacher frequently uses 5E Learning Cycle approach with satisfactory success.	Teacher regularly and effectively uses 5E Learning Cycle approach; assesses and extends prior knowledge.
Teacher primarily uses demonstrations and structured activities.	Teacher uses demonstrations and attempts open-ended activities and guided inquiry.	Teacher uses demonstrations and open-ended activities and occasionally attempts teacher-initiated and student-initiated inquiries.	Teacher uses all stages of inquiry grid and consistently selects teacher-initiated and student-initiated inquiries on the basis of the lesson.
Teacher plans instruction based on whole-class instruction.	Teacher plans whole-class instruction but occasionally uses small-group instruction.	Teacher plans whole-class instruction and regularly uses cooperative learning groups.	Teacher effectively plans for whole-class instruction as needed and frequently uses cooperative learning groups as appropriate.
Teacher tells students that doing prescribed activities is like what real scientists do.	Teacher begins to distinguish between school-based science and authentic science.	Teacher clearly distinguishes between school-based science and authentic science.	Teacher helps students to distinguish between school-based science and authentic science.

Communication			
Noninquiry Approach	*Exploring Inquiry*	*Transitioning to Inquiry*	*Practicing Inquiry*
Teacher rarely allows students to share information with one another through small-group discussions and reflections.	Teacher occasionally allows students to share information with one another through small-group discussions and reflections.	Teacher frequently expects students to share information with one another through small-group discussions and reflections.	Teacher consistently expects students to share information with one another through small-group discussions and reflections.

Communication			
Noninquiry Approach	*Exploring Inquiry*	*Transitioning to Inquiry*	*Practicing Inquiry*
Teacher speaks mainly from the front of the room.	Teacher usually speaks from the front of the room and occasionally moves about.	Teacher frequently moves about the room, speaking from different areas.	Teacher effectively moves about the room, speaking from different areas to monitor and enhance learning.
Teacher communicates by standing above and over students.	Teacher occasionally communicates to students by kneeling by or sitting on a student seat to make level eye contact.	Teacher frequently communicates to students by kneeling by or sitting on a student seat to make level eye contact.	Teacher consistently communicates to students by kneeling by or sitting on a student seat to make level eye contact.
Communication is directed from teacher to student.	Communication is usually from teacher to student but also from student to student.	Communication is occasionally from teacher to student but frequently from student to student.	Communication effectively varies from teacher to student and from student to student according to the goals of the lesson.

Engagement of Students			
Noninquiry Approach	*Exploring Inquiry*	*Transitioning to Inquiry*	*Practicing Inquiry*
Teacher engages students through rapid-fire oral questioning and discussions.	Teacher engages students through oral discussions and open-ended questions.	Teacher engages students through open-ended discussions and investigations.	Teacher engages students through open-ended discussions, investigations, and reflections.
Minimal student engagement; provides activities to verify science content.	Moderate student engagement.	Frequent student engagement.	Frequent self-engagement by students; teacher challenges students to share responsibility for their own learning.
Students are mostly passive learners; teacher uses hands-on activities confined to a single period.	Students are occasionally active learners; teacher uses hands-on activities and attempts open-ended investigations.	Students are mostly active learners; teacher uses hands-on activities and attempts open-ended investigations and encourages student-directed explorations over extended periods.	Students are consistently active; teacher uses hands-on and minds-on activities that encourage open-ended, student-initiated investigations and explorations.
Teacher solicits information from students to get correct answer.	Teacher solicits information from students to assess their understanding.	Teacher solicits information from students to assess their understanding and adjust instruction.	Teacher frequently and effectively solicits information from students to assess their understanding and

(Continued)

Table 9.1 (Continued)

Engagement of Students			
Noninquiry Approach	Exploring Inquiry	Transitioning to Inquiry	Practicing Inquiry
			adjust instruction; challenges evidence and claims from their investigation; encourages curiosity, openness to new ideas, and skepticism.
Teacher does not plan or find time for scientific investigations.	Teacher occasionally plans and makes time for investigations.	Teacher frequently plans and allocates time for investigations.	Teacher consistently plans and allocates time for frequent, ongoing investigations.

Classroom Organization			
Noninquiry Approach	Exploring Inquiry	Transitioning to Inquiry	Practicing Inquiry
Student desks are arranged in rows with seating assigned by teacher; focus toward front of class; teacher's desk in front center of class.	Student desks are usually arranged in rows or in groups assigned by teacher for occasional group work; teacher's desk to the side of classroom.	Student desks are arranged in groups assigned by teacher and students for cooperative learning groups; teacher's desk at side or in back of classroom.	Teacher and students share decisions around room design and seating arrangements to maximize student interactions, work, and discussions.
Supplies and materials are locked away; teacher permission is needed for students to access items.	Some supplies and materials are readily available for students to access on own; teacher permission needed for students to access certain items.	Many supplies and materials are readily available for students to access on own; teacher permission needed for students to access certain items.	Most supplies and materials are readily accessible for students to access on own; teacher permission needed for students to access certain items.
Classroom does not contain centers or areas for students to work independently; room arrangement remains the same for entire school year.	Classroom occasionally contains centers; room arrangement changes occasionally.	Classroom regularly contains centers and areas for independent work; room arrangement changes on the basis of topic being studied.	Classroom contains centers and areas for students to work or read independently; room arrangement changes regularly.
Walls are usually bare with a few commercially-made posters displayed.	Posters and some student work displayed on walls.	Some posters, but mostly student work displayed on walls.	Walls are filled with work representing all students in the class at various stages of completion.

Questioning Skills			
Noninquiry Approach	Exploring Inquiry	Transitioning to Inquiry	Practicing Inquiry
Teacher asks mostly low-level, recall, and knowledge-level questions.	Teacher asks recall and comprehension-level questions, poses application- and evaluation-level questions.	Teacher poses higher-level and open-ended questions.	Teacher uses all levels of questioning and adjusts level to individual students.
Teacher uses questions to impart knowledge and solicit a desired response from students.	Teacher uses questioning skills to initiate discussion.	Teacher uses questioning skills to assess prior knowledge and initiate interactions between teacher and students and among students.	Teacher uses questioning skills to assess prior knowledge, facilitate discussions among students, and construct knowledge.
Teacher leads individual students to answer questions correctly, provides correct answer when not given.	Teacher leads student to answer questions correctly, attempts prompting strategies.	Teacher frequently uses probing and prompting techniques.	Teacher consistently uses probing and prompting techniques to groups of students.
Teacher rarely asks open-ended questions.	Teacher attempts to pose open-ended questions.	Teacher frequently poses open-ended questions.	Teacher consistently and effectively uses open-ended questions.
Teacher does not use wait-time strategies.	Teacher occasionally uses wait-time strategies.	Teacher frequently uses wait-time strategies.	Teacher consistently and effectively uses wait-time strategies.
Teacher follows up students' answers by repeating student answer, saying "Okay," or going on to next question.	Teacher attempts to follow up students' answers with positive reinforcement before going on.	Teacher frequently provides praise and positive reinforcement and follows up students' answers with additional probing questions.	Teacher consistently provides praise and positive reinforcement and follows up students' answers with additional probing and engaging questions.
Teacher provides answers when students cannot answer questions.	Teacher attempts rephrasing techniques when students cannot answer questions.	Teacher frequently uses prompts and rephrasing techniques when students cannot answer questions.	Teacher consistently and effectively uses prompts and rephrasing techniques when students cannot answer questions.

Assessment Procedures			
NonInquiry Approach	Exploring Inquiry	Transitioning to Inquiry	Practicing Inquiry
Teacher frequently uses worksheets to assess learning; students record data on teacher-designed lab sheets.	Teacher reduces use of worksheets to assess learning; attempts having students record data on student-designed lab sheets.	Teacher seldom uses worksheets to assess learning; students record data on student-designed lab sheets or journals with limited success.	Teacher seldom uses formative assessments to guide teaching; students record data on student-designed lab sheets and journals successfully.

(Continued)

Table 9.1 (Continued)

Questioning Skills			
Noninquiry Approach	*Exploring Inquiry*	*Transitioning to Inquiry*	*Practicing Inquiry*
Teacher mostly uses objective-type testing to assess learning, factual information, and discrete knowledge.	Teacher uses objective testing and attempts to implement authentic assessments.	Teacher varies assessment to include objective items, portfolios, rubrics, and other performance assessments.	Teacher consistently and effectively uses multiple assessment methods to assess and monitor students' understandings and progress.
Teacher assesses students using content information only.	Teacher assesses students using content and science process skills.	Teacher assesses students using content, science process skills, and problem-solving skills.	Teacher assesses students using content, science process skills, nature of science, and scientific abilities and attitudes.
Teacher assesses to determine what students do not know; chooses assessments that are easy to grade.	Teacher chooses assessments that are most appropriate for the instruction; pilots multiple ways for student to demonstrate competence.	Teacher chooses assessments that are most appropriate for inquiry instruction; allows for multiple ways for student to demonstrate competence.	Teacher assesses to determine what students do not understand; chooses assessments that are most appropriate for inquiry instruction; allows for multiple ways for student to demonstrate competence.

Professional Development			
Noninquiry Approach	*Exploring Inquiry*	*Transitioning to Inquiry*	*Practicing Inquiry*
Teacher takes professional development workshops on solely content-related topics.	Teacher takes professional development workshops on inquiry topics; reads books on scientific inquiry.	Teacher engages workshops or college-level courses on inquiry instruction, participates in inquiry discussion groups.	Teacher does workshops; reads and writes articles on inquiry-based instruction; serves as mentor for new teachers; leads support groups.
Teacher participates mainly in one-day workshops based on content topics.	Teacher occasionally participates in ongoing university-sponsored inquiry workshops and support groups.	Teacher regularly participates in ongoing university-sponsored inquiry professional development sessions and support groups.	Teacher participates in ongoing inquiry by working with local or university level scientists or by developing original inquiry investigations.

Professional Development			
Noninquiry Approach	Exploring Inquiry	Transitioning to Inquiry	Practicing Inquiry
Teacher is not concerned with learning about inquiry strategies.	Teacher attempts to use Internet resources, videos, and software to search for inquiry articles and best practice strategies.	Teacher regularly uses Internet resources, videos, and software to search for inquiry articles and best practice strategies.	Teacher frequently uses Internet resources, online discussions, videos, and software to enhance practice of inquiry strategies.
Teacher works primarily as an individual.	Teacher works with another teacher to share inquiry strategies and activities.	Teacher works in collaboration with other teachers to develop and share inquiry strategies.	Teacher collaborates with colleagues in study groups sharing units, articles, and success stories; works across disciplines and grade levels.
Teacher takes "one-shot," fragmented professional development workshops for instruction only on content topics.	Teacher begins to see connections between inquiry and research-based strategies.	Teacher seeks professional development on inquiry and research-based strategies.	Teacher frequently engages in ongoing professional development on research-based strategies.

Using Questioning Skills in Inquiry

In a classroom atmosphere conducive to good questions and questioning, students realize a shared responsibility for their learning.

—Francis Hunkins

Got questions? Children naturally ask lots of questions. When children ask questions, they are pondering new phenomena and seeking modes to create meaning from their experiences. In science, questions foster children's natural curiosity and guide them in making observations and forming explanations. In constructivist classrooms, teachers pose questions to assess children's understandings and points of view on topics or concepts being studied. Questions open the door to a child's mind and imagination. Thus if answers to science are discovered through the questions we ask, then questions become our most formidable means to attain scientific literacy.

This chapter explores two types of questions. The first are the *investigative questions* students raise as part of their explorations. The second are *verbal questions* teachers pose during lessons or discussions. Teachers cannot underestimate their need to develop good questioning skills. Both kinds of questions are essential in developing learner-centered classrooms. When used properly, questions can access prior knowledge, encourage explorations, and engage students in critical thinking.

In Chapter 3, we read about a fourth-grade class exploring the properties of ice. Some of the inquiries may have included:

- How long does it take water to freeze?
- What are the "bubbles" in the ice hand?
- Why does the ice hand melt in the water?
- Why do the fingers get pointy when they melt?

- Why does water expand while freezing?
- Why is the ice smooth in some spots and rough in others?
- How do icebergs form?
- Will the ice hand melt faster if we stirred the water in the pan?
- Why does ice float in water?
- Does cold ice melt more slowly in cold water than in warm water?
- Why is the ice white in the thick part and clear in the thin part?

WHY YOU CAN'T INVESTIGATE
A "WHY" QUESTION

When students raise questions, it is important for the teacher to distinguish between *information-seeking* and *investigation-performing* questions. The questions in the previous section consist of both information-seeking questions, which call for a scientific explanation, and investigation-performing questions, which invite a statement to be tested. Generally, questions beginning with "why" are information-seeking questions and beckon an explanation. Often students need to consult a teacher, an outside resource, or an "expert" to answer their "why" questions. Many elementary school teachers point out that they sometimes feel uncomfortable teaching science because they are expected to answer students' "why" questions.

In the following example, Mrs. DeSain's third-grade class is studying bats. In this unit, Mrs. DeSain begins with a KWL exercise. The students share what they know about bats and then begin to raise questions about bats. Their questions include the following:

- Where do bats live?
- What do bats eat?
- Why do bats live in caves?
- How do bats use sonar to locate objects?
- Why do bats hang upside down?

Throughout the unit students will read about and discuss bat behavior. They will use their textbooks, resources from the school and community libraries, and the Internet to answer their questions. Mrs. DeSain may also know a person in the area who makes bat houses or is considered an expert on bats. Although Mrs. DeSain may design this unit to be very student-centered, the children probably will not conduct actual investigations with live bats. For that reason, the students' questions fall into the category of information-seeking questions.

Investigation-performing questions, on the other hand, generally begin with "does," "how can," "how come," "what if," or "I wonder." In understanding students' questions, different phrasing indicates different purposes. In the ice hand story, it was important to determine (a) which questions could be answered only by doing further research in the library or by asking an expert, and (b) which questions had to be revised and rewritten to change an information question to an investigation question. For that reason, Ms. Perlo sorted the student questions into three groups:

(1) questions ready for investigating, (2) questions needing revision, and (3) questions that needed an expert to answer (see Figure 10.1, which also appears in Chapter 6).

A good investigation question

1. Invites a statement to be tested,

2. Leads the student to think of solutions to solve the question,

3. Specifies the variable affecting the outcome of the investigation and the variable being measured,

4. Leads to new information that the student did not know prior to asking the question, and

5. Relates and applies to real-world situations beyond the classroom.

When the question does not meet the criteria, the teacher needs to provide assistance in revising the question. For example, one fourth grader asked, "How fast do large ice cubes melt?" With the help of the teachers, the question was reworded to read, "How does the size of the ice cube affect its melting rate?"

Similarly, an information-seeking question raised by another student was, Why do the thin fingers melt faster than the palm? Although this is an interesting question, the question needs to be reworded into an investigation-performing question, such as, How does the surface area of the ice cube affect the melting rate? By rewording the question from "Why" to "How does," the student has created a starter question that leads to an investigation.

Figure 10.1   Sorting Students' Questions

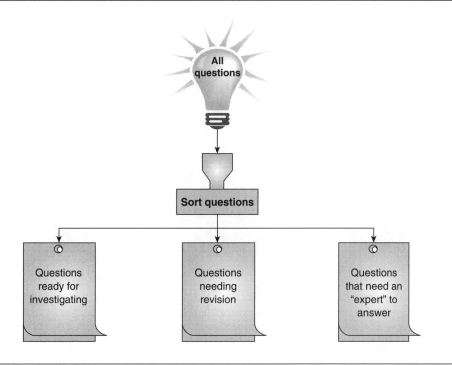

CLASSROOM QUESTIONS

Let's now turn our attention to the teacher who poses questions during a classroom discussion. Questions can be put forward to students for many reasons:

- To engage and motivate in conversation or discussion
- To provide direction to a conversation or discussion
- To assess students' prior knowledge
- To uncover students' naïve conceptions
- To stimulate and challenge higher-level thinking skills
- To focus, clarify, or guide a discussion
- To prompt a student to a particular answer
- To process information
- To have students defend or justify a position
- To keep students on task
- To pose problems and guide problem solving
- To seek solutions to problems
- To assess student progress
- To prepare for an upcoming quiz or test
- To reflect on and review material of a lesson

Questions are an essential part of a teacher's lesson. Some teachers ask as many as 200 to 300 questions a day! Posing questions to students is a vital aspect of teaching, but merely firing a barrage of questions does not necessarily make for a good inquiry lesson. A lesson overpacked with questions is like a lesson on amphetamines. Imagine a discussion led by a middle school science teacher standing at the front of a room of 24 seventh graders. His lesson plan includes using a series of questions to guide a lesson on nutrition. The lesson begins with the teacher passing out crackers and having the students place them in their mouths and chew them. (Teacher and student names are fictitious.)

Mr. Poole: Okay. The first question I would like to ask is, What's happening to the cracker as it enters your mouth? Does anyone know? Can anyone tell me? Angela?

Angela: It's getting chewed.

Mr. Poole: Okay. Good. It's getting chewed. Anything else?

Angela: It's going to your stomach.

Mr. Poole: Okay. Before we get to the stomach, what's happening in your mouth? Ryan, do you know?

Ryan: There's that spit stuff working on it. [Class laughs]

Mr. Poole: That's called saliva, Ryan.

Ryan: Yeah, saliva, that's what I meant.

Mr. Poole: Okay, saliva moistens the cracker. Then what happens? Anyone? Tomeka?

Tomeka: It goes to your stomach?

Mr. Poole: No, before that. What happens?

Tomeka: It goes down your esophagus?

Mr. Poole: Right, your esophagus. What about the esophagus? What happens after the esophagus? Anyone know? How about you, Harold?

Harold: Your stomach?

Mr. Poole: Right, your stomach. What goes on there? [Pointing to Ginny]

Ginny: It breaks down the food into . . .

Mr. Poole: [Interrupting] Well, actually the food started breaking down in your mouth. What does your stomach do? Anyone? [Pointing] Rachel?

Rachel: Uh, that's where the food, uh, goes into your body.

Mr. Poole: Not quite. Michael, do you know?

Michael: I think the stomach adds some kind of acids and chemicals that break down the cracker.

Mr. Poole: Right. The stomach adds digestive acids to break down the cracker into energy that your body uses.

As you can see, Mr. Poole's questioning technique is quite unstructured. Most of his questions are at a low-level recall or knowledge level. He also asks a number of "guess what I'm thinking of" questions. The way Mr. Poole poses the questions creates an atmosphere in which students try to anticipate what answer he wants. When Mr. Poole doesn't hear the answer he is looking for, he calls on another student until his "correct" answer is given. Although the teacher posed many questions to the class, this does not represent an inquiry lesson. In addition, Mr. Poole did not provide sufficient time for students to accurately answer several of his questions. He repeatedly interrupted the students in the middle of their answers, communicating that he's asking a question only to get the right answer, not to allow students to express their understanding and possible misconceptions. Unfortunately, teachers today are hard-pressed to pack a great deal of learning into the school calendar. Could this be one reason why so many teachers are pressured to use a rapid-fire approach when asking questions?

WAIT-TIME

Mary Budd Rowe (1974, 1987, 1996) is a noted educator for her research on *wait-time*. Wait-time is the length of time a teacher waits between the end of the student's response (to a teacher's question) and the beginning of the teacher's next question. Rowe reports that teachers typically wait about one second following a student's answer before repeating the student's answer, asking the student a follow-up question, or calling on a different student. Her research further indicates that when teachers practice short wait-time techniques (one second), students tend to give simple and short answers at a low-recall level. Rowe suggests that by pausing to wait three to five seconds after a student's response, desirable behaviors often result. Rowe, as well as Tobin and Capie (1981), reports that as the use of wait-time increases, so do

- The number of student responses
- The number of unsolicited but appropriate responses
- The use of higher levels of logical thinking
- The incidence of speculative thinking
- The number of questions students ask
- Students supporting their answers with evidence, logic, and details
- Student-to-student communication and exchanges
- The number of positive responses
- The students' confidence in their ability to construct explanations

By waiting, with an uninterrupted pause of five seconds or longer, Rowe reports that the length of the student responses increased by three to seven times!

Rowe (1974, 1987, 1996) also reports that teachers who use longer wait-times have additional time to think about students' answers and focus more on students' responses. This allows teachers to concentrate more on understanding the reasoning and points of view of their students.

In one study, Rowe asked teachers to identify five of their best and five of their slowest students. When observing the wait-time techniques of those teachers, Rowe found that teachers waited significantly less time for slower students than they did for brighter students. After reviewing the data, teachers surprisingly admitted they did not expect the slower student to provide the correct answer, so they went on to another student. In the lesson with Mr. Poole, we can see that he did not use effective wait-time techniques; thus, many of the students' responses were brief.

ANSWERING QUESTIONS AND QUESTIONING ANSWERS

Teachers probably ask hundreds of thousands of questions over the course of their careers. Knowing how to ask questions and when it is appropriate to give an answer to a question are important aspects of a learner-centered classroom. To illustrate this point, let's consider a sixth-grade physical science class. (Teacher and student names are fictitious.)

Mr. Rivers has 15 stations set up around the room. Each station has an activity that demonstrates one or more science process skills. The purpose of the lesson is to have students engage in activities to gain an understanding of those skills. By doing the activity and then determining which science skills were being emphasized, the students are constructing an understanding of science process skills.

The students work in pairs, rotating from station to station. One station has a Cartesian diver (see Figure 10.2). A Cartesian diver is made of an eyedropper partially filled with water so that the tip of the eyedropper just floats at the top of a

Figure 10.2   Cartesian Diver

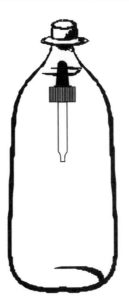

two-liter, clear plastic bottle also filled with water (see Resource F on how to make a Cartesian diver).

At this station, the students are instructed to gently squeeze the sides of the bottle and observe what happens to the "diver." Next, they must devise an illustration or a model to explain how the Cartesian diver works.

In one group, Tim and Bernie indicated that they didn't have the faintest idea what was going on inside the bottle. The answer is relatively simple, and Mr. Rivers assumed that both students had enough understanding of volume and pressure to solve the "mystery." He decided to pose several prompting questions to guide them to an understanding.

Mr. Rivers: When you squeeze the bottle, what happens to the diver?

Tim: It goes down.

Mr. Rivers: Good. Now, as you squeeze the bottle, what happens to the volume inside the bottle?

Bernie: What do you mean?

Mr. Rivers: Well, as you squeeze the bottle, does the volume inside the bottle increase, decrease, or remain the same?

Bernie: I'm not sure.

Mr. Rivers: Okay, let's try this. [Reaching for a can of soda] If I were to crush the can, what would happen to the soda inside the can?

Bernie: It would come out.

Mr. Rivers: Very good. Why does the soda come out?

Bernie:	Because you squeezed the can and there's less room inside the can for the soda.
Mr. Rivers:	[Silence]
Tim:	So, since there is less room in the can, the soda has nowhere to go but to spill out, right?
Mr. Rivers:	Right! Now can you use that to answer what happens to the volume when you squeeze the Cartesian diver?
Tim:	The volume decreases?
Mr. Rivers:	Are you sure?
Tim:	Yeah, the volume decreases!
Mr. Rivers:	Okay, now if the volume of the bottle decreases, what happens to the pressure in the bottle when you squeeze it?
Bernie:	It probably increases.
Mr. Rivers:	It does increase, you're right. Now, because the volume inside the bottle decreases, what happens to the water inside the bottle?
Bernie:	It goes up the little diver?
Mr. Rivers:	How do you know?
Bernie:	I saw it go up.
Mr. Rivers:	You mean, you observed the water going up.
Bernie:	Yeah.
Mr. Rivers:	What did you observe that told you the water was going up the diver?
Tim:	I saw the water go up.
Mr. Rivers:	[Silence]
Tim:	The little level thing went up higher in the diver, so that probably means the water is rising up into the diver.
Mr. Rivers:	Good observation! Now, as the water rises up into the diver, what happens to the diver?
Tim:	It goes down because it has more water in it and it weighs more, so that makes it sink to the bottom of the bottle.
Mr. Rivers:	[Silence]
Tim:	And so when I stopped squeezing the bottle, the pressure went back to normal, and the volume of the bottle increased, forcing the water back out of the diver, and the diver went back up!
Mr. Rivers:	Good job! So what did you need me for? You knew the answer.
Bernie:	I didn't think I did.

This brief lesson demonstrates the effective use of wait-time and the power of posing questions to elicit a student's prior knowledge. What goes through Mr. Rivers's mind the moment a student asks him a question? In that split second just after the question is asked, at the start of a student's answer, he might ask himself, "Does this student have any idea in his or her head how to answer this question?" If the answer is no, he probably feels it doesn't make any sense to try to coax an answer out of the student. Instead, he provides a direct and appropriate answer. Posing a question to try to "pry" an answer out of someone's head when the information isn't there creates a frustrating situation for both the teacher and the student. If the teacher thinks, however, that the student has some prior knowledge or experience that can be used to answer the question, then prompting and probing questions are more appropriate than providing an answer.

As "gatekeepers" of their own knowledge, students are constantly balancing their personally held rationalizations with scientific verifications. We have seen how indispensable a teacher's questioning skills are in facilitating this tenuous stability. According to Lucas, Broderick, Lehrer, and Bohanan (2005):

> Questioning is indeed robustly rooted in children's everyday ways of thinking about the world, but serious classroom support is required if these children's questions are to become productive guides to scientific inquiry. Similarly, children are apt at generating justifications to support their actions or points of view in an argument. However, they often regard their actions or beliefs as unproblematic, even self-evident. In contrast, scientific inquiry demands a separation between belief and evidence, so that each can be considered apart and their relations made explicit. (p. 39)

TYPES OF QUESTIONS

During the Cartesian diver discussion, the questions the teacher asked were important in directing and focusing the thinking processes of the students. His questions also directed the students toward an intended goal: understanding how the diver works. In classroom discussions, the teacher's questions can be classified into four types:

1. *Clarifying questions* require students to make their thoughts and understanding more explicit. We ask clarifying questions when students fall short of providing a reasonable explanation. Clarifying questions ask the student to restate his or her understanding, elaborate, or articulate a particular position on a topic. Teachers often pose clarifying questions by asking such things as:

What do you mean by that?

Can you be more specific?

What's the significance of that?

2. *Focusing questions* require students to narrow their answers and provide more specific responses. We ask focusing questions when students provide elusive, vague, or generalized answers. Teachers often pose focusing questions by asking:

Can you give me an example of that?

What pattern do you see?

How does this apply to another situation?

3. *Probing questions* require a student to justify a response, support a point of view, or analyze a situation to make further generalizations, formulate outcomes, or state a cause-and-effect description. They are aimed at correcting, improving, or expanding a student's original response to a question. Teachers ask probing questions when students' answers are flimsy or partially explained or when they feel students know more than they are actually answering. Probing questions encourage students to clarify answers by providing more evidence or providing supporting details. They also cause students to reason and respond at elevated cognitive levels. Teachers often pose probing questions by asking:

What if you tried adding more soap solution?

What do you think will happen if you used a larger marble?

What do you mean by that?

What are you thinking about when you say that?

What do you think you should do next?

Do you agree or disagree?

4. *Prompting questions* require students to provide answers that are guided by questions asked by the teacher. We ask prompting questions when we want a student to come to a particular conclusion. Prompting questions often contain clues or hints to guide the student to answering correctly. Sometimes a teacher will use a prompting question as a follow-up question when a student cannot answer an original query correctly. Rather than say that the student did not answer correctly, a teacher can follow up the answer with a prompting question that is simpler or more direct. This kind of question is reworded from the original question, with hints and suggestions added. When a student's response seems to be scattered or off topic, the teacher can pose a prompting question that tends to lead to an obvious answer. Some examples of prompting questions are:

Don't you think you should try it again?

Have you thought about trying to increase the angle of the ramp?

Have you tried using more paper clips?

What can you do to the Bugs-o-Copter to make it fall faster?

In a way, a prompting question is like a life preserver. When a student seems to be "drowning" in an idea, we throw him or her help to make sense of his or her understanding. Many savvy teachers know when and how to pose a prompting question, saving the student from embarrassment.

Taking another slant on posing questions, Furtak and Ruiz-Primo (2005) suggest a three-step approach, called the Questioning Cycle. According to them:

The teacher begins by *eliciting* a response from students that reveals the state of the students' understanding. Next, the teacher *recognizes* the response by reflecting it back to the students or asking another follow-up question. The third step involves taking some form of *action* to help the student move towards the essence of the activity or concept. The process can be thought of as a cycle to reflect the ongoing nature of informative questioning throughout inquiry activities. (p. 22)

INTERACTION OF QUESTIONING

Looking back on Mr. Poole's lesson on nutrition, a distinct communication pattern emerges. The interaction between the teacher and the student starts with the teacher asking a question and a student responding with an answer. The teacher goes on to ask another student a question, expecting a particular answer. The pattern shows the direction of communication from teacher to student and back to the teacher again (see Figure 10.3). This type of questioning limits the interaction to just two participants: the teacher and the student being questioned.

Redirectioning, on the other hand, is a technique used by teachers to involve many students in a discussion. During redirectioning, the teacher calls on one student and asks another student to build on the comments from the first student. Redirection encourages students to listen and become aware of other students' comments. Not

Figure 10.3 Teacher-to-Student Interaction in Questioning

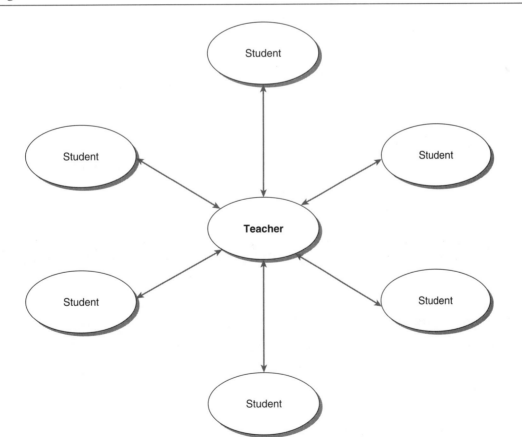

Figure 10.4   Redirecting Interaction in Questioning

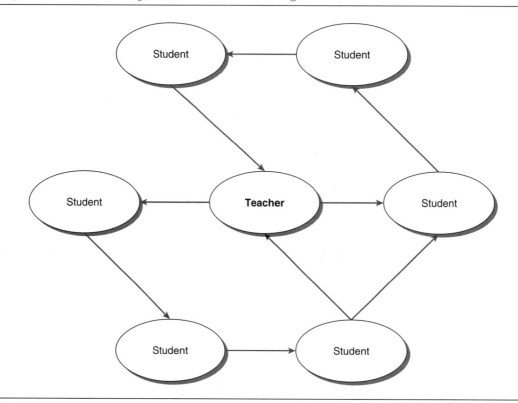

only must students listen to their peers, but they must also must analyze and be able to react to previous comments. During redirectioning, the teacher is no longer the conduit of the conversation. A typical questioning pattern would look something like this (see Figure 10.4):

The discussion may sound something like this. (Teacher and student names are fictitious.)

Mr. Lopez: In your leaf experiment, why did you give the plants all the same amount of water? Jason?

Jason: Because if you changed the amount of water, some plants would get a lot of water and some just a little, and that might affect the results of your experiment.

Mr. Lopez: Margaret, is Jason right?

Margaret: Yeah, you have to give all your plants the same amount of water to make it a fair experiment.

Mr. Lopez: [Silence]

Ann: I think that if you changed the amount of water you give each of the plants, it would change the outcome of the experiment, and you want only one variable to affect the outcome.

Margaret: That makes the amount of water one of the controlled variables in the experiment.

Michael: But what about amount of sunlight the plant receives, shouldn't that be the same too?

Margaret: Yes. That makes the amount of sunlight another one of the controlled variables in the experiment.

In another example of redirectioning, the teacher can say, "I'm going to ask Michelle a question, then I'm going to ask a boy a follow-up question." By prefacing the question to Michelle with that statement, the boys are prompted to ask themselves "Am I going to be called on next?" This technique helps keep all the boys attentive and listening to Michelle's answer.

Sometimes, a student knows the answer, but he or she lacks experience in communication. We might hear a student say "I know the answer, I just can't explain it." Sometimes, that can mean "I don't know what you are talking about" or "I need help." In these situations, consider providing prompting questions to help the student to think about his or her own thinking.

To include *all* students in the questioning process, teachers should distribute questions equally and equitably throughout the class. As an exercise, go into another teacher's room and observe which children are called on to answer a question. Make a diagram of the classroom's seating arrangement and label each desk with the gender of the student sitting at it.

Throughout the lesson, place a tally mark in the corresponding desk box for each time the teacher poses a question to that student. Also, write the name of the student in the box when, and only when, the teacher calls on the student by name. This will show you three things: (1) the frequency with which the teacher calls on boys versus girls, (2) the degree to which the teacher personalizes the class by calling on students by name, and (3) which areas of the room get the most attention. If there are 28 students in the class and only five have names filled in their boxes, chances are that the teacher does not personalize questions by calling on students by name.

In addition, draw a line to indicate the movement of the teacher throughout the lesson. Do you observe the teacher moving about the room or staying in one location? Does the teacher call on students sitting directly in front of him or her? Because teachers often call on students in their immediate vicinity, it is often suggested they move about the room and ask questions from the back of the room to students in the front. As your observation techniques advance, tally how the teacher responds following an answer. Does the teacher repeat the answer? Provide positive reinforcement? Say "Okay"? Ask a follow-up question? Or say nothing and go on to the next question?

Every classroom will contain a few students who are shy or afraid of giving wrong answers. Initiate questions with nonvolunteering students by letting them know you are going to ask the question. To avoid any undue embarrassment, get their attention first by calling on them by name. Pose questions that are fairly straightforward and easy to answer. Following an answer, wait a few seconds, and if there is no further response, provide positive reinforcement by saying, "Yes, that's right! Good answer. Thank you."

QUESTIONS FOR REFLECTION AND DISCUSSION

1. A fourth-grade class is starting a thematic unit on whales. What information-seeking questions can the teacher expect students to ask?

2. The same class later will be starting a unit on butterflies. What information-seeking and investigation-performing questions can the teacher expect students to ask?

Inquiry Investigations

The following are examples of how teachers can provide elementary and middle school children with opportunities to elicit questions from an exploration. Each lesson provides discrepancies to spark interest in science. But before we go any further, it's time for a second disclaimer. In reading the lessons, some may say that the content level is minimal. Some may say it's even trivial. To that I would agree. However, the purpose of the investigations is not to focus on physical or life science content; the purpose is to provide opportunities for students to investigate and raise questions from open-ended explorations. These lessons may be most beneficial to do in the early part of the school year without overwhelming students with learning an enormous amount of new facts and concepts. The sole purpose is to offer straightforward, uncomplicated, and easy to set up explorations (with some based on the 5E format) that allow students to enhance their appreciation for inquiry, especially when the students may have limited experience in designing ways to test their own questions. If you decide to use these lessons in your own classroom, college course, or summer institute, you will need to modify and supplement these examples with additional content and assessments appropriate for your grade level and district standards. Consider discussing how the examples develop one's ability to do and understand scientific inquiry. Consider discussing how you would modify the lesson for a lower or higher grade level. Also discuss how you would assess student learning for each lesson. Most important, use the lessons to raise your capacity to generate questions and, of course, your Inquiry Quotient.

BUGS-O-COPTERS

In *Bugs-o-Copters*, students will (a) explore concepts in forces and motion, and (b) design investigations to test how one variable affects the motion, direction, or falling rate of a Bugs-o-Copter. Teachers can use Bugs-o-Copters to introduce science process skills or the inquiry cycle. Because the activity is highly motivational and requires little prior content knowledge, it can be used as a "kick-off" to the school year and a motivator for learning science.

Title of Lesson: *Bugs-o-Copters*

Grade Levels: 5–8

Essential Question: How does the Bugs-o-Copter's ear length affect the falling rate?

Estimated Time: 30–60 minutes

Lesson Objectives:

- Students will observe and record the rate of descent of the Bugs-o-Copter.
- Students will determine how the surface area of the ears affects the friction between the Bugs-o-Copter and the air.

Correlation with the *National Science Education Standards* (NSES): As a result of this activity, all students will:

- Identify questions that can be answered through scientific investigations (NRC, 1996, p. 145)
- Design and conduct a scientific investigation (p. 145)
- Develop descriptions, explanations, predictions, and models using evidence (p. 145)
- Understand that the motion of an object can be described by its position, direction of motion, and speed. That motion can be measured and represented on a graph (p. 154)

Concepts/Terms: resistance, friction, motion, force, aerodynamics, gravity

Science Skills Used: observing, communicating, inferring, interpreting data, predicting, controlling variables, experimenting, collecting and recording data, constructing models

Background: Gravity naturally causes the Bugs-o-Copter to fall to the ground; however, as the Bugs-o-Copter falls, the air pushes up against the ears. The angle of the ears causes the air to move sideways, causing a simple thrusting motion. As the air molecules hit the underside of the ears, this causes a small amount of friction, counteracting the rate of fall caused by gravity. The larger the surface area of the ears, the more friction will occur, and the slower the Bugs-o-Copter will spin (or fall). Students will design ways to change the aerodynamics of the Bugs-o-Copter by changing the shape or size of each of the ears or changing the amount or position of the paper clip.

In Bugs-o-Copters, students seem to move very quickly through the steps of the investigation. In seconds, they move from the "question" phase to the "implementation" phase of the plan. The intermediate steps of inquiry (identifying the manipulated and the responding variables) often occur without the student consciously thinking about them as important features of the investigation. The teacher should facilitate students' becoming aware of their thinking process (metacognition) even though it may seem like a natural or unconscious process. Exploring the Bugs-o-Copters is such a simple activity that we often overlook this. By reinforcing these mental steps in the elementary and middle school years, teachers help students to understand and appreciate the thinking processes during an inquiry and apply their thinking when faced with more complex tasks in high school.

Misconceptions: Students associate how the Bugs-o-Copter works with how a actual helicopter works. Be sure to clarify the difference at the end of the lesson.

Materials: (for each student)
- 1 short-eared Bugs-o-Copter
- 1 long-eared Bugs-o-Copter
- Scissors
- Several small and large paper clips

Safety Concerns: None, but watch students who stand on a chair to drop the Bugs-o-Copter from a higher level.

Grouping Arrangements: Allow students to work individually.

Preparation/Prior Setup: Have one short-eared and one large-eared Bugs-o-Copter cut out in advance.

Procedure

Engage: Assess prior knowledge by posing the question, What do you know about spinning objects? Demonstrate various spinning objects: tops, gyroscopes, pinwheels, windmills, a globe spinning on its axis, or a maple seed.

Explore: Show students how to cut out the short-eared Bugs-o-copter. Fold the ears in opposite directions. Place a paper clip at the feet and hold Bugs-o-Copter (feet down) from an outstretched arm. Release and observe the rate of fall and direction of the spin. Repeat the dropping several times. Encourage students to record their observations and questions in their science journals. Allow students to cut out the long-eared Bugs-o-Copter. Before they drop the long-eared version, encourage them to make a prediction about how it will drop compared with the short-eared version. Have them record that prediction in their journals. As students drop their two Bugs-o-Copters, have them think about and record further questions to investigate. Direct them to write "what if" and "I wonder" questions in their journals or on a T-chart.

Explain: Lead a discussion on the falling rates of the two Bugs-o-Copters. Explain how the surface area affects the amount of friction between the air and the ears and thus the rate of descent. Predict what would happen if you dropped Bugs-o-Copters on the Moon, where there is no air and less gravity. Predict what would happen if you dropped Bugs-o-Copters in a vacuum jar.

Extend: Ask students to share their "what if" questions to investigate. Post the questions on poster paper. Revise any "why" questions into investigative questions. Identify the manipulated and responding variables for each question or inquiry. Allow students to plan and carry out their experimental designs for the questions. Questions may include the following:

- Does the number of paper clips affect the falling rate?
- What would happen if I place a paper clip on the ears of the Bugs-o-Copter?

- Does the thickness of the paper affect how the Bugs-o-Copter will spin?
- What would happen if I made a Bugs-o-Copter out of poster board instead of paper?
- What if I cut out the outline (shape) of the ears?
- Does the shape of the ears affect how the Bugs-o-Copter falls?
- What if I put the paper clips in a different location?
- How can I get both the short-eared and the long-eared Bugs-o-Copters to hit the floor at the same time?
- What if I change the direction the ears are folded?
- How would cutting slits in the ears affect the spinning?
- Will the way the ears are folded affect how the Bugs-o-Copter will spin?
- How can I make the Bugs-o-Copter spin in the opposite direction?
- Which Bugs-o-Copter, the short-eared or long-eared, makes more spins before hitting the floor?
- Would the Bugs-o-Copter spin in the opposite direction in the Southern Hemisphere than in the Northern Hemisphere?
- If I attach the feet of Bugs-o-Copter to a string and suspend it, upside down, from the ceiling and attach a paper clip at the head of Bugs-o-Copter (see Figure 11.1), and then place a small fan at low speed below Bugs-o-Copter, can I make the Bugs-o-Copter spin upside down? How can I change the direction of the spinning?

Evaluate: Provide time for students to report the results of their investigations. Have each student make a three-minute oral presentation to the class. Provide a rubric for making an effective oral presentation.

Figure 11.1   Photo of Bugs-o-Copter (hanging upside down)

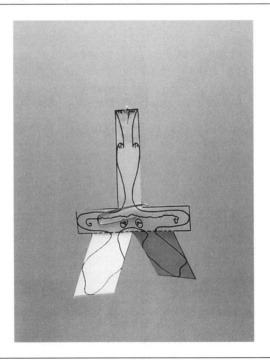

CLAYBOATS

In *Clayboats*, students will design boats made of clay and determine the best shape to hold the most pennies, ceramic tiles, or small washers as "cargo." Students will also investigate other materials for making boats.

Title of Lesson: *Clayboats*

Grade Levels: 4–6

Essential Questions: How can you make a boat from a ball of clay? Can you make a boat from other materials, such as a sheet of aluminum foil?

Estimated Time: 45–90 minutes

Lesson Objectives:
- Students will construct their own floating containers (clay or aluminum foil boats) to investigate the concept of floating.
- Students will predict the number of cargoes (pennies, ceramic tiles, or small washers) the boat will hold without sinking, and then test their boats.
- Students will explain that displacement is a concept involved in whether an object will float or sink.

Correlation with the NSES: As a result of this activity, all students will:
- Develop descriptions, explanations, predictions, and models using evidence (NRC, 1996, p. 145)
- Communicate scientific procedures and explanations (p. 148)

Concepts/Terms: solid, float, sink, capacity, displacement

Science Skills Used: observing, predicting, collecting data, recording data, explaining results

Background: An object floats or sinks because of the amount of liquid (water) it displaces. An object that displaces more water weight than its own weight will float. A one-ton ship will float when it displaces more than one ton of water.

Misconceptions: When you change the shape of a substance such as clay, you change its mass. Objects float or sink because of their weight (mass).

Materials:
- Plastic tubs (one per group)
- Plasticine or water-resistant clay
- Roll of aluminum foil
- Various toy boats
- Pennies, ceramic tiles, or small washers as "cargo"
- Water
- Paper towels

Safety Concerns: None, but watch students as they test their boats in the water.

Grouping Arrangements: Allow each student to construct and test his or her own boat.

Preparation/Prior Setup: Before using, test the clay in water. Some types of clay soften and dissolve when placed in water. Plasticine is usually available in local hobby stores.

Procedure

Engage: Ask students to share their experiences with different objects that float or sink. Show students a lump of clay. Ask students to predict what will happen when you drop the lump of clay into a tub of water. Demonstrate what happens when you drop the clay in a tub of water (it sinks).

Explore: Pass out an equal-sized lump of clay to each student. Challenge students to redesign the clay so it will float when placed in water. Allow students to come to the water tubs in small groups to test their boats. Avoid congestion around the tubs. Challenge students to modify the clayboat so it will hold the greatest number of pennies or tile cargoes. Have students predict and record their number before testing. Record the actual number of pennies the clayboat held before sinking.

Explain: Compare boat shapes and the number of pennies each held. Did some shapes hold more pennies than others? Why? Explain how displacement relates to the boats' ability to float. Introduce the concept of buoyancy. Why is it easier to float in saltwater than fresh water?

Elaborate: Challenge students to design a boat made from a different material (such as aluminum foil). How many pennies can the aluminum foil boat hold before sinking? Test other plastic toy boats to determine how much weight they can hold before sinking. How does the amount and mass of water displaced compare with the mass of the boat and pennies (cargoes)?

Evaluate: Describe the best shape of a boat to hold the most amount of pennies.

EGG OSMOSIS

In *Egg Osmosis*, students will observe the effect of osmosis, water moving across a membrane from a high concentration to a lower concentration. Later, they will design an investigation to test the effect of putting additives in water and its effect on the osmosis process.

Title of Lesson: *Egg Osmosis*

Grade Levels: 6–8

Essential Question: What is osmosis?

Estimated Time: 90 minutes

Lesson Objectives:

- Students will set up a model to demonstrate water moving across a semi-permeable membrane.

- Students will test the effect of putting additives in water and determine effects on the osmosis process.

Correlation with the NSES: As a result of this activity, all students will

- Ask a question about objects and events in the environment (NRC, 1996, p. 122)
- Plan and conduct simple investigations (p. 122)
- Employ simple equipment and tools to gather data and extend the senses (p. 122)
- Use data to construct reasonable explanations (p. 122)
- Communicate investigations and explanations (p. 122)

Concepts/Terms: diffusion, osmosis, semipermeable membrane, high concentration, low concentration, solution, hypertonic solution, hypotonic solution, isotonic solution

Science Skills Used: observing, collecting data, explaining results, experimenting

Background: Water passes through the membrane (osmosis) and enters the egg. The increase of volume of liquid inside the egg causes the yolk to move up and ooze out the straw.

Materials for the Engage Demonstration:

- 1 bottle of perfume

Materials for Each Student:

- 1 egg
- 1 plastic cup
- 1 clear straw
- 1 pin
- Wax or a candle
- Matches

Materials for the Follow-up Investigation:

- Chicken eggs
- Regular or kosher salt
- Sugar or corn syrup
- Artificial sweeteners
- Vinegar

Safety Concerns: Have students wash their hands before and after handling raw eggs to avoid possible salmonella contamination. Some students may have problems working with a sharp pin.

Grouping Arrangements: Allow each student to make his or her own egg osmosis model.

Preparation/Setup: None

Procedure

Engage: Open a bottle of perfume in the front of the room. Ask students, what do you smell? Explain the concepts of diffusion (the movement of molecules from a higher to a lower concentration).

Explore: Pass out an egg to each student. Instruct them to use a pin or small knife to chip away at the bottom (most rounded part) of a raw egg. Ask them to gently remove the outer shell and expose the thin membrane just inside the shell. If any students chip through the membrane, that's okay; they should continue chipping. They can seal the punctured section later with dripping candle wax. Have the students expose about one square centimeter of unpunctured membrane, and seal any punctured sections of the membrane with candle wax. On the top side of the egg (narrowest end), ask the students to puncture a hole with the pin through the shell *and* membrane. The hole should be just large enough to insert a straw. Have them place a straw, about four inches long, into the top hole so the straw is about one or two inches inside the egg. They should use candle wax to seal the straw around the hole. Have them place the egg in a paper cup, fill the paper cup about halfway with water, and set it and the egg aside. After 24 hours, observe what happened.

Explain: Explain the process of osmosis. Provide diagrams to illustrate the process. Compare diffusion with osmosis. Introduce appropriate terms: osmosis, semipermeable membrane, diffusion.

Extend: Design an investigation to test the effect of an additive to the water on the rate of osmosis. Consider the following investigative questions:

- What would happen to the rate of osmosis if various amounts of sugar or corn syrup were added to the water? (Place eggs in separate containers with 100% corn syrup, 75% corn syrup and 25% water, 50% corn syrup and 50% water, 25% corn syrup and 75% water, and 100% water.)
- What would happen to the rate of osmosis if various amounts of artificial sweeteners were added to the water?
- What would happen to the rate of osmosis if various amounts of salt were added to the water?
- What would happen to the rate of osmosis if the straw were not placed through the top of the egg?
- What would happen if a chicken or an ostrich egg were submerged in a container of vinegar for two days? (The vinegar, or acetic acid, dissolves the calcium in the eggshell, leaving the egg white [albumin] and the yolk encased in the membrane.)
- What would happen to the size and mass of a decalcified egg if it were placed in water? In corn syrup? In combinations of water and corn syrup?
- What happens to onion cells when viewed under a microscope and a concentrated salt solution is introduced to the cells?

Evaluate: Students can make a drawing to illustrate the process of osmosis. Students can make a drawing to illustrate three types of solutions—hypotonic, hypertonic, and isotonic—showing the concentration of water molecules inside and outside the cell. Specific terms can be provided by the teacher to be included in the illustration.

INVESTIGATING LIQUIDS

In *Investigating Liquids*, students will explore how different liquids appear on different surfaces. Students will also discover the principles of surface tension and cohesion.

Title of Lesson: *Investigating Liquids*

Grade Levels: 6–8

Essential Question: How do different liquids appear on various surfaces?

Estimated Time: 45–60 minutes

Lesson Objectives:

- Students will observe, test, and record the properties of various liquids on different surfaces.
- Students will understand the principle of cohesion and evaporation.

Correlation with the NSES: As a result of this activity, all students will:

- Think critically and logically to make the relationships between evidence and explanations (NRC, 1996, p. 145)
- Communicate scientific procedures and explanations (p. 148)
- Develop an understanding that a substance has characteristic properties (p. 154)
- Understand that substances often are placed in categories or groups when they react in similar ways (p. 154)

Concepts/Terms: cohesion, evaporation, surface tension

Science Skills Used: observing, communicating, predicting, inferring, interpreting data, experimenting, constructing models

Background: The water and alcohol drops will appear differently on the wax paper. Water, having a greater force of cohesion, will form a high, round drop. The alcohol, having less cohesion, will form a low, flat drop. Both drops will form flatter drops on the aluminum foil.

Misconceptions: Students may think that the color of the liquid affects its behavior or properties.

Materials: (for a group of two or three students)

- 1 small plastic cup one-quarter filled with water and two drops of red food coloring
- 1 small plastic cup one-quarter filled with 70% isopropyl alcohol and two drops of blue food coloring
- 2 eyedroppers (one in each cup)
- 1 sheet of wax paper (about 10 × 10 inches)
- 1 sheet of aluminum foil (about 10 × 10 inches)
- 1 sheet of clear plastic wrap (about 10 × 10 inches)
- 1 sheet of paper towel
- 1 piece of clear glass or mirror
- Various rulers, timers, magnifying lens, and Styrofoam trays (optional)

Safety Concerns: Isopropyl alcohol is flammable. Keep away from any open flame. Using safety goggles is suggested.

Grouping Arrangements: Place students in groups of two's or three's.

Preparation/Prior Setup: In one set of cups, pour 10-20 mL of water. Add two drops of red food coloring. In the second set of cups, pour 10-20 mL of 70% rubbing alcohol. Add two drops of blue food coloring. Place an eyedropper in each cup.

Procedure

Engage: Assess prior knowledge by posing the following questions: What do you know about puddles? Where do you find puddles? (for example, on cars and sidewalks after rain, under air conditioners, on ceilings, under dripping faucets). Make a concept map of students' prior understanding.

Draw a cross-section of a puddle. Draw a bird's-eye view of a puddle. Compare drawings.

Explore: Allow students to explore and "mess about" by making and mixing drops of the two liquids on the wax paper and aluminum foil. Compare and contrast the drops and puddles. Mix drops together. On the aluminum foil, add a drop of red liquid to the blue. Then add a drop of blue to the red. Repeat the same procedure on the wax paper. Why do the liquids act differently on the aluminum foil than on the wax paper? Have students record their observations in their journals or on a T-chart. Pose the following questions:

- How do the size, shape, and behavior of the blue and red liquids compare?
- Do the drops or puddles look differently on the wax paper than on the aluminum foil?
- What would happen if you made drops on the paper towel?
- What happens when you add the blue liquid to the red liquid?
- What happens when you place drops on the clear plastic wrap? On the Styrofoam tray?

Make a diagram or chart to compare differences. Place observations on poster paper and share with the class.

	Red	*Blue*
Smell	no smell	strong smell
Swish in plastic cup	liquid stays up on side	liquid drips down
Drops on side of glass	forms drops	no drops
Splash test	forms ripples	forms ripples
Ink test	draws ink out of pen	does not draw ink out
Puddle races	moves slowly	moves quickly
On wax paper		
On aluminum foil		
On Styrofoam plate		
Red drop on blue		
Blue drop on red		

Explain: Discuss the behavior of the red and blue liquids on the different surfaces. Build a model to explain how drops behave. Contrast cohesion versus adhesion. Explain why waxing your car causes puddles to form. Pose the questions: Does a puddle need a depression or hole to form? Where do puddles go after a rain?

Extend: Have additional materials available: motor oil, corn syrup, liquid soap, vinegar, glycerin, mineral oil, thermometers, kosher salt flakes, ice, aluminum plates, paper plates, glass plates, Styrofoam plates, different U.S. coins, overhead light source, rubber comb, piece of wool or rabbit's fur. Allow students to design their own investigations from their original liquid explorations.

Students can consider the following investigations or ones of their own designs:

- Do the liquids act differently on the shiny side than on the dull side of aluminum foil?
- How do other liquids behave on wax paper, aluminum foil, and clear transparent wrap?
- Place the differently colored liquids on an inclined glass plate. How do red and blue drops compare in drop races? How do they compare with other liquids?
- Predict how many drops of red and blue liquid will fit on the head of a penny. Predict how many drops of red liquid will fit on the tail of a penny. Predict how many drops of red liquid will fit on the head of a nickel. On a dime. On a quarter.
- Test the effect of height on "splat-ability" (dropping liquids from different heights). Test the effect of different surfaces on "splat-ability."
- Do the red drops evaporate faster or slower than the blue drops?
- How does sunlight affect the time it takes for water drops to evaporate?
- Are the liquid "puddles" attracted by static electricity?

Evaluate: Would a water spider be able to stand easier on the red liquid or on the blue liquid? Explain your answer.

SCIENCE PROCESS SKILL STATIONS

In *Science Process Skill Stations*, students will develop an ability to use basic science skills, the tools used in carrying out scientific experiments and investigations. Students will work in pairs and rotate to each station in any order, follow the directions provided, complete the task, and record all data and measurements in their science journals.

Title of Lesson: *Science Process Skill Stations*

Grade Levels: 3–6

Essential Question: What are science process skills?

Estimated Time: 45–60 minutes

Lesson Objectives:
- Students will follow directions and complete a task
- Students will collect and record data or measurements for each task

Correlation with the NSES: As a result of this activity, all students will
- Employ simple equipment and tools to gather data and extend the senses (NRC, 1996, p. 122)
- Use data to construct reasonable explanations (p. 122)
- Communicate investigations and explanations (p. 122)

Science Skills Used: observing, classifying, communicating, measuring, inferring, predicting, hypothesizing, interpreting data, experimenting, and constructing models

Background: Teachers should be familiar with the definition and description of each science skill. Teachers should also be familiar with the behaviors associated with each skill. Consult a science resource for additional information.

Safety Concerns: None

Grouping Arrangements: Allow students to work in pairs.

Preparation/Prior Setup: Provide students with the directions for each task or place the task directions at each station. Label each station by its number. Provide paper towels for stations using water.

Station 1: The Penny

Materials:

- 2 eyedroppers
- 1 small cup of water
- Assorted pennies (U.S., Canadian, new, old)
- Other assorted coins (nickel, dime, quarter)
- Paper towels

Procedure:

1. Fill the eyedropper with water.

2. Hold the dropper over the penny. Gently squeeze the eyedropper.

Questions to Investigate:

- How many drops of water do you think can fit on the head of a penny? Record that number in your science journal.
- Use an eyedropper to drop water on the head of a clean, dry penny. Record the number of drops the penny can hold before spilling over the side. Was there a difference between the number of drops you thought the penny could hold and the actual number?

Inquiring Further:

- Will the penny hold more or fewer drops on the head or the tail side?
- Will the penny hold more or fewer drops if it is dirty and oily?
- Will a Lincoln penny hold more or fewer drops than a "wheat" penny?
- Will a U.S. penny hold more or fewer drops than a Canadian penny?
- How many drops will a nickel hold?
- How many drops will a quarter hold?

Station 2: The Cartesian Diver

Materials:

- 1 Cartesian diver (Instructions for building a diver can be found in Resource F.)

Procedure:

1. Gently squeeze the sides of the bottle. What happens to the diver?

2. Explain in a brief paragraph how the Cartesian diver works. Include an illustration or model to explain what's happening.

Inquiring Further:
- How is the Cartesian diver like a submarine?
- How is the Cartesian diver like a swim bladder of a fish?

Station 3: Milk Cartons

Materials:
- 6 milk cartons, labeled 1–6, each containing one small object, such as: a rubber ball, a AAA dry cell battery, a domino, a marble, a small Styrofoam ball, or a penny
- 6 clear plastic bags, each containing one of the contents of the milk cartons

Procedure:
1. Without opening the cartons (although shaking is allowed), place each bag in front of the milk carton that you think shares the same object.
2. Record your conclusions by matching the item to the carton number.
3. Before leaving the station, remove the bags from the front of the milk cartons.

Station 4: Screws

Materials:
- 1 clear bag of 15 assorted screws and bolts
- 1 Styrofoam or paper plate (the kind with dividers into three sections, 1 large and 2 small)

Procedure:
1. Place all the screws in the large area of the Styrofoam plate.
2. Divide the screws into two groups.
3. Place each group in the smaller areas of the plate.
4. Explain in your journal why you divided the screws the way you did.

Inquiring Further:
- What other properties can you use to divide the screws?

Station 5: Magnets

Materials:
- 1 magnet
- A container of 10–15 assorted magnetic and nonmagnetic objects

Procedure:
1. Look at all the objects in the container.
2. Individually, predict whether or not you think each object will be attracted to a magnet.
3. Record your predictions by writing in your science journal "Magnetic" or "Not magnetic" alongside the name of the object.
4. Share your predictions with your partner.
5. One at a time, test each object to see whether it is magnetic or not.
6. Make a data table and record your results.

Inquiring Further:
- Test 10–15 other objects in the classroom.
- Record whether they are magnetic or not.

Station 6: Float or Sink

Materials:
- 1 half-gallon container of water
- 10–15 assorted objects to be tested (e.g., candle, domino, button, metal washer, plastic washer, cork, sponge, paper clip, pumice, small rock)
- Paper towels

Procedure:
1. Look at all the objects in the container.
2. Individually, write whether you think each object will float or sink when placed in a tub of water.
3. Record your predictions by placing in your science journal an "F" or "S" alongside the name of the object.
4. Share your predictions with your partner.
5. One at a time, test each object to see whether it floats or sinks.
6. Make a data table and record your results.

Inquiring Further:
- What would happen if you tested the objects in saltwater?
- What would happen if you tested the objects in rubbing alcohol?

Station 7: Touch Squares

Materials:
- 1 touch square sheet (see Resource G)
- 1 hand timer or a clock or watch with a second hand

Procedure:
1. One partner will be the "timer" and the other will be the "toucher."
2. When the timer says, "Go," the toucher will touch each square in numerical order from 1 to 15 using his or her dominant hand.
3. The timer will record the number of seconds it takes the toucher to touch all 15 squares in order.
4. Repeat Step 2 five times. Record each trial in your science journal.
5. Switch roles with your partner.
6. Find your average reaction time.
7. Who had the faster reaction time?

Inquiring Further:
- What would happen to your reaction time if you used your nondominant hand?

- Do girls have a faster reaction time than boys?
- Do students have a faster reaction time than teachers?

Station 8: Reaction time

Materials:

- 12-inch ruler

Procedure:

1. Have the first partner make a horizontal "C" with his or her index finger and thumb.

2. The other partner will hold a ruler with the "0" end just above the partner's gap in the C.

3. When the ruler is dropped, the first partner will catch the ruler with his or her finger and thumb.

4. Record the number where the ruler was caught.

5. Repeat this five times.

6. Find your average.

7. Exchange roles with your partner.

8. Compare reaction times.

Inquiring further:

- What would happen to your reaction time if you used your nondominant hand?
- Do girls have a faster reaction time than boys?
- Do students have a faster reaction time than teachers?

Station 9: Bubbles

Materials:

- 12-inch ruler or centimeter ruler
- 1 small cup of bubble solution (made from liquid soap)
- 1 small cup of water
- Several straws

Procedure:

1. Spread some bubble solution on the table top.
2. Dip a straw into the bubble solution and place the soapy end of the straw on the surface of the table.
3. Gently blow to form a bubble on the table top.
4. Keep blowing until the bubble pops and leaves a ring on the tabletop.
5. Use a ruler to determine the distance across the ring (the diameter).
6. Practice blowing a bubble three more times.
7. After three practices make three more bubble rings.
8. Record your results and find the average distance.
9. Compare your average to your partner's average.

Inquiring Further:

- What if you used different soap brands? (e.g., Ivory, Joy, Palmolive, or a generic brand)
- How does adding glycerin or corn syrup affect the size of the bubble?
- Does the wetness of the table top affect the size of the bubble?
- How can you blow a bubble inside a bubble?
- How can you make a chain of bubbles like a caterpillar?

Station 10: Mystery Box

Materials:

- 1 shoebox containing 1 small marble and 2 wooden square blocks glued to the bottom of the box. (Glue the blocks so they are flush against opposite walls of the box as shown in Figure 11.2.) Tape the lid of the box shut.

Procedure:

1. Tilt the mystery box back and forth. Listen to the sound that is made.

2. Inside the box are two small square blocks. Without opening the box, determine where the two blocks are located.

3. Draw a diagram or model to show where you think the two blocks are located.

Inquiring Further:

- Glue a magnet inside another mystery box. Tape the lid of the box shut. Use a compass to determine where the magnet is located.

Figure 11.2 Interior of Mystery Box

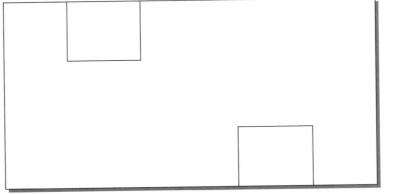

STIRRING THE ALPHABET

In *Stirring the Alphabet*, students will explore concepts in refraction and reflection and design investigations to explore the interaction of light with other materials.

Title of Lesson: *Stirring the Alphabet*

Grade Levels: 5–8

Essential Question: How does light interact with objects?

Estimated Time: 30–60 minutes

Lesson Objectives:

- Students will observe and record the transmission of light as it interacts with matter, such as a lens, a hollow tube, or a mirror.
- Student will formulate questions to investigate.
- Students will distinguish between refraction and reflection.

Correlation with the NSES: As a result of this activity, all students will:

- Identify questions that can be answered through scientific investigations (NRC, 1996, p. 145)
- Design and conduct a scientific investigation (p. 145)
- Use appropriate tools and techniques to gather, analyze, and interpret data (p. 145)
- Develop descriptions, explanations, predictions, and models using evidence (p. 145)
- Think critically and logically to understand the relationships between evidence and explanations (p. 145)
- Understand that light interacts with matter by transmission (including refraction), absorption, or scattering (including reflection) (p. 155).

Concepts/Terms: light, refraction, reflection, absorption, rays

Science Skills Used: observing, communicating, inferring, interpreting data, experimenting, constructing models

Background: As the light travels through the stirring rod (the lens), light is refracted and the image is inverted. The uppercase letters are symmetrical (top to bottom), so inverted letters appear to look uninverted. All lowercase letters and words are not symmetrical, so they appear inverted. The color of the word, being either red or blue, has nothing to do with the appearance of the inversion. By placing a line under the statement and viewing the statement through a stirring rod, you can see that all the words and letters actually do invert.

Misconceptions: Students may think that the color determines whether the letters will invert or not.

Materials: (for each student)

- 6-inch clear glass stirring rod
- 6-inch piece of flexible vinyl tubing with a ¼-inch inside diameter
- Strip of paper with the words: HIDE the BIKE from DEBBIE
- Optional materials: mirrors, triangular prisms, various sized plastic cylinders with different diameters, clear plastic straws, four-color pens, clear water, blue-colored water, red-colored water, test tubes with stoppers, red and blue overhead acetate sheets, 3-D glasses

Safety Concerns: None, but watch to make sure no glass rods are dropped and broken.

Figure 11.3   Photo of Stirring Rod on Paper

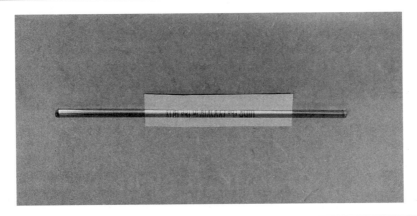

Grouping Arrangements: If space and materials permit, allow students to work individually.

Preparation/Prior Setup: Prepare 1x4 inch paper strips with the statement "HIDE the BIKE from DEBBIE." The uppercase words HIDE, BIKE, and DEBBIE should be in red. The lowercase words "the" and "from" should be in blue. Place a stirring rod, a 6-inch piece of flexible tubing, and a strip of "HIDE the BIKE from DEBBIE" paper in a small baggie. Have the optional materials ready to prompt other questions and inquiries.

Procedure:
- Tell students to place the stirring rod directly on the letters of the strip of paper, so the rod is lying over the words and statement (see Figure 11.3).
- Ask the students, What do you observe? Tell students to share their observations with a partner.
- Tell students to roll the stirring rod up and down across the strip of paper. What do they observe now? Have students share their observations again with a partner and then with the entire class.
- Tell students to raise the stirring rod about one-half inch above the letters. What do they observe now?
- Encourage students to test the flexible plastic tubing. Does the tubing make the letters invert? What would happen if the stirring rod were placed inside the flexible tubing?
- Prompt students to use a mirror. Does a mirror make the letters invert?
- Pose the following questions to students:
  When looking through the stirring rod, why are some letters inverted and others not?
  Does the color have anything to do with the inversion of the letters?
  How can you use a four-color pen to find out if the color of the words makes a difference?
  Why do lowercase letters invert and the uppercase do not?
  What is it about the letters that make them appear to invert?
  Which uppercase letters invert? Which lowercase letters invert?
  Do numbers invert?

Would the tubing invert the letters if a stirring rod were placed in it?
How does the diameter of the rod determine the focal length?
What would happen if you filled a straw with water? Would it make the letters invert?
Do the lenses in your eyeglasses invert letters?

For Further Investigations:

1. Provide sets of four test tubes to each group of students. Test tube A contains red-colored water and a stopper. Test tube B contains blue-colored water and a stopper. Test tube C contains clear water and a stopper. Test tube D is empty with a stopper. Prompt students to look at the red and blue words through the four different tubes and investigate their questions. Have students use drawings to record their findings and evidence. Use the evidence to form explanations. Have students communicate their findings and form a model about light on the basis of the explanations.

2. Look at the words on the strip of paper through a red and a blue overhead acetate sheet. Can you see the red letter through a red sheet? What do the red letters look like through a blue sheet? Look at the letters through 3-D glasses. Close one eye at a time. Can you see any difference? (Note: You may have to use your computer and printer to vary the color level and adjust the quality of the intensity of the red and blue letters to match the acetate sheet and 3-D glasses.)

Assessment Strategies:

- Have students use a three-column chart to make a list of observations, questions, and explanations during the investigation.
- Have students make a Venn diagram to compare and contrast refraction and reflection.
- Have students write their first name in "code" so it appears upright when viewed through a stirring rod.
- Have students explain how the lens in their eye works. Why is the image formed on the retina inverted? If that is true, why don't we see all images upside down?
- Have students write a reflection in their student journals about the observations made and the questions raised, and explanations formulated.
- Prepare multiple-choice questions containing misconceptions as distracters.
- Use a *Science Inquiry Monitoring Chart* (see Chapter 8) to record observed inquiry skills during the investigation.
- Provide strips of paper, each containing a term or phrase about refraction and reflection. Have students then use the strips to prepare a concept map on "The interaction of light with materials" and explain the order of the map.

The assessment for this exploration can also be divided into pre-, during-, and post-activity assessments:

Pre-lesson Assessment Strategies:

1. On a separate sheet of paper or in their science journals, ask students to write down what they know about the words refraction and reflection. Have students read their responses aloud. Prepare a concept map of their

responses (prior understandings) on a large sheet of poster paper. Record their responses in one color. Keep the paper posted visible in the room. During the exploration, allow students to add statements to the concept map using a second color. After the exploration, repeat the task and add new responses (newly constructed knowledge) to the concept map with a third color to show pre- and post-understandings of the concept.

2. Fill a large, two-liter glass beaker with water. Look at a face through the beaker. Describe the appearance of the face. Why does the face look distorted? Pose the question: What would you predict the face would look like if the beaker were empty?

During the Lesson Assessment Strategies:

1. Tell students to record their observations, questions, and explanations on a three-column chart (provided, see Figure 11.4) or in their science journals.

2. Use the science inquiry monitoring chart (see Chapter 8) to record observed inquiry skills.

Post-Lesson Assessment Strategies:

1. Explain how the lens in your eye works. Why is the image on your retina said to be inverted? If that is true, why don't we see all images upside down?

2. Provide strips of paper each containing a term or phrase about refraction and reflection. Have students use the strips to prepare a concept map and explain the order of the map.

3. Have students write a reflection in their science journals about the observations, explanations, and models formulated.

4. Have students make a Venn diagram to compare and contrast refraction and reflection.

5. Have students write their first name in "code" so it appears upright when viewed through a stirring rod.

6. Provide multiple-choice questions containing the misconception as a distracter. For example:
   When viewed through a raised stirring rod, letters appear inverted because
   a. the light rays stop moving.
   b. the light rays are bent.
   c. the light rays bounce back.
   d. of the color of the letters.

   A flat mirror produces an image that is
   a. right-side up.
   b. upside down.
   c. smaller than the actual size.
   d. larger than the actual size.

7. Place a pencil in a glass filled three-fourths with water. Ask students to describe the appearance of the pencil. Why does the pencil appear to be broken? (see Figure 11.5)

Figure 11.4   Recording Chart

Recording Chart		
Observations	*Questions*	*Explanations*

Figure 11.5   Pencil in a Glass of Water

8. Hold the pencil vertically in the center of the glass. Make an observation. Place the pencil against the edge of the glass. Compare the first situation to the second. Fill a second glass with regular Wesson oil. Place a clear stirring rod into the glass. Compare this situation with the pencil in the water.

9. Pose the following situation: Paulo likes to go spear fishing. He goes down to the local bay and sees a fish swimming in the water. Paulo tries to spear the fish but keeps missing. What concept about light is Paulo not considering while he is spear fishing?

10. Place a penny in the bottom of a glass beaker three-fourths filled with water. Place a second penny on the table alongside the beaker. Have students make observations and write an explanation of what they observe.

THE THING

In *The Thing*, students will act as anthropologists removing a "preserved" specimen from a plaster of paris "rock." Students will give a three- to five-minute oral presentation to explain the classification scheme developed for The Thing.

Title of Lesson: *The Thing*

Grade Levels: 6–8

Essential Questions: How do anthropologists makes inferences from fossils and preserved specimens? How are new specimens classified according to the existing taxonomy system?

Estimated Time: 3–5 days

Lesson Objectives:

- Students will remove a specimen from a plaster of paris "rock" and identify the characteristics of the specimen
- Students will use the present taxonomy system to develop a means to classify The Thing and assign a scientific name to the specimen
- Students will provide a rationale for their scientific name and present their new classification of the specimen to the class

Correlation with the NSES: As a result of this activity, all students will:

- Use appropriate tools and techniques to gather, analyze, and interpret data (NRC, 1996, p. 145)
- Develop descriptions, explanations, predictions, and models using evidence (p. 145)
- Think critically and logically to infer relationships between evidence and explanations (p. 145)
- Communicate scientific procedures and explanations (p. 145)
- Understand that species acquire many unique characteristics through biological adaptation, which involves the selection of naturally occurring variations in populations (p. 158)

Concepts/Terms: classification, taxonomy, invertebrates, anthropology, fossils, sedimentary rock, impressions, phylum, class, genus, species

Science Skills Used: observing, measuring, communicating, inferring, collecting data, recording data, explaining results, constructing models

Background: Fossils provide a story to animals and plants existing long ago. Anthropologists carefully remove specimens from the surrounding rock to expose the remains or imprint of the organism. Students need prior experience with measuring mass and length. This may be the first time students have used a classification key. Additional instruction may be necessary.

Misconceptions:

- Fossils can be found in all types of rock.
- Fossils are pieces of dead plants and animals that have not decayed.

Materials:

- Plaster of paris "rock" containing The Thing (1 per group)
- Plastic kitty litter pan (1 per group)
- Small hammers, screwdrivers, or chisels
- PAM cooking spray
- Eye goggles (1 pair per student)
- Dilute ammonium chloride (optional)
- Eyedroppers
- Small brushes or toothbrushes
- Cloth and paper towels
- Triple beam balances
- Measuring rulers
- Colored pencils or crayons
- Resources on invertebrate classification

Safety Concerns: Students should wear protective eye goggles while chipping the plaster of paris. The teacher should demonstrate the proper procedure for chipping and using dilute ammonium chloride.

Grouping Arrangements: Students will work in pairs.

Preparation/Prior Setup: Several days before the start of the unit, the teacher will make "rock" samples for each group containing The Thing (see Figure 11.6). (This particular object was originally found and purchased in a toy store in upstate New York. The object was chosen for the activity because of the characteristics resembling several invertebrates. The Thing is black [like a spider], has three body parts [like an insect], has 10 legs [like a crustacean], and has spiny skin [like an echinoderm]). Although the exact same toy may not be available in stores in your area, you can substitute other unusual-looking, plastic animals. Rocks are made by mixing a small batch of plaster of paris, following the directions on the package. Fill the bottom third of a half-gallon cardboard milk carton with the plaster of paris. Coat the outer body of The Thing with PAM cooking spray. The spray will allow easy removal of the plaster from the specimen. Place The Thing on top of the plaster of paris and cover the specimen completely with the remaining amount of plaster. Be sure The Thing is covered with at least one-half inch of plaster. Set aside to harden. Make enough samples for each group of students. Brown food coloring and gravel can be added to the "rock" for effect.

Procedure

Introduce students to the task. Tell students they will play the role of anthropologists. Samples of rock have been discovered in the jungles of Brazil and it's believed that the samples contain a species of animal that has been extinct for 50 million years. Their task is to carefully remove the specimen from the rock and make calculations and measurements concerning the new species. Students may use a brush and dilute ammonium chloride to dissolve pieces of the plaster of paris from the specimen.

Figure 11.6   Photo of The Thing

Because students tend to smash the rock with a hammer, the teacher should provide directions and guidance for the proper technique for chipping away the plaster. Instruct students on the proper technique anthropologists use to remove fossils and specimens from rock.

Students will list the characteristics of the specimen and find similarities to insects, crustaceans, arachnids, and echinoderms.

Students will use the present taxonomy system to develop a means to classify the new specimen. If necessary, a new phylum or class may be developed and assigned to the specimen. Each group will devise an appropriate scientific name of the organism and present their new classification to the annual convention of the *American Invertebrate Association*. Students will give a three- to five-minute oral presentation to the class describing how they classified The Thing.

Prompting Questions

Select fragments of the plaster from the pan that contain impressions of the specimen. Ask students to examine the impressions. Pose the question, How are the fragments like the rock surrounding the fossil? Have students identify the body part of the specimen from the impression in the fragment.

Explain how sediments form sedimentary rock. Pose the questions, Why are fossils only found in this type of rock? Why aren't fossils found in metamorphic or igneous rock?

Resource A

Resources for Teachers

When you make a commitment to become an inquiry-based teacher, you make a commitment to promote your intellectual and professional development throughout your entire, ongoing teaching career. Professional growth can come in the form of reading; attending workshops, summer institutes, or seminars; taking graduate-level courses; or collaborating and exchanging ideas through support groups and online forums.

For some, this book is the beginning of an exploration into inquiry. For others, it is one of many resources shaping the construction of your understanding of inquiry. The purpose of this section is to familiarize science teachers with some of the many resources available on inquiry-related topics at the elementary and middle school levels. Organized by topics, this annotated bibliography serves to provide suggested reading and resources for ongoing professional growth. Each resource is assigned one or more suggested levels:

PS (preservice)

N (novice)

P (professional)

M (mastery)

For those leading a summer workshop or institute on inquiry or those developing a library of inquiry-based science resources, it is suggested to make available to participants as many of the following resources as possible. For other science- and inquiry-related books and resources, you may also easily search through NSTA Recommends (http://www2.nsta.org/recommends/), an online list of recommended books and resources on a variety of topics in science education and teaching. Several of the annotated bibliographies for the following resources were taken from NSTA Recommends.

Highly recommended books, identified with a "thumbs-up" icon (👍), have been selected as a starting point for professional reading or creating a library collection on scientific inquiry.

PRINT RESOURCES ON
INQUIRY-BASED TEACHING

8 Essentials of Inquiry-Based Science, K-8 (2006)
Elizabeth Hammerman
Corwin Press, ISBN 1-4129-1499-X

The book provides eight important components for developing inquiry-based programs and professional development opportunities. Level = P, M

Inquiry-Based Learning: Using Everyday Objects (2003)
Amy Edmonds Alvarado and Patricia Herr
Corwin Press, ISBN 0-7619-4680-2

The authors present an interdisciplinary theme, "Object-Based Learning," hands-on instructional strategies that promote active learning in Grades 3–8. After an introduction to object-based inquiry, the authors provide ways to plan and assess active learning. Sample lessons are offered in language arts, science, social studies, and math. Level = PS, N, P

👍 *Becoming a Reflective Educator: How to Build a Culture of Inquiry in the Schools* (2nd ed., 2002)
Timothy Reagan, Charles Case, and John Brubacher
Corwin Press, ISBN 0-7619-7553-5

Although this book is not specifically for science teachers, through examples and case studies, it paints a picture of school culture, inquiry, and reflective practice. The book is appropriate for teacher-leaders, science department heads, curriculum supervisors, and administrators. Level = P, M

Integrating Inquiry Across the Curriculum
Richard Audet and Linda Jordan, Editors
Corwin Press, ISBN 1-4129-0617-2

A collection of articles from experts on best-practice strategies and research-based suggestions to integrate inquiry throughout the core academic areas: social studies, science, history, mathematics, and language arts. Assessment is discussed, as is teaching inquiry to special needs students and second language learners. Level = N, P, M

Children's Inquiry: Using Language to Make Sense of the World (1999)
Judith Wells Lindfors
Teachers College Press, ISBN 0-8077-3836-0

With an in-depth look at inquiry as a classroom culture, this is an excellent resource for experienced elementary school teachers integrating language development and collaborative dialogue with scientific inquiry. Level = P, M

👍*Doing Good Science in Middle School: A Practical Guide to Inquiry-Based Instruction* (2004)
Olaf Jorgenson, Jackie Cleveland, and Rick Vanosdall
National Science Teachers Association, ISBN 0-87355-232-6

A practical, "how-to" guide for middle level science. The book offers suggestions for implementing the 5E model as well as discussions of classroom management, safety, integration with math and technology, and 10 developmentally appropriate inquiry activities. Level = PS, N, P

👍*Inquiry and the National Science Education Standards: A Guide for Teaching and Learning* (2000)
National Research Council
National Academy Press, ISBN 0-309-06476-7

A comprehensive guide for implementing inquiry in the science classroom. Excellent reading to accompany the National Science Education Standards. Contains useful strategies for teachers and numerous vignettes as examples. Level = PS, N, P

👍 *Inquiring Into Inquiry Learning and Teaching in Science* (2000)
James Minstrell and Emily Van Zee, Editors
American Association for the Advancement of Science, ISBN 0-87168-641-4

An excellent and comprehensive collection of articles that will appeal to the experienced inquiry teacher or teacher-leader. Level = P, M

Inquiry Teaching in the Sciences (2004)
Barry Fox, Terri Grosso, and Phyllis Tashlik
Teachers College Press, ISBN 0-8077-4565-0

With a blend of pedagogical suggestions and vignettes, this book follows middle and high school science teachers through their inquiry-based units. Level = PS, N, P

Organizing Wonder: Making Inquiry Science Work in the Elementary School (1998)
Jody Hall, with Carol Callahan, Helen Kitchel, Patricia Pierce, and Pedie O'Brien
Heinemann, ISBN 0-325-00045-X

Hall, in collaboration with the other authors/teachers, presents seven steps in encouraging students to engage in science through inquiry investigations. Each of the four collaborating authors provides classroom vignettes that describe students conducting scientific investigations. The foreword was written by Dr. Wynne Harlen, internationally renowned for her work and research in inquiry-based learning. Level = N, P

Beyond the Science Kit: Inquiry in Action (1996)
Wendy Saul and Jeanne Reardon, Editors
Heinemann, ISBN 0-435-07102-5

Saul and Reardon, in collaboration with other authors/teachers, present essays that show teachers how to use science kits as starting points for engaging students in inquiry investigations. Each of the collaborating authors provides classroom case studies and vignettes that describe how inquiry happens in the classroom. One essay provides an alternative to the typical science fair: "A Kids' Inquiry Conference." Level = N, P

Nurturing Inquiry: Real Science for the Elementary Classroom (1999)
Charles Pierce
Heinemann, ISBN 0-325-00135-9

This book looks into one teacher's classroom and shows how inquiry is sustained throughout the entire school year. Part 1 introduces the reader to how Pierce prepares his room, the student, and himself for an inquiry-based unit of study. Part 2 explains how the "fire" is sustained through the year, and Part 3 provides assessment strategies that complement inquiry instruction. Level = N, P

👍 *Inquiry at the Window: Pursuing the Wonder of Learners* (1997)
Phyllis Whitin and David Whitin
Heinemann, ISBN 0-435-07131-9

In this book, teacher Phyllis Whitin shows the reader how an event as simple as observing birds outside a classroom window led to an ongoing investigation about behavior and eating habits. As the students conduct their investigations, the author paints a picture of the importance to any inquiry investigation of making observations and recording data. The study shows how one science inquiry can lead to an interdisciplinary focus. Level = N, P

The Challenge and Promise of K-8 Science Education Reform (Foundations Monograph Series, Vol. 1, 1997)
National Science Foundation

A free beginner's guide (available at http://www.nsf.gov/ in PDF format) to science education reform and the importance of inquiry. Provides introductory reading on leadership, curriculum, instruction, assessment, and professional development. Level = PS, N

👍 *Inquiry: Thoughts, Views, and Strategies for the K–5 Classroom* (Foundations Monograph Series, Vol. 2, 1999)
National Science Foundation

A free monograph primer (available at http://www.nsf.gov/ in PDF format) on science inquiry. Provides introductory information on inquiry teaching. Level = PS, N

👍 *Primary Science: Taking the Plunge* (2nd ed., 2001)
Wynne Harlen, Editor
Heinemann, ISBN 0-325-00386-6

One of the best books on how to help children raise questions, observe and record their work, and plan scientific investigations. The authors' considerable experience in constructivist principles and inquiry-based instruction makes this book practical as well as research based. The chapters on "children's questions" and "planning investigations" are especially helpful. This book has ongoing usefulness; you will refer to it repeatedly. Level = PS, N, P, M

👍 *Teaching and Learning Primary Science* (2nd ed., 1993)
Wynne Harlen
Paul Chapman, ISBN 1-85396-185-X

With a research-based approach, Harlen takes the reader through the development of how children learn science and the ideas they bring to classrooms. In this second edition, the roles of language and process skills are addressed in relation to how they facilitate children's thinking in science. Additional topics include the role of the teacher and assessment strategies. This book is an excellent follow-up to Harlen's *Primary Science: Taking the Plunge*, listed immediately above. Level = PS, N, P, M

Teaching High School Science Through Inquiry: A Case Study Approach (2005)
Douglas Llewellyn
Corwin Press, ISBN 0-7619-3938-5

Although the book is written for Grades 9–12, middle school teachers may find the case studies appropriate for their students. Level = PS, N, P

Theme Immersion: Inquiry-Based Curriculum in Elementary and Middle Schools (1994)
Maryann Manning, Gary Manning, and Roberta Long
Heinemann, ISBN 0-435-08806-8

For teachers who have established inquiry-based classrooms and want to take the next step of integrating inquiry with thematic units, this is an excellent resource. According to the authors, theme immersion is an "in-depth study of a topic, issue or question." By combining inquiry and a thematic approach, the authors provide practical suggestions for planning and implementing theme immersion units. Level = N, P, M

Developing Inquiry-Based Science Materials (2001)
Hebert Their, with Bennett Daviss
Teachers College Press, ISBN 0-8077-4123-X

This volume focuses on the process of designing and implementing a material-based science program. Other topics, such as guiding students through inquiries, constructivism, and assessment, provide interesting reading for experienced teachers, teacher-leaders, and science curriculum coordinators. Level = P, M

Inquiry and Learning: Realizing Science Standards in the Classroom (1996)
John Layman
The College Board, ISBN 0-87447-547-3

A brief overview for teachers new to inquiry. Appropriate for upper elementary and middle level teachers. Level = PS, N

PRINT RESOURCES ON INQUIRY INVESTIGATIONS

Taking Inquiry Outdoors: Reading, Writing, and Science Beyond the Classroom Walls (2000)
Barbara Bourne, Editor
Stenhouse, ISBN 1-57110-302-3

Vignettes and reflections by elementary and middle school master teachers and educators who use the natural environment as an extension of the classroom. Their journals and stories provide enriching ways to integrate inquiry-based science with reading, writing, and listening skills. Level = N, P, M

Inquiry Into Action (2nd ed., 2005)
American Chemical Society, ISBN 0-8412-3935-4

Seven sets of physical science investigations for students in Grades 3–6. Topics include chemical changes, states of matter, density, mixtures, and solutions. Each set of investigations includes a correlation with the national standards, background information for the teacher, step-by-step instructions, and activity sheets for students. Level = PS, N, P

Biology Investigations: Standards-Based Labs, Assessments, and Discussion Lessons (2006)
Martin Shields
Jossey-Bass, ISBN 0-7879-7652-0

> Chapters 1 and 2 provide an overview of inquiry and constructivism. Chapters 3–9 provide investigations on the cell, heredity, evolution, interdependence, living systems, the behavior of organisms, and social perspectives in science. Although designed for Grades 7–12, middle school teachers with average and high-ability students will find the investigations appropriate for their classes. Level = N, P, M

Science as Inquiry (2000)
Jack Hassard
Good Year Books, ISBN 0-673-57731-7

> An excellent resource for upper elementary and middle school teachers looking for a complete guide to direct active learning and project-based activities. Contains Web sites and assessment strategies to promote inquiry-based learning. Level = PS, N

The Pillbug Project (1999)
Robin Burnett
NSTA Press, ISBN 0-87355-109-5

> According to NSTA, this book is organized around 10 days of practical activities that help children explore, through inquiry, an organism's life cycle. Level = PS, N, P, M

PRINT RESOURCES ON CONSTRUCTIVISM

Constructivism in Education (1995)
Leslie Steffe and Jerry Gale, Editors
Lawrence Erlbaum, ISBN 0-8058-1096-X

> This book is recommended for those with an established understanding of constructivism. The chapters provide extensive background into the research and philosophy of constructivist principles. The introductory chapter by von Glasersfeld is interesting reading. Level = P, M

Using the Learning Cycle to Teach Physical Science: A Hands-On Approach for the Middle Grades (1996)
Paul Beinherz and Marylou Dantonio
Heinemann, ISBN 0-435-08376-7

> After a brief description of the learning cycle, the authors provide sample lessons on seven physical science topics ranging from Bernoulli's principle to surface tension. Level = N, P

Targeting Students' Science Misconceptions: Physical Science Activities Using the Conceptual Change Model (1994)
Joseph Stepans
Idea Factory, ISBN 1-885041-00-4

The book begins with a brief discussion on misconceptions and conceptual change, followed by sample lessons on 15 physical science topics ranging from matter to light and color. Level = N, P

The Learning Cycle: Elementary School Science and Beyond (1997)
Edmund Marek and Ann Cavallo
Heinemann, ISBN 0-435-07133-5

The authors provide a theoretical framework that includes references to the work of Piaget, Ausubel, and Vygotsky. Whether you use the 3E or 5E format, the Learning Cycle includes strategies for integrating constructivism and inquiry into your science lessons. The book also includes sample science lessons for elementary classrooms that could easily be extended to the middle level grades. Level = PS, N, P

👍 *In Search of Understanding: The Case for Constructivist Classrooms* (2nd ed., 1999)
Jacqueline Brooks and Martin Brooks
Association for Supervision and Curriculum Development, ISBN 0-87120-211-5

This book is a worthwhile starting point for reading about constructivism and its application to teaching. Although the book applies to all content areas, science teachers in particular will find this book helpful in gaining a baseline understanding of constructivism. The book is easy to read and is filled with practical suggestions for classroom practice. Level = N, P

👍 *What Children Bring to Light: A Constructivist Perspective on Learning in Science* (1994)
Bonnie Shapiro
Teachers College Press, ISBN 0-8077-3375-X

This book helps teachers understand the historical development of constructivism and become better listeners by providing several case studies of children explaining and exploring their perceptions of light, reflection, absorption, and vision. The case studies also provide a look into multiple intelligences and how a child's perception affects his or her understanding of physical science concepts. Level = P, M

👍 *How Children Learn: Science in the Classroom* (2005)
National Research Council
National Academy Press, ISBN 0-309-08950-6

A "must-have" book for everyone interested in developing an understanding of the learning process within a science context. An excellent supplement to *How People Learn: Brain, Mind, Experience, and School*. Level = P, M

The Practice of Constructivism in Science Education (1993)
Kenneth Tobin, Editor
Lawrence Erlbaum, ISBN 0-8085-1878-2

Part 1 describes the nature of constructivism, including observations by authors Tobin and von Glasersfeld. Part 2 identifies teaching and learning in science and mathematics, and Part 3 provides the perspective of teachers learning to change. The book is recommended for those who have a basic understanding of constructivism. It is an excellent resource but probably shouldn't be the first book you read on constructivism. Level = P, M

👍 *Learning Science and the Science of Learning* (2002)
Rodger Bybee, Editor
Heinemann, ISBN 0-87355-208-3

An easy-to-read yet comprehensive volume on learning in science. Includes 12 articles by experts in the field on topics such as designing curriculum, assessing learning, and planning professional development. Level = N, P

👍 *Science Teaching and Development of Thinking* (2002)
Anton Lawson
Wadsworth/Thomson, ISBN 0-534-04851-X

A comprehensive text, for the experience inquiry teacher, on the nature of science, the construction of knowledge, the learning cycle, assessment, and other timely issues in science education. This book belongs on the shelf for every science teacher serious about the theory and practice of inquiry. Includes information on recent brain and memory research as it relates to learning science. Level = P, M

PRINT RESOURCES ON SCIENCE STANDARDS

Standards in the Classroom: An Implementation Guide for Teachers of Science and Mathematics
Richard Audet and Linda Jordan
Corwin Press, ISBN 0-7619-3857-5

This book makes the connection between national standards and the 5E Learning Cycle. It explains topics in assessment, developing standard-based curricula, evaluating instructional materials, and curriculum mapping. Level = N, P, M

Exemplary Science in Grades 5-8: Standards-Based Success Stories (2006)
Robert Yager
NSTA Press, ISBN 0-873552628

A collection of 15 stories of standards-based teaching. Level = N, P, M

Pathways to the Science Standards: Guidelines for Moving the Vision Into Practice, Elementary School Edition (1998)
Lawrence Lowery, Editor
National Science Teachers Association, ISBN 0-87355-161-3

A practical guide for implementing the vision of the National Science Education Standards at the elementary school level. Level = N, P, M

Pathways to the Science Standards: Guidelines for Moving the Vision Into Practice, Middle School Edition (1998)
Steven Rakow, Editor
National Science Teachers Association, ISBN 0-87355-166-4

A practical guide for implementing the vision of the National Science Education Standards at the middle school level. Level = N, P, M

PRINT RESOURCES ON SCIENCE LITERACY, HISTORY OF SCIENCE, AND THE NATURE OF SCIENCE

Atlas for Science Literacy (2001)
American Association for the Advancement of Science
Oxford University Press, ISBN 0-87168-668-6

According to NSTA Recommends, "The *Atlas of Science Literacy* may be the most significant and comprehensive contribution to science education since the publication of the Standards." It is a "must have" for science educator or curriculum developers. Developed from the Project 2061 publication *Benchmarks for Science Literacy*, the *Atlas* provides a visual overview of the guidelines for science literacy in mathematics, physical sciences, and social sciences for grades K–12. Level = P, M

Benchmarks for Science Literacy (1993)
American Association for the Advancement of Science
Oxford University Press, ISBN 0-19-508986-3

Hallmark publication of national guidelines for achieving scientific literacy by 2061. Level = N, P, M

Every Child a Scientist: Achieving Scientific Literacy for All (1998)
National Research Council
National Academy Press

A brief, yet essential, booklet (also available as an e-book) on how to use the National Science Education Standards to improve a school's science program. Topics include why we need science, the vision for quality education, using the Standards, and taking steps toward education reform. Level = PS, N, P

The Nature of Science (2nd ed., 1991)
Frederick Aicken
Heinemann, ISBN 0-435-08310-4

An introduction to the nature of science, plus essays on topics in science and a chronological table, make this book an interesting read. Level = PS, N, P, M

Science for All Americans (1990)
American Association for the Advancement of Science
Oxford University Press, ISBN 0-19-506771-1

An introduction to science literacy, plus elaborations on the areas and topics from *Benchmarks for Science Literacy* (listed above). Level = PS, N, P, M

Science Literacy for the Twenty-first Century (2003)
Stephanie Marshall, Judith Scheppler, and Michael Palmisano, Editors
Prometheus Books, ISBN 1-59102-020-4

Essays on scientific literacy by Stephen Gould, Howard Gardner, James Trefil, Rodger Bybee, and others. An epilogue by Leon Lederman. Level = P, M

Science Matters: Achieving Scientific Literacy (1991)
Robert Hazen and James Trefil
Anchor Books, ISBN 0-385-26108-X

An introduction to science literacy, plus essays on 150 topics in science from "absolute zero" to "X-rays." Level = N, P, M

The Structure of Scientific Revolutions (3rd ed., 1996)
Thomas Kuhn
University of Chicago Press, ISBN 0-226-45807-5

This is considered one of the most influential books on the discovery of science. Experienced science teachers will find an interesting and intellectual link between Kuhn's model of how science evolves and the process of scientific inquiry. Excellent reading for the serious inquirer. Level = P, M

Achieving Scientific Literacy (1997)
Rodger Bybee
Heinemann, ISBN 0-435-07134-3

Bybee offers a vision for improving science instruction, focusing on achieving scientific literacy using a standards-based approach. Topics include defining scientific literacy, establishing national standards, and creating a vision for the future. Level = N, P, M

👍 *Scientific Inquiry and Nature of Science: Implication for Teaching, Learning, and Teacher Education* (2006)
L. B. Flick and N. G. Lederman, Editors
Springer, ISBN 1-4020-5150-6

This is an excellent resource that explains the meaning of scientific inquiry and nature of science. Other articles include: addressing students with disabilities, technology to support inquiry, assessment, and implications to classroom teaching. A recommended book for those teachers who consider themselves "students" of inquiry. Level = P, M

PRINT RESOURCE ON DEMONSTRATIONS AND DISCREPANT EVENTS

👍 *Invitations to Science Inquiry* (2nd ed., 1987)
Tik Liem
Science Inquiry Enterprises, ISBN 1-878106-21-X

This book contains more than 400 quick and easy means to get your students "fired up" with science. All the discrepant events include lists of materials necessary to complete the demonstrations, the procedures to follow, questions to pose after the demonstrations to stimulate inquiry, and an explanation of the scientific concepts involved. Demonstrations are provided for life, earth, and physical sciences. This will become the most used book in your professional library. Level = PS, N, P, M

PRINT RESOURCES ON ASSESSMENT

👍 *Classroom Assessment and the National Science Education Standards* (2001)
National Research Council
National Academy Press, ISBN 0-309-06998-X

This volume accompanies the National Science Education Standards and provides background for classroom assessment aligned to the Standards. Offers strategies to strengthen an inquiry-based assessment program and compares formative and summative assessment measures. Level = N, P, M

Seamless Assessment in Science: A Guide for Elementary and Middle School Teachers (2006)
Sandra Abell and Mark Volkmann
Heinemann, ISBN 0-325-00769-1

One of the most comprehensive, practical, "how-to" books linking the 5E Learning Cycle and assessment. Examples for Grades 1–3, 4–5, and 6–8 in life, physical, and earth and space science. Level = PS, N, P

Everyday Assessment in the Science Classroom (2003)
J. Myron Atkin and Janet Coffey, Editors
National Science Teachers Association, ISBN 0-87355-217-2

A collection of 10 articles pertaining to science assessment, from experts in the field. The chapter titled "Assessment of Inquiry" provides an overview for assessing inquiry investigations. Level = P, M

Learning and Assessing Science Process Skills (3rd ed., 1995)
Richard Rezba, Constance Sprague, Ronald Fiel, H. James Funk, James Okey, and Harold Jaus
Kendall Hunt, ISBN 0-8403-8430-0

This book takes readers through a step-by-step approach to increasing their understanding of basic skills, such as observing, communicating, classifying, measuring, inferring, and predicting. Part 2 includes integrated skills needed to conduct a scientific investigation. The chapters follow a self-paced, individualized process that provides hands-on activities to practice each skill. The new edition also provides assessment strategies for each science skill. Level = PS, N, M

Active Assessment for Active Science: A Guide for Elementary School Teachers (1994)
George Hein and Sabra Price
Heinemann, ISBN 0-435-08361-9

This is a clear and straightforward approach to designing alternative, authentic, or performance assessments. In Chapter 1, the authors build a case for active assessment by describing the growing trend in science education. Forms of assessment used to evaluate student progress are discussed: tests ("pre" and "post"), questionnaires, concept maps, embedded activities, self-evaluations, and portfolios. Chapter 3 provides some realistic and practical suggestions for those just getting started, as well as tips for managing the transition from traditional to alternative assessment procedures. Other chapters, such as those on interpreting children's work and using rubrics, also will be useful to the reader. Level = PS, N, P

👍 *Teaching, Learning & Assessing Science, 5-12* (3rd ed., 2000)
Wynne Harlen
Paul Chapman Publishing, ISBN 1-85396-449-2

This edition provides a framework for constructivist learning and assessment of children's ideas. An excellent text for teachers of children ages 5 through 12. Although many references are from the United Kingdom, Harlen has an international reputation that applies to all countries. Level = P, M

Science Educator's Guide to Laboratory Assessment (2002)
Rodney Doran, Fred Chan, Pinchas Tamir, and Carol Lenhardt
NSTA Press, ISBN 0-87355-210-5

The first four chapters of this book provide the reader with a rationale for assessment and for developing and implementing alternative and performance assessments. The second four chapters provide examples of performance assessments in biology, chemistry, earth science, and physics. Although the book is geared toward a secondary school audience, middle school teachers will find the examples helpful when designing hands-on assessments for inquiry-based units. Level = N, P, M

Rubrics for Assessing Student Achievement in Science Grades K–12 (2004)
Hays Lantz
Corwin Press, ISBN 0-7619-3101-5

Chapters 1–3 provide a background for assessment in science education and why rubrics are important in assessing student work. The next four chapters present examples of rubrics for grades K–1, 2–3, 4–6, and 7–12. Level = PS, N, P, M

Assessing Student Understanding in Science: A Standards-Based K–12 Handbook (2001)
Sandra Enger and Robert Yager
Corwin Press, ISBN 0-7619-7649-3

This book presents assessment based on six domains: concept, process, application, attitude, creativity, and the nature of science. Rubrics are provided along with examples of assessments in Grades K–4, 5–8, and 9–12. Level = N, P, M

👍 *Weaving Science Inquiry and Continuous Assessment: Using Formative Assessment to Improve Learning* (2003)
Maura O'Brien Carlson, Gregg Humphrey, and Karen Reinhardt
Corwin Press, ISBN 0-7619-4590-3

Chapter 1 addresses the uniqueness of continuous assessment. Chapter 2 deals with facilitating assessment within the context of inquiry, while Chapter 3 provides explanations and examples within the inquiry classroom. Chapters 4 and 5 present ways of analyzing student work and addressing the realities of inquiry assessment. Level = N, P, M

PRINT RESOURCES ON GENERAL SCIENCE TOPICS

👍 *Understanding Models in Earth and Space Science* (2003)
Steven Gilbert and Shirley Watt Ireton
NSTA Press, ISBN 0-87355-226-1

Understanding Models is an excellent and comprehensive resource on the use of models and model building in science. Chapter 6, "Inquiry and Model Building," focuses exclusively on inquiry. Level = N, P, M

Science Through Multiple Intelligences: Patterns That Inspire Inquiry (1999)
Robert Barkman
Zephyr Press, ISBN 1-56976-096-9

Contains inquiry science activities and projects that encourage multiple intelligences and align to the National Science Education Standards. Level = PS, N, P

Science for All Children: A Guide to Improving Elementary Science Education in Your School District (1997)
National Science Resource Center
National Academy Press, ISBN 0-309-05297-1

This book offers a recipe for science education reform. In Part 1, a vision for developing an exemplary elementary school science program is discussed with reference to the latest research on how children learn science. In Part 2, specific references to inquiry include selection of instructional materials, professional development, assessments, and building support. Part 3 includes case studies of eight school districts implementing the recommendations of the National Science Resource Center. Level = P, M

MULTIMEDIA RESOURCES ON INQUIRY

A Private Universe (DVD) (1987)
Produced by Matthew Schneps and the Science Media Group of the Harvard-Smithsonian Center for Astrophysics; distributed by Astronomical Society of the Pacific, 390 Ashton Avenue, San Francisco, CA 94112
Order online at http://www.learner.org/collections/mathsci/teachers/pup/

This DVD is distributed to science educators courtesy of the NASA-SAO Education Forum on the Structure and Evolution of the Universe. According to Annenberg, "From its famous opening scene at a Harvard graduation, this classic of educational research brings into sharp focus the dilemma facing all educators: Why don't even the brightest students truly grasp basic science concepts?" This award-winning program traces the problem through interviews with eloquent Harvard graduates and professors and Heather, a bright middle school student who has some strange ideas about the orbits of the planets. Equally fitting for education methods classes, teacher workshops, and presentations to the public, it is an essential resource for any educational video collection. Level = PS, N, P, M

Search for Solutions (DVD) (2003)
Available free and online from www.teachingtools.com

The DVD contains 10 programs about scientists, exploration, and the discovery process. Appropriate for upper middle school students. Level = N, P, M

ONLINE RESOURCES ON INQUIRY

Doing Science: The Process of Scientific Inquiry (2006)
National Institutes of Health
http://science.education.nih.gov/customers.nsf/middleschool.htm

An NIH Curriculum Supplement Series for teachers in Grades 7–8. Written in cooperation with the Biological Sciences Curriculum Study (BSCS), the resource provides an introduction to inquiry and the National Science Education Standards, the 5E model, and sample lessons for middle school students. An excellent resource, plus it's free! Order online or download from the Web site. See the Web site above for this and other NIH curriculum supplements.

Exploratorium Institute for Inquiry
http://www.exploratorium.com/IFI/index.html

According to the Exploratorium, the Institute for Inquiry was "created in response to widespread interest in inquiry-based science instruction. The Exploratorium Institute for Inquiry provides workshops, programs, online support, and an intellectual community of practice that affords science reform educators a deep and rich experience of how inquiry learning looks and feels." Level = PS, N, P, M

👍 *Inquiry Strategies for Science and Mathematics Learning: It's Just Good Teaching*
NWREL (Northwest Regional Educational Laboratory)
http://www.nwrel.org/free/jgt.asp

According to NWREL, this document "provides the rationale for using inquiry-based teaching and offers specific strategies teachers can use in the classroom to facilitate their students' learning of concepts and skills. . . . A list of resources, including print materials, on-line sources, and organizations, enables teachers to explore additional tools to support their efforts in creating an inquiry-based classroom." Level = PS, N

Annenberg/CPB
http://www.learner.org

> The premier Web site for professional development resources and videos in science and mathematics. The lists on the site include schedules of distance-learning video series. Programs include Science Firsthand (Grades 7–9); Case Studies in Science Education (K–8); Science K–6: Investigating Classrooms; The Science of Teaching Science; For K–8 Science Education; Minds of Our Own (elementary and middle level); and Private Universe Teacher Workshops (Grades K–12). Level = PS, N, P, M

PBS TeacherSource
http://www.pbs.org/teachersource/sci_tech.htm

> Resources for elementary and middle school teachers in a variety of school settings focus on standards-based and inquiry-based science instruction. Level = PS, N, P

PROFESSIONAL ORGANIZATIONS

☝ National Science Teachers Association

The NSTA provides professional development resources, national and regional conferences, online discussions, and much more for K–16 science teachers. When an elementary or middle school teacher becomes an NSTA member, he or she receives the elementary school journal, *Science and Children*, or the middle school journal, *Science Scope*; online newsletters and support; plus *NSTA Reports*, a monthly newspaper on recent science events and topics. Level = PS, N, P, M

Resource B

Eighteen Concept Statements

Formative Assessments	Summative Assessments	Elaborate
Portfolios	Monitoring Charts	Explain
Concept Maps	Engage	Evaluate
Self-Evaluations	Prior Knowledge	Explore
Analytical Rubrics	Holistic Rubrics	National Science Education Standards
Objective Test Items	Inquiry-Based Instruction	Higher-Order Thinking Skills

Resource C

Inquiry Self-Assessment
Response Grids

1. Curriculum

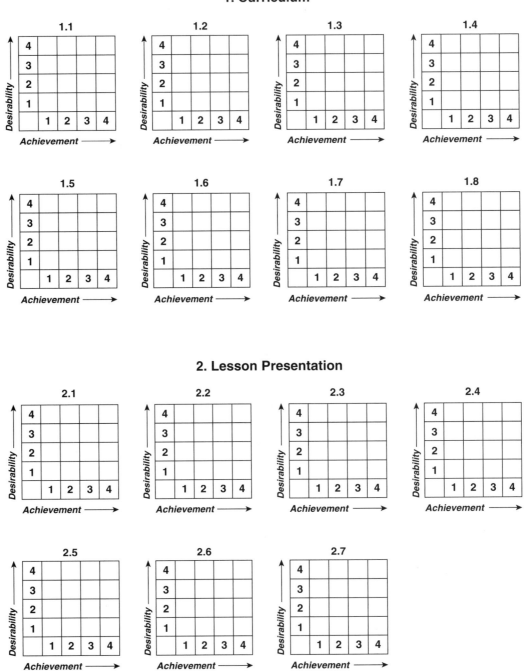

2. Lesson Presentation

3. Communication

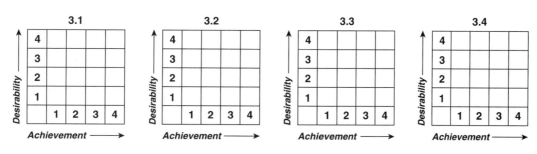

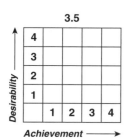

4. Engagement of Students

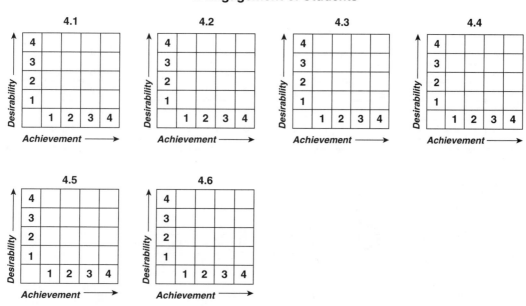

5. Classroom Organization

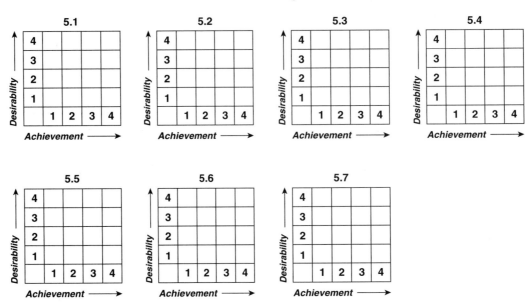

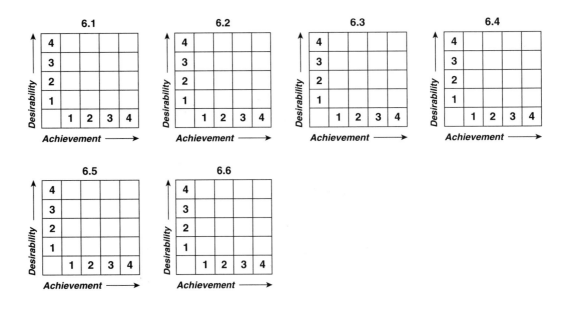

6. Questioning Skills

7. Assessment Procedures

7.1

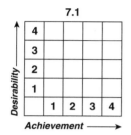

7.2

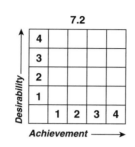

7.3

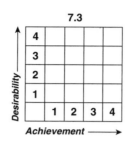

7.4

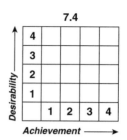

7.5

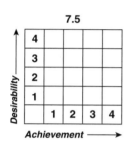

8. Professional Development

8.1

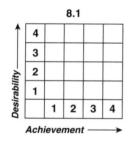

8.2

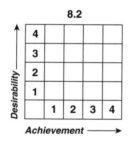

8.3

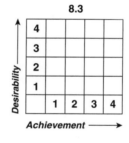

8.4

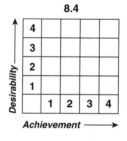

8.5

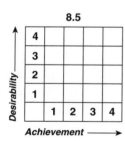

Resource D

Inquiry Self-Assessment
Summary Matrix

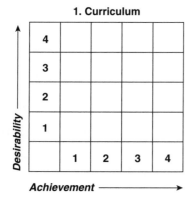

1. Curriculum

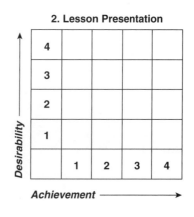

2. Lesson Presentation

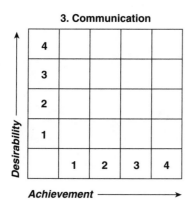

3. Communication

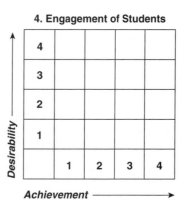

4. Engagement of Students

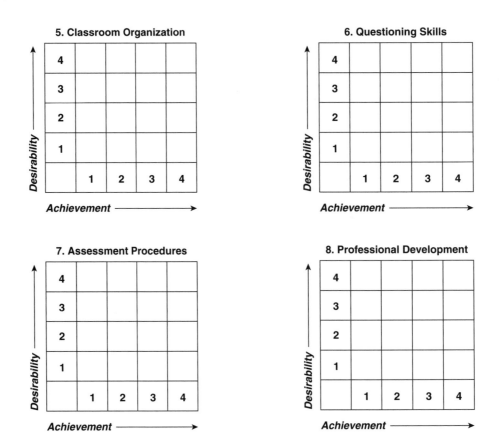

5. Classroom Organization

Desirability ↑
4
3
2
1
    1   2   3   4
Achievement →

6. Questioning Skills

Desirability ↑
4
3
2
1
    1   2   3   4
Achievement →

7. Assessment Procedures

Desirability ↑
4
3
2
1
    1   2   3   4
Achievement →

8. Professional Development

Desirability ↑
4
3
2
1
    1   2   3   4
Achievement →

Resource E

Diagrams for Short-Eared and Long-Eared Bugs-o-Copters

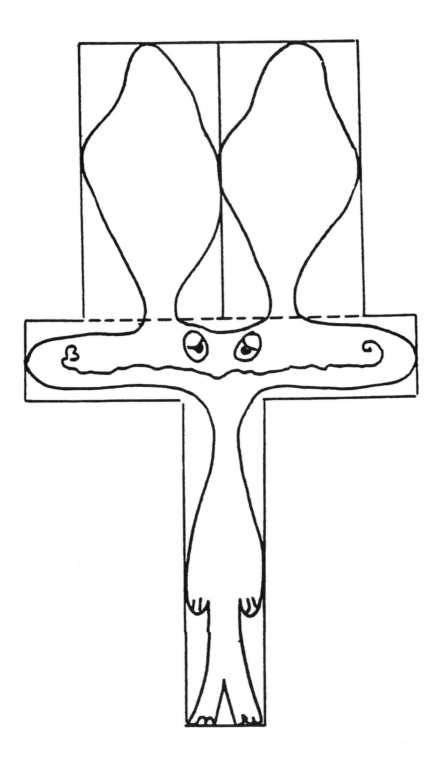

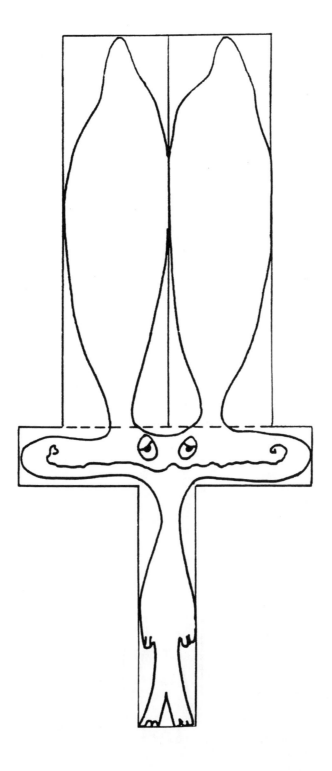

Resource F

How to Make a Cartesian Diver

1. Remove the screw top, label, and base from a clear plastic 2-liter soda container.

2. Fill the 2-liter container with water and set it aside. Leave a little bit of room to insert the eyedropper.

3. Fill a separate large glass (about 6–8 inches tall) with water.

4. Fill an eyedropper with enough water (about half full) so the dropper just floats when placed in the glass of water. The rubber top of the eyedropper should just break the surface of the water.

5. Remove the eyedropper from the glass and place it in the 2-liter container.

6. Replace the screw top on the container.

7. Gently squeeze the sides of the container and observe what happens to the eyedropper (diver).

Resource G

Touch Squares

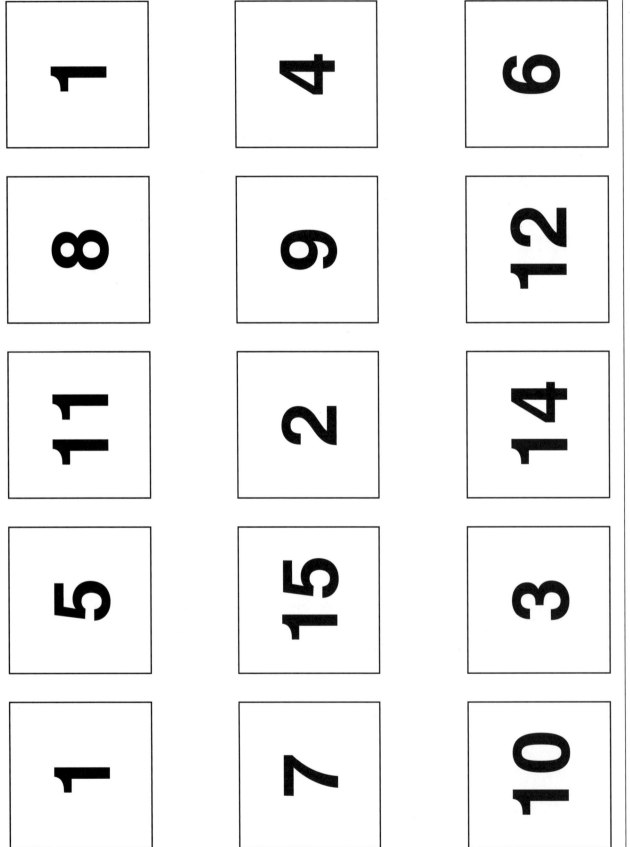

References

Abraham, M. (1997). *The learning cycle approach to science instruction* (Monograph No. 9701). Norman, OK: National Association for Research in Science Teaching.

Adams, D., & Hamm, M. (1998). *Collaborative inquiry in science, math and technology.* Portsmouth, NH: Heinemann.

Amaral, O., Garrison, L., & Duron-Flores, M. (2006). Taking inventory. *Science and Children, 43*(4), 30-33.

American Association for the Advancement of Science. (1990). *Science for all Americans.* Washington, DC: Author.

American Association for the Advancement of Science. (1993). *Benchmarks for science literacy.* Washington, DC: Author.

Atkin, J. M., & Karplus, R. (1962). Discovery or invention. *The Science Teacher, 29*(2), 121-143.

Atwater, M. (1994). Research on cultural diversity in the classroom. In D. Gabel (Ed.), *Handbook of research on science teaching and learning* (pp. 558-576). New York: Macmillan.

Ausubel, D. (1968). *Educational psychology: A cognitive view.* New York: Holt, Rinehart and Winston.

Ausubel, D., Novak, J., & Hanensian, H. (1978). *Educational psychology: A cognitive view.* New York: Holt, Rinehart and Winston.

Barell, J. (2003). *Developing more curious minds.* Alexandria, VA: Association for Supervision and Curriculum Development.

Barkman, R. (1999). *Science through multiple intelligences: Patterns that inspire inquiry.* Tucson, AZ: Zephyr Press.

Barman, C. (1996). How do students really view science and scientists? *Science and Children, 33*(1), 30-33.

Barman, C. (1997). Students' view of scientists and science: Results from a national survey. *Science and Children, 34*(1), 18-23.

Barman, C., & Kotar, M. (1989). The learning cycle. *Science and Children, 26*(7), 30-32.

Beisenherz, P., & Dantonio, M. (1996). *Using the learning cycle to teach physical science.* Portsmouth, NH: Heinemann.

Bell, B., & Gilbert, J. (1996). *Teacher development: A model from science education.* London: Falmer.

Bennett, C. (2001). Genres of research in multicultural education. *Review of Educational Research, 71*(2), 171-217.

Biological Sciences Curriculum Study (BSCS). (1970). *Biology teacher's handbook.* New York: John Wiley.

Bodrova, E., & Leong, D. (1996). *Tools of the mind: The Vygotskain approach to early childhood education.* Englewood Cliffs, NJ: Prentice Hall.

Bodzin, A., & Gehringer, M. (2001). Breaking science stereotypes. *Science and Children, 38*(4), 36-41.

Bourne, B. (Ed.). (2000). *Taking inquiry outdoors: Reading, writing, and science beyond the classroom walls.* Portland, ME: Stenhouse.

Bransford, D., Brown, A., & Cocking, R. (Eds.). 2000. *How people learn: Brain, mind, experience, and school.* Washington, DC: National Academy Press.

Brooks, J., & Brooks, M. (1999). *In search of understanding: The case for the constructivist classrooms.* Alexandria, VA: Association for Supervision and Curriculum Development.

Buhrow, B., & Upczak Garcia, A. 2006. *Ladybugs, tornadoes, and swirling galaxies: English language learners discover their world through inquiry.* Portland, ME: Stenhouse.

Bybee, R. (1997). *Achieving scientific literacy: From purposes to practices.* Portsmouth, NH: Heinemann.

Bybee, R. (Ed.). (2002). *Learning science and the science of learning.* Arlington, VA: NSTA Press.

Chamot, A., & O'Malley, J. M. (1994). *The CALLA handbook: Implementing the cognitive academic language learning approach.* Reading, MA: Addison-Wesley.

Colburn, A. (2004). Inquiring scientists want to know. *Educational Leadership, 62*(1), 63-66.

Colburn, A., & Clough, M. (1997). Implementing the learning cycle. *The Science Teacher, 64*(5), 30-33.

Costenson, K., & Lawson, A. (1986). Why isn't inquiry used in more classrooms? *The American Biology Teacher, 48*(3), 150-158.

DeBoer, G. (1991). *A history of ideas in science education.* New York: Teachers College Press.

DeBoer, G. (2000). Scientific literacy: Another look at its historical and contemporary meaning and its relationship to science education reform. *Journal of Research in Science Teaching, 37*(6), 582-602.

Dewey, J. (1900). *The school and society.* Chicago: University of Chicago Press.

Dewey, J. (1902). *The child and the curriculum.* Chicago: University of Chicago Press.

Dewey, J. (1916). *Democracy and education.* New York: Macmillan.

Driscoll, M. (1994). *Psychology of learning for instruction.* Boston: Allyn & Bacon.

Duit, R., & Treagust, D. (1995). Students' conceptions and constructivist teaching approaches. In B. Fraser & H. Walberg (Eds.), *Improving science education* (pp. 46-69). Chicago: National Society for the Study of Education.

Dyasi, H., & Worth, K. (n.d.). *Inquiry.* Retrieved October 23, 2006, from http://cse.edc.org/products/inquiryscienceelemclassroom/inquiry.asp

Edwards, C. (1998). Promoting student inquiry. *The Science Teacher, 65*(7), 18-20.

Exploratorium. (n.d.). What is inquiry? San Francisco, CA. Retrieved August 11, 2006, from http://www.exploratorium.edu/ifi/about/philosophy.html

Fathman, A., & Crowther, D. (Eds.). (2006). *Science for English Language Learners: K-12 Classroom Strategies.* Washington, DC: National Science Teachers Association Press.

Flick, L.B., & Lederman, N. G. (2006). Introduction. In L.B. Flick & N.G. Lederman (Eds.), *Scientific inquiry and the nature of science: Implications for teaching, learning, and teacher education* (pp. ix-xvii). Dordrecht, The Netherlands: Springer.

Furtak, E., & Ruiz-Primo, M. (2005). Questioning cycle: Making students' thinking explicit during scientific inquiry. *Science Scope, 42*(4), 22-25.

Gagne, R. (1970). *The conditions of learning* (2nd ed.). London: Holt-Saunders.

Gardner, H. (1983). *Frames of mind: The theory of multiple intelligences.* New York: Basic Books.

Gardner, H. (1999). *Intelligence reframed: Multiple intelligences for the 21st century.* New York: Basic Books.

Gilbert, S., & Watt Ireton, S. (2003). *Understanding models in earth and space science.* Arlington, VA: NSTA Press.

Goleman, D., Boyatzis, R., & McKee, A. (2002). *Primal leadership: Realizing the power of emotional intelligence.* Boston: Harvard Business School.

Gonzalez-Espada, W. (2004). Multicultural education: Helping all students succeed in science. *Electronic Journal of Literacy Through Science, 3*(12), 5.

Hargreaves, A., & Fink, D. (April, 2000). The three dimensions of reform. *Educational Leadership, 57*(7), 30-34.

Hart, D. (1994). *Authentic assessment.* Reading, MA: Addison-Wesley.

Haury, D. (1993). Teaching science through inquiry. *ERIC/CSMEE Digest.* (ERIC Document Reproduction Service No. ED 359048) Retrieved July 20, 2006, from http://www.ericdigests.org/1993/inquiry.htm

Hein, G., & Price, S. (1994). *Active assessment for active science.* Portsmouth, NH: Heinemann.

Herman, J., Aschbacher, P., & Winters, L. (1992). *A practical guide to alternative assessment.* Washington, DC: Association for Supervision and Curriculum Development.

Hester, J. (1994). *Teaching for thinking*. Durham, NC: Carolina Academic Press.

Holliday, W. (2006). A Balanced Approach to Science Inquiry Teaching. In L.B. Flick, & N. G. Lederman (Eds.), *Scientific inquiry and the nature of science: Implications for teaching, learning, and teacher education* (pp. 201-217). Dordrecht, The Netherlands: Springer.

Hunkins, F. (1995). *Teaching thinking through effective questioning* (2nd ed.). Norwood, MA: Christopher-Gordon.

Johnson, D., Johnson, R. T., & Holubec, E. (1984). *Circles of learning*. Washington, DC: Association for Supervision and Curriculum Development.

Karplus, R., & Thier, H. (1967). *A new look at elementary school science*. Chicago: Rand McNally.

Kuhn, T. (1996). *The structure of scientific revolutions* (3rd ed.). Chicago: University of Chicago. (Originally published 1962)

Lawson, A., Abraham, M., & Renner, J. (1989). *A theory of instruction: Using the learning cycle to teach science concepts and thinking skills* (Monograph No. 1). Manhattan, KS: National Association for Research in Science Teaching.

Lederman, N. G. (2006). Syntax of nature of science within inquiry and science instruction. In L. B. Flick, & N. G. Lederman (Eds.), *Scientific inquiry and the nature of science: Implications for teaching, learning, and teacher education* (pp. 301-317). Dordrecht, The Netherlands: Springer.

Lederman, N., & Lederman, J. (2004). Revising instruction to teach the nature of science. *The Science Teacher, 71*(9), 36-39.

Lederman, N. G., Abd-El-Khalick, F., Bell, R. L., & Schwartz, R. S. (2002). View of Nature of Science Questionnaire (VNOS): Toward Valid and Meaningful Assessment of Learners' Conceptions of Nature of Science. *Journal of Research in Science Teaching, 39*(6), 497-521.

Liem, T. (1987). *Invitations to science inquiry*. Chino Hills, CA: Science Inquiry Enterprises.

Llewellyn, D. (1998, November). *Are you an inquiry teacher?* Paper presented at the 103rd Annual Conference of the Science Teachers Association of New York State, Ellenville, NY.

Llewellyn, D. (2004). *Teaching high school science through inquiry: A case study approach*. Thousand Oaks, CA: Corwin Press.

Llewellyn, D. (2006). Building professional learning communities. *NSTA Reports, 17*(4), 10-11.

Llewellyn, D. (2007). Making the most of concept maps. *Science Scope, 30*(5), 74-77.

Lorsbach, A., & Tobin, K. (1992). *Constructivism as a referent for science teaching*. (Monograph No. 30). Retrieved July 20, 2006, from http://www.exploratorium.edu/IFI/resources/research/constructivism.html

Lucas, D., Broderick, N., Lehrer, R., & Bohanan, R. (2005). Making the grounds of scientific inquiry visible in the classroom. *Science Scope, 29*(3), 39-42.

Macrina, F. (1995). *Scientific integrity*. Washington, DC: American Society of Microbiology.

Marek, E., & Cavallo, A. (1997). *The learning cycle*. Portsmouth, NH: Heinemann.

Martin, R., Sexton, C., & Gerlovich, J. (1999). *Science for all children: Lessons for constructing understanding*. Needham Heights, MA: Allyn & Bacon.

Maxwell, J. C. (1998). *The 21 irrefutable laws of leadership*. Nashville, TN: Thomas Nelson.

McClough, M., & Olsen, J. (November, 2004). The nature of science: Always part of the science story. *The Science Teacher, 71*(9), 28-31.

McComas, W. (2004). Keys to teaching the nature of science. *The Science Teacher, 71*(9), 24-27.

McDuffie, T. (2001). Scientists: Geeks and nerds? *Science and Children, 38*(8), 16-19.

Minstrell, J., & Van Zee, E. (Eds.). (2000). *Inquiring Into Inquiry Learning and Teaching in Science*. Washington, DC: American Association for the Advancement of Science.

National Center for Improving Science Education (NCISE). (1992). *Assessment in science education: The middle years*. Washington, DC: Author.

National Research Council (NRC). (1996). *National science education standards*. Washington, DC: National Academy Press.

National Research Council. (1998). *Every child a scientist: Achieving scientific literacy for all*. Washington, DC: National Academy Press.

National Research Council. (2000). *Inquiry and the national science education standards: A guide for teaching and learning*. Washington, DC: National Academy Press.

National Research Council. (2001). *Classroom assessment and the national science education standards*. Washington, DC: National Academy Press.

National Research Council. (2006). *Learning to think spatially*. Washington, DC: National Academies Press.

National Science Teachers Association. (1978). *Guidelines for self-assessment*. Washington, DC: National Science Teachers Association Press.

National Science Teachers Association. (1998). NSTA position statement—The national science education standards: A vision for the improvement of science and learning. *Science Scope, 65*(5), 32-34.

National Science Teachers Association. (2000). *Inquiry and the National Science Education Standards: A guide for teaching and learning*. Washington, DC: National Academies Press.

Novak, J. (1977). *A theory of education*. Ithaca, NY: Cornell University Press.

Novak, J. (1998). *Learning, creating and using knowledge: Concepts maps as tools in schools and corporations*. Mahwah, NJ: Lawrence Erlbaum.

Novak, J., & Gowin, D. (1989). *Learning how to learn*. New York: Cambridge University Press.

Ogle, D. (1986). K-W-L: A teaching model that develops active reading of expository text. *The Reading Teacher, 39*(6), 564-570.

Pellegrino, J., Chudowshy, N., & Glaser, R. (Eds.). (2001). *Knowing what students know: The science and design of educational assessment*. Washington, DC: National Academy Press.

Phillips, D. C., & Soltis, J. (1991). *Perspectives on learning* (2nd ed.). New York: Teachers College Press.

Piaget, J. (1970). *The science of education and the psychology of the child*. New York: Orion.

Popper, K. (1972). *Objective Knowledge: An Evolutionary Approach*. New York: Oxford University Press.

Posner, G., Strike, K., Hewson, P., & Gertzog, W. (1982). Accommodation of a scientific conception: Toward a theory of conceptual change. *Science Education, 66*, 211-227.

Riley, R. (1999). *Excelencia para todas*. Address by U.S. Secretary of Education on the progress of education for Hispanic Americans and the challenges of a new century. Washington, DC: U.S. Department of Education.

Rowe, M. B. (1974). Wait-time and rewards as instructional variables. *Journal of Research in Science Teaching, 11*, 263-279.

Rowe, M. B. (1987). Using wait-time to stimulate inquiry. In W. Wilen (Ed.), *Questions, questioning techniques, and effective teaching* (pp. 95-106). Washington, DC: National Education Association.

Rowe, M. B. (1996). Science, silence, and sanctions. *Science and Children, 34*(1), 35-37.

Sagan, C. (1996). *The demon-haunted world*. New York: Ballantine.

Scheurich, J., & Skrla, L. (2003). *Leadership for equity and excellence*. Thousand Oaks, CA: Corwin Press.

Schwab, J. (1962). The teaching of science as enquiry. In *The Teaching of Science* (pp. 1-103). Cambridge, MA: Harvard University Press.

Schwartz, R., & Crawford, B. (2006). Authentic Scientific Inquiry as Context for Teaching Nature of Science. In L. B. Flick, & N. G. Lederman (Eds.), *Scientific inquiry and the nature of science: Implications for teaching, learning, and teacher education* (pp. 331-355). Dordrecht, The Netherlands: Springer.

Sergiovanni, T. (1996). *Leadership for the schoolhouse*. San Francisco: Jossey-Bass.

Shamos, M. (1995). *The myth of scientific literacy*. New Brunswick, NJ: Rutgers University Press.

Shiland, T. (1999). Constructivism: The implications for laboratory work. *Journal of Chemical Education, 76* (1), 107-109.

Songer, N., Lee, H., & Kam, R. (2001, April). *Technology-rich inquiry science in urban classrooms: What are the barriers to inquiry pedagogy?* Paper presented at the annual meeting of the American Educational Research Association, Seattle, WA.

Sprung, B., Froschl, M., & Campbell, P. (1987). *What will happen if—Young children and the scientific method*. New York: Educational Equity Concepts.

Sutman, F. X. (1996). Science literacy: A functional definition. *Journal of Research in Science Teaching, 33*(5), 459-460.

Sutman, F. X. (2001). Mathematics and science literacy for all Americans. *Enc focus, 8*(3), 20-23.

Thomas, W., & Collier, V. (1995). Language minority student achievement and program effectiveness. *California Association for Bilingual Education Newsletter, 17*(15), 19-24.

Tobin, K., & Capie, W. (1981). *Wait-time and learning in science* (AETS Outstanding Paper for 1981). Burlington, NC: Carolina Biological Supply Company.

Trautman, N., McKinster, J., & Avery, L. (2004, April). *What makes inquiry so hard?* Paper presented at the National Association for Research in Science Education, Vancouver, BC, Canada.

Trefil, J. (2003). Two modest proposals concerning scientific literacy. In S. Marshall, J. Scheppler, & M. Palmisano (Eds.), *Scientific literacy for the twenty-first century* (p. 150-160). Amherst, NY: Prometheus Books.

U.S. Department of Education. (2000). *Before it's too late*. Washington, DC: U.S. Department of Education, National Commission of Mathematics and Science Teaching for the 21st Century.

Vygotsky, L. (1962). *Thought and language* (E. Hanfmann and G. Voker, Trans.). Cambridge, MA: MIT Press. (Original work published 1934)

Vygotsky, L. (1978). *Mind in society: The development of higher psychological processes*. Boston: Harvard University Press.

Vygotsky, L. (1979). Consciousness as a problem in the psychology of behavior. *Soviet Psychology, 18*(1), 67-115. (Original work published 1924)

Watson, J. (1968). *The double helix: A personal account of the discovery of the structure of DNA*. Kingsport, TN: Kingsport Press.

Watts, M. (1991). *The science of problem-solving*. Portsmouth, NH: Heinemann.

Whitin, P., & Whitin, D. (1997). *Inquiry at the window: Pursuing the wonders of learners*. Portsmouth, NH: Heinemann.

Wiggins, G. P., & McTighe, J. (1998). *Understanding by design handbook*. Alexandria, VA: Association for Supervision and Curriculum Development.

Wolfe, P. (December, 1998). Revising effective teaching. *Educational Leadership, 11*, 61-64.

Wood, D., Bruner, J., & Ross, G. (1976). The role of tutoring in problem-solving. *Journal of Child Psychology and Psychiatry, 17*, 89-100.

Youngson, R. (1998). *Scientific blunders*. New York: Carroll & Graf.

Index